T0379987

REPRESENTING MEDIEVAL GENDERS AND SEXUALITIES IN EUROPE

Transcending both academic disciplines and traditional categories of analysis, this collection illustrates the ways genders and sexualities could be constructed, subverted and transformed. Focusing on areas such as literature, hagiography, history, and art history, from the Anglo-Saxon period to the early sixteenth century, the contributors examine the ways men and women lived, negotiated, and challenged prevailing conceptions of gender and sexual identity. In particular, their papers explore textual constructions and transformations of religious and secular masculinities and femininities; visual subversions of gender roles; gender and the exercise of power; and the role sexuality plays in the creation of gender identity. The methodologies which are used in this volume are relevant both to specialists of the Middle Ages and early modern periods, and to scholars working more broadly in fields that draw on contemporary gender studies.

*Elizabeth L'Estrange is lecturer in the History of Art
at the University of Birmingham, UK.*

*Alison More is a researcher in the Department of History
at Radboud University in the Netherlands.*

Representing Medieval Genders and Sexualities in Europe

Construction, Transformation, and Subversion, 600–1530

Edited by Elizabeth L'Estrange and Alison More

Routledge
Taylor & Francis Group

LONDON AND NEW YORK

First published 2011 by Ashgate Publishing

Published 2016 by Routledge
2 Park Square, Milton Park, Abingdon, Oxon OX14 4RN
711 Third Avenue, New York, NY 10017, USA

Routledge is an imprint of the Taylor & Francis Group, an informa business

Copyright © 2011 The editors and contributors

British Library Cataloguing in Publication Data
Representing medieval genders and sexualities in Europe :
    construction, transformation, and subversion, 600-1530.
    1. Sex role--Europe--History--To 1500. 2. Sex role--
    Religious aspects--Christianity. 3. Masculinity--
    Religious aspects--Christianity. 4. Masculinity--Europe--
    History--To 1500. 5. Women--Europe--History--Middle
    Ages, 500-1500. 6. Sex role in literature--History--To
    1500. 7. Sex role in art--History--To 1500. 8. Sex--
    Europe--History--To 1500.
    I. L'Estrange, Elizabeth. II. More, Alison.
    305.3'094'0902-dc22

Library of Congress Cataloging-in-Publication Data
Representing medieval genders and sexualities in Europe : construction, transformation, and subversion, 600-1530 / edited by Elizabeth L'Estrange, Alison More.
        p. cm.
    Includes bibliographical references and index.
    ISBN 978-1-4094-0987-8 (hardcover : alk. paper)
        1. Gender identity--Europe--History--To 1500. 2. Sex customs--Europe--History--To 1500. 3. Gender identity--Europe--History--To 1500--Sources. 4. Sex customs--Europe--History--To 1500--Sources. 5. Europe--Social life and customs. 6. Europe--Social conditions--To 1492. 7. Europe--Intellectual life. 8. Europe--Religious life and customs. 9. Art and society--Europe--History--To 1500. 10. Popular culture--Europe--History--To 1500. I. L'Estrange, Elizabeth. II. More, Alison, 1975-

HQ14.R47 2011
305.304'0902--dc22

                                                                        2011001429

ISBN 9781409409878 (hbk)

Contents

List of Illustrations

Notes on Contributors

JENNIFER BORLAND is an assistant professor of Art History at Oklahoma State University, specializing in medieval art and architecture. She received her PhD, entitled 'Unstable Women: Transgression and Corporeal Experience in Twelfth-Century Visual Culture' in art history from Stanford University in 2006. Her research and teaching interests range from medieval theories of corporeality and vision, to audience and reception, representations of gender, and medical and scientific imagery. She is the author of 'The Forested Frontier: Commentary in the Margins of the Alhambra Ceiling Paintings', in *Medieval Encounters*, 14 (2008) and 'The Immediacy of Objects: Reassessing the Contribution of Art History in Feminist Medieval Studies', *Medieval Feminist Forum*, 44 (2008). Forthcoming projects include articles on gynaecological manuscripts containing images of the *foetus-in-utero*, and a *Sheela-na-gig* sculpture from the Nuns' Church at Clonmacnoise, Ireland. She is also working on a study of the late medieval illustrated manuscripts of Aldobrandino of Siena's *régime du corps*, a popular late medieval regimen of health.

JENNIFER CAVALLI is a PhD candidate in the Department of History, Indiana University, studying gender, female religiosity and court culture in Renaissance Italy. She has a particular interest in the role of female communities in self-formation and the convergence of religious and secular virtues on gendered identity. She has taught classes on Western civilization and the Renaissance and served as editorial assistant for *The Medieval Review*. Her doctoral dissertation examines female networks and convent culture in late fifteenth- and early sixteenth-century Italy and is entitled 'Between the Court and the Convent: Isabella d'Este and Female Communities in the Renaissance'.

FIONA S. DUNLOP is Research Associate of the Centre for Medieval Studies, University of York. She is the author of 'The Rule of Youth and the Rule of the *Familia* in Henry Medwall's *Nature'*, in *The Medieval Household in Christian Europe, c. 850–c. 1550*, ed. Cordelia Beattie, Anna Masklakovic and Sarah Rees Jones (Turnhout: Brepols, 2003); 'Making Youth Holy: Holiness and Masculinity in *The Interlude of Youth'*, in *Holiness and Masculinity in the Middle Ages*, ed. Patricia H. Cullum and Katherine J. Lewis (Cardiff: University of Wales Press, 2004); and *The Late Medieval Interlude: The Drama of Youth and Aristocratic Masculinity* (York: York Medieval Press, 2007). Her research interests include medieval and early modern drama, gender and the history of childhood. She teaches English at Bootham School, York.

ELIZABETH L'ESTRANGE obtained her PhD from the School of Fine Art, History of Art and Cultural Studies at the University of Leeds in 2004. She was then based at the University of Liège in Belgium, where she held post-doctoral fellowships from the Leverhulme Trust and the Fonds national de recherche scientifique in the History of Art. She is now lecturer in History of Art at the University of Birmingham. Her research interests are in fifteenth- and early sixteenth-century art, especially books of hours, women's patronage at the French court, representations of maternity and constructions of the gaze. She has published a number of articles on devotional manuscripts and the patronage of Anne of France and Anne of Brittany; she is also the author of 'Gazing at Gawain: Reconsidering Tournaments, Courtly Love, and the Lady Who Looks', *Medieval Feminist Forum*, 44 (2008). Her first monograph, *Holy Motherhood: Gender, Dynasty and Visual Culture in the Later Middle Ages* (Manchester: Manchester University Press, 2008), received the 2010 Society for Medieval Feminist Scholarship's First Book Prize. Current projects include a monograph co-authored with Kathleen Wilson-Chevalier on Queen Claude of France and the early Reform in France.

AISLINN LOCONTE obtained her PhD from Oxford University and has held the post of Senior Lecturer in Art History at Roehampton University. She specializes in Italian Renaissance art and architecture. Her particular research interests include Neapolitan art and urbanism, women and visual culture in early modern Europe, court culture, the writings of Giorgio Vasari and art historiographies. She has published articles on royal women's patronage of art and architecture in Angevin Naples and has contributed to the catalogue of the critically acclaimed exhibition 'The Art of Italy in the Royal Collection: Renaissance and Baroque'. She is currently preparing a monograph entitled *Patronage, Art and Power: Royal Women in the Late Medieval and Early Modern Kingdom of Naples*.

ALISON MORE is a researcher for the project 'Religious Orders and Identity Formation in Late Medieval and Early Modern Europe' at Radboud University in Nijmegen. Her particular focus is on preaching and the reception of sermons in houses of later medieval religious women. She has previously held the position of Assistant Professor at the Franciscan Institute and School of Franciscan Studies at St. Bonaventure University. Her doctoral thesis, '"*Milites Christi in hortis liliorum Domini*"? Hagiographic Constructions of Masculinity and Holiness in Thirteenth-Century Liège' was obtained from the University of Bristol in 2005. Her research interests include the changing devotional climate of the high Middle Ages, with a particular focus on the new religious movements that developed at this time. She is working on an edition of Beguine rules for the Brepols series *Disciplicina Monastica*.

CASSANDRA RHODES obtained her PhD entitled, 'King, Mother, Soldier, Whore. Multiple Performances of Virginity in Anglo-Saxon Prose Saints' Lives: The Heterogeneity of an Ideal' from the University of Manchester in 2007. Her research interests are grounded in notions of medieval gender, particularly representations of male virginity as depicted in hagiographic texts. She is also interested in examining an apparent difference in visual representations of saints, particularly female saints, between miniatures found in Anglo-Saxon manuscripts and those in their continental counterparts. She has taught classes in Old English, as well as Anglo-Saxon and later medieval literature.

FRANCESCA CANADÉ SAUTMAN is Professor of French at Hunter College and The Graduate Center of CUNY. She has published on medieval and early modern studies, Francophone literature, folklore, ethnic studies, gender and queer theory. She is the author of *La Religion du quotidien: Rites et croyances de la fin du Moyen Age* (Florence: Olschki, 1995), the co-editor with Pamela Sheingorn of *Same-Sex Love and Desire Among Women in the Middle Ages* (New York: Palgrave, 2001) and, with Giuseppe Di Scipio and Diana Conchado, of *Telling Tales: Medieval Narratives and the Folk Tradition* (New York: Palgrave, 1998). She has been an editorial board member for the *Encyclopedia of Sex and Gender*, was co-founding editor of *Marvels and Tales* from 1987 to 1994, and editor of *Medieval Folklore* from 1991 to 1994. Recent articles on medieval studies include, with Hamid Bahri, 'Crossing History, Dis-Orienting the Orient; Amin Maalouf's Uses of the "Medieval"', in *Medievalisms in the Postcolonial World*, ed. Nadia Altschul and Kathleen Davis (Baltimore: The Johns Hopkins University Press, 2009) and 'Sacred Commodity, Commodifying the Sacred: Reckoning with Wine in Late Medieval French Culture', in the special issue of *Mediaevalia*, entitled *In Vino Veritas* (2010). She is currently working on a book on gender, community and violence in late medieval Flanders and the French North.

HELEN SWIFT is Fellow and Tutor in Medieval French at St Hilda's College, Oxford. Her research interests straddle the late medieval and early modern periods, exploring the poetics of vernacular literature between 1350 and

1550, in particular defences of women, as in her book *Gender, Writing, and Performance: Men Defending Women in Late Medieval France (1440–1538)* (Oxford: Oxford University Press, 2008). Recent articles have engaged with the codicological context of these defences, or have used tools of modern critical theory to help articulate contemporary understandings of intertextuality, from the *Roman de la rose* to Alain Chartier. A future book project is planned on Martin le Franc.

List of Abbreviations

AASS	*Acta Sanctorum quotquot Toto Orbe Coluntur*, ed. Jean Bolland, et al., 67 vols (Antwerp and Brussels: Société des Bollandistes, 1643–1940)
BHL	*Bibliotheca hagiographica latina antiquae et mediae aetatis*, ed. Henricus Fros, 2 vols (Brussels: Société des Bollandistes, 1898–1901)
EETS e.s.	Early English Text Society, Extra Series
EETS o.s.	Early English Text Society, Original Series
ET	English Translation
PL	J.P. Migne, ed., *Patrologia cursus completus: series latina*, 221 vols (Paris: Migne, 1841–64)

Preface and Acknowledgements

The role of gender, long ignored by traditional scholarship, has provided many and valuable insights into medieval and early modern society. More recent scholarly discussion has moved towards questioning the definition of the category itself. This present volume can be placed in that tradition. Inspired by a series of formal and informal discussions, including a meeting of the Gender and Medieval Studies Conference on 'Genders and Sexualities' held at the University of Leeds in 2005, it has grown and transformed in ways that we did not initially imagine. For this, thanks are due first and foremost to our contributors for the fascinating ways in which they have responded to and developed the theme of gender construction, transformation and subversion in their various topics. We would also like to thank the following people for their support and advice during the writing and editing process: Rosalind Brown-Grant, Katharine Burkitt, George Ferzoco, Shanda Hunter-Trottier, Robert King, Stephen King, John More, Margaret More, Cathy McClive, Catherine Mooney, Carolyn Muessig, Eleanor Pridgeon, Monica Sandor and the anonymous reviewers and our editor at Ashgate, Erika Gaffney.

Working with such a rich variety of topics, sacred and secular, and with a chronological range that extends from the Anglo-Saxon to the early modern period, has taught us much both as editors and scholars. More importantly, however, it has also highlighted the many exciting directions that studies of medieval and early modern genders and sexualities are taking and it is hoped that this volume will inspire further debate and analysis in this field.

1

Representing Medieval Genders and Sexualities in Europe: Construction, Transformation, and Subversion, 600–1530

Elizabeth L'Estrange and Alison More

The point of new historical investigation is to disrupt the notion of fixity, to discover the nature of the debate or repression that leads to the appearance of timeless permanence in binary gender representation.[1]

In the 1986 article quoted above, Joan W. Scott advocated the use of gender as a category for (re)analyzing the way a variety of academic disciplines, from history and literature to politics and the social sciences, could be approached and scholars' findings nuanced. Some twenty-five years later, Scott's article is 'one of the most cited historical works of its time'.[2] Although the concept of a 'category of analysis' may, and has, been brought into question,[3] Scott's insistence on the importance of disrupting 'the notion of fixity' and normalized binary oppositions has become a central concern for scholars of sexuality and gender. This approach has been nuanced further in the light of Judith Butler's exploration of the performative nature and materiality of gender, as well as of the role of language and biological sex in gender construction.[4] Furthermore, the work of feminist scholars such as Patricia Hill Collins has drawn attention to the importance of examining the ways in which race and class intersect with gender.[5] The findings of scholars discussing such issues have resulted in a wider and more theoretical approach to gender that draws on cultural and linguistic studies as well as anthropology, as a way of examining the multiplicities of sexualities and genders. Engaging with such innovations, scholars are now applying similar critical historiographical and analytic techniques to the study of the Middle Ages and the early modern period, as collections such as *Gender and Difference in the Middle Ages, Constructing Medieval Sexuality, Presenting Gender: Changing Sex in Early Modern Culture* and *Gender and Christianity in Medieval Europe* demonstrate.[6]

In the present volume, scholars of history, art history, religion and literature continue this engagement with theoretical gender studies, exploring the 'nature of the debate' as highlighted by Scott. They analyze sources from England to Italy via the Low Countries, and from the Anglo-Saxon period to the early sixteenth century. Their essays question and explore the fixity and cultural dependence of medieval and early modern genders and sexualities through the specific themes of construction, transformation and subversion. Although some of the texts, genres and images discussed may be familiar (saints' lives, tomb sculpture, the *querelle des femmes*, humanist letters, female rulers and images of women), the authors offer new and alternative readings of their material by emphasizing the ways in which genders and sexualities were and are constructed by various discourses (visual, linguistic, religious) and how those discourses – and thus the genders they claim to describe – could be transformed or subverted. In particular, the contributors examine not only how sex and gender constructions served a prevailing social order and patriarchal hierarchy, but also how men and women were themselves able to question, manipulate or break down such hierarchies, normalized responses and binary oppositions through their commissions, writings, interpretations or self-presentations.

From Women's Studies to Gender Studies and Beyond

The discipline of 'gender studies' is often described as a trajectory, which developed from both the American Civil Rights movement and from the 'women's studies' movement that emerged from Second Wave Feminism of the 1970s and 1980s. Initially, the terms 'women' and 'gender' were so closely linked that they seemed synonymous.[7] The aim here is not to retrace the history of these terms through a literary review but rather to highlight some of the ways in which 'women's' and then 'gender studies' have developed as a discipline, particularly in relation to those areas of scholarship that are intrinsic to the contributions to this volume, such as masculinity studies, religious studies, literature and art history.[8]

The concept of 'gender' has been subject to many interpretations. As early as the fourth century, the grammarian Servius pointed out that, '[g]enders are named this way because of that which they generate'.[9] While he stated that there were only two biological genders, he conceded that the category of grammatical gender was constructed on the basis of either assigned or authoritative social usage.[10] As gender theories have become considerably more complex since Servius' time, most scholars would disagree with his idea of two 'natural' genders, but would apply his idea of assigned or authoritative constructs to gender roles as well as to grammatical gender.[11] In the 1970s, studies such as Ann Oakley's *Sex, Gender and Society* alerted scholars to the role of social factors in constructing differences between masculine and feminine.[12] In subsequent scholarship, both the concept of gender and theories about its construction have been, and continue to be, problematized. The ever-evolving debate on the nature of gender means that there is no scholarly consensus on the extent to which society or even biological sex affects and informs gender roles. Instead, it is now widely agreed that gender is not a fixed norm, and many critics argue that it is not bound by binary oppositions.[13] Rather, gender is understood to be a socially constructed, performative and changing heuristic or hermeneutic category, which determines and allows us to find latent meaning in behaviours, texts, images and social structures.[14]

If we accept the view that gender is performative, then the terms 'masculinity' and 'femininity' have neither ontological nor hegemonic significance. Consequently, readings informed by gender require a complex process of decoding that includes an historically specific approach to the ways in which genders and sexualities were both understood and constructed in the past.[15] Medieval texts such as chronicles and hagiography contain numerous examples of men and women who question the societal ideal by taking on roles normally reserved for the opposite sex. Notably, stories of woman who disguised themselves as men in order to enter the 'more perfect' form of religious life were common.[16] Some of these tales were undoubtedly written to chastize clerics for their decadence, while others, such as the tale of the ill-fated 'Pope Joan' who gave birth in a public procession, emphasized the necessity of maintaining traditional gender roles.[17] It is important to recognize, however, that neither the masculine gender role nor its associated characteristics are exclusive to men. In some cases, even those born male were not always portrayed as 'masculine'. This is evident in studies such as Sean Tougher's analysis of Byzantine eunuchs, which explores the phenomenon of fluctuating or multiple gender identities and the ways in which they were intertwined with social position.[18]

Societal changes not only affect the ways in which gender roles are idealized and perceived, but also the social roles available to men or women. For the Middle Ages, studies such as Monica Green's exploration of the provision of women's medicine and healthcare or Martha Howell's examination of how gender roles adapted to economic developments, explore how changing public needs have dictated gendered norms.[19] In the same way, Mathew Kuefler's discussion about an emerging ideal of Christian masculinity acknowledges that gender constructions do not occur independently of each other, or of social, economic or religious contexts.[20] Consequently, such studies demonstrate the need for a deeper understanding of gender pluralities, facilitating a move from 'femininity' to 'femininities' and 'masculinity' to 'masculinities'.

Gender: A Category of Analysis

Recognition of the plurality of genders and sexualities has led, perhaps first and foremost, to a reframing of the initial aims of feminist historians: redressing the absence of women from the historical record. As Butler and Gillian Beer have both noted, 'women' does not constitute a pre-existing, homogeneous, stable group ready for analysis and, as a result of such thinking, the very possibility of writing or reclaiming 'women's' history has been queried.[21] For the Middle Ages in particular, this has led to critiques of early ground-breaking studies such as Caroline Walker Bynum's *Holy Feast and Holy Fast*, and Christiane Klapisch-Zuber's *Women, Family and Ritual in Renaissance Italy* that emphasized emotive response, corporeality, childbearing, food and the domestic sphere as defining aspects of womanhood.[22] These associations were recast by feminist authors as providing women with means of empowerment in so far as they were qualities or abilities not possessed by men. Although these works have gone a long way towards highlighting how certain forms or experiences of devotion came to be labelled 'feminine', the empowering or subversive aspects of these corporeal and maternal constructions of the 'feminine' gender, derive, ultimately, from dominant masculine classical and medieval discourses about the female sex, as David Aers has cogently argued.[23] Furthermore, perceptions of gender are often shaped by relationships *between* the sexes. The essays in volumes such as *Gendered Voices: Medieval Saints and their Interpreters* or *Gendering the Master Narrative: Women and Power in the Middle Ages* illustrate the ways in which the sexes perceive and interact with one another, allowing a more nuanced understanding of the ways in which gendered roles could be constructed, subverted and transformed.[24]

Scholars have thus moved away from the tendency to study women in a vacuum and have sought instead to analyze how categories become established and reified, deconstructing what Scott called the appearance of 'timeless permanence in binary gender representation'.[25] Similarly, this has also involved a shift away from the dichotomy in which 'empowerment' discourses were countered by those that stressed the inevitable reassertion of patriarchy, and thus 'women's' inevitable victimization.[26] Attention to women's varied social roles – different combinations of, for example, marital statuses (single, married, widow), lifestyle choice (nun, beguine, the decision to remain a widow), profession, religion and class – can shed new light on the position of women in society without casting them in the role of victims of patriarchy or as exceptions overcoming the odds. Thus, the essays in *Women and Power in the Middle Ages*, *Aristocratic Women in Medieval France*, and *Singlewomen in the European Past* have focused on questions of agency and women's ability to exercise authority and power *within* the constraints of patriarchy.[27] Such an approach reveals – and acknowledges – not only the limitations for women within a society that constrained them economically, socially and sexually, but also the possibilities for alternative responses and the different ways in which women's social roles could allow them to manipulate, transform or subvert traditional hierarchies.[28]

In this volume, the essays by Francesca Canadé Sautman (Chapter 4: Constructing Political Rule, Transforming Gender Scripts) and Aislinn Loconte (Chapter 7: Constructing Female Sanctity in Late Medieval Naples) continue this investigation by showing how aristocratic women could exercise successful rule in the thirteenth and fourteenth centuries by harnessing the power granted to them as queens and countesses, and by manipulating the gender roles they were expected to play for their own ends. In her essay, Loconte shows how images on a funerary monument were used to construct and ultimately transform the image of Queen Sancia of Naples. Although Sancia's commitments as a ruler prevented her from entering a Franciscan convent, the queen was able to take advantage of her position of power to become a patron and advocate for the order. Her funerary monument, commissioned by her niece, depicted Sancia as the powerful queen, protector and patron she had been during her lifetime. Yet the representation on her tomb also transformed the image of Sancia as a secular ruler by associating her with two spiritually powerful – and above all holy – women, Clare of Assisi and the Blessed Virgin Mary. Loconte shows how, in a further play on gender, the monument used eucharistic imagery to suggest an association between Sancia and Christ, in one case even depicting Sancia in a Christ-like role surrounded by Franciscan nuns in what appears to be a 'feminized' version of the Last Supper. Through images, the queen is transformed: instead of remaining a powerful, secular figure, her visual identification with Christ also endows her with spiritual power. The image of Sancia in the place of Christ could be seen as an audacious form of *imitatio Christi*, yet it also confers a measure of religious authority on Sancia's secular rule and her actions.

Whereas Loconte deals with how power, gender and imagery could be used to negotiate a transformation between secular and religious spheres, Sautman discusses the intersections between gender and the exercise of power. Here she examines the examples of Joan and Margaret, two thirteenth-century countesses of Flanders, to show how, despite the perceived frailty of their sex, these women occupied prominent, powerful, positions usually reserved for men. Sautman nuances existing approaches to the reigns of these countesses, particularly in relation to the exercise of power, authority and warfare. She shows that, although gendered topoi were used in many attempts to subvert the countesses' rule, both women strategically applied their administrative strengths to subvert and transform the role of ruler. Her analysis suggests that the rule of Joan and Margaret was in fact part of a *longue durée* of female administrator-rulers in Flanders, one which parallels, and sometimes even replaces, that of the warrior-prince.

The fate of the male warrior-prince is also central to Fiona Dunlop's essay (Chapter 10: Mightier than the Sword) which is one of three essays in this volume, along with those of Alison More (Chapter 3: Convergence, Conversion and Transformation) and Cassandra Rhodes (Chapter 2 'What, after all, is a male virgin?'), that engage with the ever-growing field of masculinity studies. In fact, despite the forty years since gender studies began to develop as a discipline with its emphasis on patriarchy and male–female relations, and despite the fact that much traditional scholarship has been written by, for and about men, it is only relatively recently that scholars have addressed masculinity as a concept in itself and men as gendered beings. In 1995, the sociologist R.W. Connell gave the name 'hegemonic masculinity' to the non-specific masculine ideal by which other interpretations or performances of gender were and are marginalized or subordinated.[29] This ideal has pervaded interpretation and scholarship across all historical periods. In the Middle Ages, masculinity held a privileged position that was supported both physiologically and etymologically in medieval narratives, which has facilitated the idealization of the masculine by modern scholars and critics. Medieval medical theories held that masculine physiology was the result of ideal conditions before birth: if a favourable combination of humours existed, a foetus would be male, less than ideal circumstances ensured that it would be female. Linguistically, man or *vir* was named for his *virtus* or manly strength. Woman or *mulier* on the other hand derived her name from her softness or decadence (*mollitia*). Scholars have, however, begun to deconstruct this hegemonic masculinity, further problematizing gender binaries and acknowledging that masculine, like feminine, gender performances can vary according to factors such as religion, race, level of education and social status.[30] For instance, Ruth Mazo Karras divided her study of medieval masculinity, *From Boys to Men*, into three separate sections: the knight, the scholar and the craftsman, and Mathew Kuefler has explored the emergence of Christian masculinity, tracing the social and cultural influences of the classical world, as well as the emerging discourse of manly ideals from the Christian world.[31] Alexandra Sheppard demonstrates the formation of various types of masculine identity in relation to and in contrast with the prevailing patriarchy and Rosalind Brown-Grant and Andrea Pearson have explored the construction of courtly, chivalric masculinity in texts and images.[32] The plurality of masculine identities revealed in these studies demonstrates that an essentialist, culturally normative, or hegemonic, ideal of masculinity is impossible: it is surely significant that the plural term 'masculinities' now appears in studies more often than its singular equivalent.

Dunlop's essay in this volume examines a transformation in the constructions of manliness among the secular nobility at the beginning of the Tudor reign. She focuses on the volatility of a masculine ideal, which here moves away from one of physical strength to one which privileges the defensive and strategic powers of the subject's mind. As aristocrats became more dependent on the crown for advancement, and as they were increasingly in competition with non-nobles, it was ever more apparent that birth right and military prowess were no longer enough to ensure social promotion. At this time, the traditional model of the manly warrior was supplemented by one of 'learning and virtuous exercise' which, though present throughout the Middle Ages, was more emphasized for religious than for knights. Dunlop demonstrates this rethinking of noble masculinity through the verse text 'He who made this hous for contemplacion', which was added to a manuscript belonging to the Percy family. The poem contains a disputation between voices advocating the virtues of various and competing models of manliness and was intended to teach the Percy heir to construct a noble masculinity based on a paradigm which privileged control of the body (*virtuus exercyse and contemplacion*) and development of the mind (*exercyse of learning*) over military strength or political ambition. Dunlop shows that the Percys' search for new ways of signifying nobility – through literacy and study – reflects a wider anxiety about the performance of noble masculinity in the late fifteenth and early sixteenth centuries.

The virility of the male saintly subjects that Rhodes and More examine is emphasized through cultivation of virtue rather than physical strength, and through chastity or virginity rather than sexual conquest. Rhodes examines the role, function and portrayal of virginity in the lives of Anglo-Saxon male saints included in Aldhelm's late-seventh-century *De Virginitate* and Ælfric's late-tenth-century *Lives of the Saints*. Although previous studies of medieval masculinity have often linked questions of gender with issues of sexuality, they have rarely considered the heterogeneity of male virginity in the Anglo-Saxon period. Using these two texts, and drawing on five tropes of male virginity evident in Anglo-Saxon hagiography, Rhodes' analysis shows that virginity was perceived as something more complex than a physical state for the male saint. Instead, it could serve as, for instance, a locus of sanctity enabling the performance of miracles, a source of physical strength in battle, or a factor contributing to tortuous martyrdom. In analyzing virginity, Rhodes presents it both as a configuration of complex behaviours and as a masculine expression of sexual identity.

An exploration of hagiographic representations of the oscillating nature of gendered categories continues in More's article where she considers how, in saints' lives, the subject's journey towards holiness is portrayed through a series of transformations. In the *vitae* of female saints, this is often conveyed as the saint overcoming the limitations of her sex and achieving manly virtue (*virtus*). However, in addition to addressing images of the traditional 'virile woman', More explores gendered imagery in hagiographic texts portraying male saints from Liège. In the *vitae* of these men, subverting, blending and transforming gender can more accurately be seen as a journey away from any expression of sexual identity. The men More examines are portrayed as distancing themselves from masculine ideals, and become increasingly identified with their feminine souls (*animae*). Yet while these male subjects are indeed depicted using increasingly feminine textual imagery, their womanliness is a sign of strength rather than weakness. The 'womanly men' portrayed in these hagiographic texts have conquered the masculine weakness of the flesh. Although they are represented as feminine, they have, in fact, moved away from sexuality entirely.

The essays by More, Dunlop and Rhodes re-affirm that men, like their female contemporaries, performed and constructed identities framed by the fluid and adaptable language of gender. The notion that genders are themselves constructed in discourse and are then mapped back onto sexed bodies has opened up a wide debate on the relationship between sex, gender and linguistic expression.[33] Though semantic categories such as gender have remained stable, societies have constructed and re-shaped their symbolic and interpretive characteristics.[34] In this volume, the contributions by Helen Swift (Chapter 6: Representing Gender Identity in the Late Medieval French *Querelle des femmes*) and Jennifer Cavalli (Chapter 9: Fashioning Female Humanist Scholarship) explore the relationship between linguistic expression, gender metaphors and sexed bodies in fifteenth- and early sixteenth-century secular texts. Cavalli's essay on the early sixteenth-century writings of Laura Cereta deals with the power of the word in the construction of identity, showing how effective subversion can be accomplished through appropriation. She illustrates the ways in which Cereta made use of the contemporary perceptions of the limitations of her sex so as to overcome them. As a woman who aspired to participate in masculine, scholarly activity, it might be logical to expect Cereta, in her writings, to make use of the 'virile woman' concept, popular in the writings of Petrarch and Boccaccio. However, instead of claiming that she overcame the limitations of her sex by transcending her femininity, Cereta brought tales of domestic experience and incorporated imagery associated with the domestic sphere into the manly realm of scholarly endeavour. She thus fashioned an alternative type of literate woman who, by emphasizing rather than effacing constructed gender difference, was able to compete with men in a field from which women were traditionally excluded.

Swift's contribution also shows how masculine imagery was not always appropriated by women, or held up as an ideal state for them. Instead, in her essay, Swift offers a close reading of the gendered language and imagery in two French texts, Martin Le Franc's *Champion des dames* (1442), and Antoine Dufour's *Les Vies des femmes célèbres* (1504) in order to show how masculine imagery could be used to praise particular transitory stages or aspects of women's behaviour. Engaging with the radical androgyny that is implied in her title-quotation, 'Pourquoy appellerions nous ces choses differentes, qu'une heure, un moment, un mouvement peuvent rendre du tout semblables?', Swift demonstrates that the categories of masculinity and femininity are little more than complex symbolic webs that are mapped onto male and female bodies. She takes a striking example from the *Champion des dames*, which performs a remarkable recuperation, in woman's favour, of Ovid's myth of Hermaphroditus and Salmacis. The Champion sets up the desideratum of being transformed biologically from a male into a female as a way of advancing what we might call a new 'modèle héroïque féminin'. Swift also analyzes how Dufour's lives of famous women represents women's behaviour in the more nuanced and performative terms of 'drag', or 'wearing' masculine or feminine characteristics as a matter of expediency. In this way she shows that both gender and biological sex are constructed and adaptable, and it therefore comes as no surprise that gender, in her analysis, cannot be presented as a fixed and attainable ideal.

Gender constructions – and their subversions and transformations – are not only manifest in language but also in visual representations. Depictions of women have long been invoked as evidence of their roles in society, particularly for the medieval and early modern periods where textual evidence is often lacking.[35] Often, such studies have echoed the victim vs empowerment approach noted above, either by failing to interrogate the masculinist or patriarchal point of view from which images of women were created, or else reiterating the inevitability of patriarchy, most notably by evoking Laura Mulvey's concept of the masculine gaze and the objectified woman.[36] Whereas Mulvey's theory was taken up by medieval and early modern feminist art-historians and helped to bring women as both subjects and objects to the fore, as a methodological approach rooted specifically in film theory, it has tended to obscure female agency. In response to this, historians of art and visual culture have begun to explore instances where women took an active role in art production as patrons and viewers – roles traditionally seen as the privilege of men. For instance, the work of Adrian Randolph on the viewing of household objects in fifteenth-century Italy, Jeffrey Hamburger's studies of German nuns as viewers and makers of art, and the monumental *Patronnes et mécènes en France à la Renaissance* have contributed to a major reconsideration of women's roles in medieval and early modern visual and manuscript culture.[37] In this volume, Loconte's essay, discussed above, and those by Elizabeth L'Estrange (Chapter 8: *Deschi da parto* and Topsy-Turvy Gender Relations in Fifteenth-Century Italian Households) and Jennifer Borland (Chapter 5: Violence on Vellum) engage with specific instances where women viewed or commissioned monumental art, religious manuscripts and secular 'domestic' art from the twelfth through to the fifteenth century. Their contributions explore how these art objects not only promoted ideologies of gender but also allowed room for women to forge alternative or subversive interpretations even while those objects may have upheld other patriarchal notions.

Borland's essay explores the performativity of gender using the imagery that accompanies a manuscript *vita* of Margaret of Antioch and reveals the symbolic instability attributed to this saint. Her analysis shows that the images which depict Margaret's story oscillate between conventional gender boundaries. Though Margaret possesses the manly strength of faith, in her *vita* she is subject to torture and portrayed in the feminized role of victim. Through her reactions to the violence inflicted on her, Margaret reveals characteristics generally considered masculine. The pictorial and linguistic devices deployed in the manuscript portray her journey as one of transformation, from victim to hero, yet, in a construction more complex than simple masculinization, the threat of Margaret's power is expressed in the straddling of both gender categories and through her apparent refusal to stay in a position that is identifiable in terms of gendered norms. Borland's attention to the defacement of certain images in the Munich manuscript also allows her to analyze the viewer's direct engagement with the *vita* and the particular tactile quality and immediacy of images in the Middle Ages. She suggests that this reciprocal understanding of viewing implicates the audience in Margaret's transgressive status.

Whereas Borland's essay focuses on religious imagery, L'Estrange's essay deals with secular images of love and motherhood that were offered to lay women on birth trays (*deschi da parto*) in early modern Italy. Yet L'Estrange, like Borland, also emphasizes the tactility and proximity involved in viewing: *deschi da parto* were intended to be handled, and served a practical function, mediating between the enclosed, female-dominated birth chamber and the 'masculine' world outside. Furthermore, these birth trays were frequently decorated with what can be described as prescriptive imagery, showing secular birth scenes and baby boys that were intended to feed the 'maternal imagination'. They were often given by men to women to help them conceive legitimate heirs and thus protect the patriline. However, L'Estrange avoids an essentialist correlation between the female recipients of these trays and their idealized images of maternity and marital love. In fact, these trays often also incorporated images of the popular 'woman on top' topos, such as Phyllis riding Aristotle which, although also ostensibly didactic in nature, hint at another set of possible, disrupting, interpretations. L'Estrange shows how the subversive potential of these topsy-turvy images would have been brought into sharp focus for the female viewer by the change in power dynamics in a household that was occasioned by a birth, where the woman was placed 'on top' in the family. She thus argues that *deschi da parto* not only constructed and upheld traditional expectations of women as wives and mothers within Tuscan families, but could also be interpreted in a more subversive way by the women who received them. As is the case for the audience of the funerary monument discussed in Loconte's essay, the images in Borland and L'Estrange's essays can be read as both depicting and encouraging the fluidity, transformation and subversion of existing gendered paradigms.

The essays presented here reveal that gender was as unstable and multifaceted in the past as it is considered to be today. The volatility which exists within the category of gender both constitute and reinforce its fragile and constructed nature. By exploring the way or ways in which gender is both rooted in and shaped by a particular social and historical context, the contributions demonstrate that multiple expressions of femininity and masculinity existed in both religious and secular society, and that they could be transformed and subverted by both men and women. By exploring the shifting and unstable paradigms of gender, our contributors have been able to find meaning in its changeability and thus to expand our understanding of its use as an analytical tool. In their critical approaches or in their material, they have sought to look beyond binary oppositions and the desire to categorize, seeking instead to tease out the multiple literary and pictorial expressions of gender construction, transformation and subversion in the medieval and early modern periods.

Notes

1. Joan W. Scott, 'Gender: A Useful Category of Historical Analysis', *The American Historical Review*, 91 (1986), 1053–75 (p. 1068).

2. On the citation of Scott, see Alexandra Sheppard and Garthine Walker, 'Gender, Change and Periodisation', *Gender and History*, 20 (2008), 453–62 (p. 455). Scott herself reflects on the importance of gender and the influence of her article in a 2010 article. See Joan W. Scott, 'Gender: Still a useful Category of Analysis', *Diogenes*, 225 (2010), 7–14.

3. On categories of analysis, see Jeanne Boydston, 'Gender as a Question of Historical Analysis', *Gender and History*, 20 (2008), 558–83.

4. Judith Butler, *Gender Trouble: Feminism and the Subversion of Identity* (London: Routledge, 1990; repr. 1999); and *Bodies that Matter: On the Discursive Limits of 'Sex'* (London and New York: Routledge, 1993). Studies which draw upon Butler include *Bodily Citations: Religion and Judith Butler*, ed. Ellen T. Armour and Susan St. Ville (New York: Columbia University Press, 2006); and Amy Hollywood, *Sensible Ecstasy: Mysticism, Sexual Difference, and the Demands of History* (Chicago: University of Chicago Press, 2002).

5. Patricia Hill Collins, *Black Feminist Thought: Consciousness and the Politics of Empowerment* (New York: Routledge, 1990, repr. 2000).

6. *Gender and Difference in the Middle Ages* ed. Sharon Farmer and Carol Braun Pasternack (Minneapolis: University of Minnesota Press, 2001); *Constructing Medieval Sexuality*, ed. Karma Lochrie, Peggy McCracken and James Schultz (Minneapolis: University of Minnesota Press, 1997); *Presenting Gender: Changing Sex in Early Modern Culture*, ed. Chris Mounsey (London: Associated University Presses, 2001); *Gender and Christianity in Medieval Europe: New Perspectives*, ed. Lisa M. Bitel and Felice Lifshitz (Philadelphia: University of Pennsylvania Press, 2008). Cf. *Saints, Scholars, and Politicians: Gender as a Tool in Medieval Studies*, ed. Mathilde van Dijk and Renée Nip (Turnhout: Brepols, 2005).

7. Scott, 'Gender', p. 1056.

8. In addition to Scott, 'Gender', see Ann Oakley, 'A Brief History of Gender', in *Who's Afraid of Feminism: Seeing Through the Backlash*, ed. Ann Oakley and Juliet Mitchell (New York: The New Press, 1997), pp. 29–55. For reviews on the development of medieval gender studies see the essays in Farmer and Pasternack, *Gender and Difference*; the essays in the special edition of *Speculum*, 68 (1993), ed. Nancy Partner which focus on medieval studies and feminism; and Bitel and Lifshitz, *Gender and Christianity*.

9. 'Genera dicta sunt ab eo quod generant', see *Commentarius in artem Donati*, ed. Heinrich Keil, *Grammatici Latini*, 7 vols (Leipzig: B.G. Teubner, 1864), iv, p. 407. Cf. Isidore of Seville, 'Etymologiarum', c. 11, par. 17–18, *PL* 82, col. 417. Scott, 'Gender', pp. 1053–54.

10.   *Commentarius in artem Donati*, pp. 407–408.

11.   Harriet Bradley, *Gender* (Cambridge: Polity, 2007), p. 14. For an extended discussion of Servius' distinction, see Julia M.H. Smith, 'Introduction: Gendering the Early Medieval World', in *Gender in the Early Medieval World: East and West, 300–900*, ed. Leslie Brubaker and Julia M.H. Smith (Cambridge: Cambridge University Press, 2004), pp. 1–19 (p. 5).

12.   Ann Oakley, *Sex, Gender and Society* (San Francisco: HarperCollins, 1972), pp. 158–72. Derek Neal offers a nuanced perspective, which emphasizes that although gender is ultimately constructed, the role of physiology in that construction should not be overlooked. See Derek Neal, *The Masculine Self in Medieval England* (Chicago: University of Chicago Press, 2008), pp. 124–28 and 150–56.

13.   Oakley later addressed the development of gender studies in her work in the late 1990s. See Ann Oakley, 'A Brief History of Gender'; cf. Alison Shaw, 'Changing Sex and Bending Gender: An Introduction', in *Changing Sex and Bending Gender*, ed. Alison Shaw and Shirley Ardener (New York: Berghahn Books, 2005), pp. 1–19; Boydston, 'Gender', p. 559.

14.   Butler, *Gender Trouble*, pp. 59–66; Denise Riley, *Am I that Name?* (Minneapolis: University of Minnesota Press, 2003); Chris Mounsey, 'Introduction', in *Presenting Gender*, pp. 11–23. Cf. Sheppard and Walker, 'Gender, Change and Periodisation', pp. 455–56. Emphasis on gender as a category of analysis has led to studies such as *Landscape and Gender: Renegotiating Morality and Space*, ed. Josephine Carubia, Lorraine Dowler and Bonj Szczygiel (London: Routledge, 2005); and *Gendering Global Transformations: Gender, Culture, Race, and Identity*, ed. Chima J. Koriehand and Philomena E. Okeke-Ihejirika (London: Routledge, 2008).

15.   Butler, *Gender Trouble*, pp. 101–107; Jeffrey Jerome Cohen, *Medieval Identity Machines* (Minneapolis: University of Minnesota Press, 2003), pp. 84–86; Bradley, *Gender*, pp. 59–74.

16.   Martha Newman, 'Real Men and Imaginary Women: Engelhard of Langheim Considers a Woman in Disguise', *Speculum*, 78 (2003), 1184–213; Elizabeth Castelli, 'I Will Make Mary Male: Pieties of the Body and Gender Transformation of Christian Women in Late Antiquity', in *Body Guards: The Cultural Politics of Gender Ambiguity*, ed. Julia Epstein and Kristina Straub (New York and London: Routledge, 1991), pp. 29–49.

17.   Newman, 'Real Men', pp. 1190–91, 1203–205; Barbara Newman, *From Virile Woman to Woman Christ: Studies in Medieval Religion and Literature* (Philadelphia: University of Pennsylvania Press, 1995), pp. 182, 239.

18.   Shaun Tougher, 'Social Transformation, Gender Transformation? The Court Eunuch 300–900', in *Gender in the Early Medieval World*, pp. 70–82.

19.   Monica Green, *Making Women's Medicine Masculine: The Rise of Male Authority in Premodern Gynecology* (Oxford: Oxford University Press, 2008); see also her 'Gendering the History of Women's Healthcare', and Martha Howell, 'The Gender of Europe's Commercial Economy, 1200–1700', both in *Gender and History*, 20 (2008), 487–518 and 519–38.

20.   Mathew Kuefler, *The Manly Eunuch: Masculinity, Gender Ambiguity and Christian Ideology in Late Antiquity* (Chicago and London: University of Chicago Press, 2001).

21.   See Butler, *Gender Trouble*, pp. 3–11, and Gillian Beer, 'Representing Women, Re-Presenting the Past', in *The Feminist Reader*, ed. Catherine Belsey and Jane Moore (London: Blackwell, 1989), pp. 77–90.

22.   See for example Bynum's *Holy Feast and Holy Fast: The Religious Significance of Food to Medieval Women* (Berkeley: University of California Press, 1987); and Klapisch-Zuber's *Women, Family, and Ritual in Renaissance Italy*, trans. Lydia G. Cochrane (Chicago: University of Chicago Press, 1985), especially her chapter on 'Holy Dolls', pp. 310–29.

23.   Aers's analysis draws on Butler's critique of Julia Kristeva's (maternal) body politics. See David Aers and Lynn Staley, *The Powers of the Holy: Religion, Politics, and Gender in Late Medieval Culture* (Philadelphia: University of Pennsylvania State Press, 1996), esp. pp. 28–39; for other critiques of the normalized place of maternity in late medieval representations, see Kathleen Biddick, 'Genders, Bodies, Borders: Technologies of the Visible', *Speculum*, 68 (1993), 389–418; Nicholas Watson, 'Desire for the Past', *Studies in the Age of Chaucer*, 21 (1999), 78–81; Ulinka Rublack, 'Female Spirituality and the Infant Jesus in Late Medieval Dominican Convents', *Gender and History*, 6 (1994), 37–57. For a discussion of images of motherhood and childbearing from the fifteenth century that aims to avoid an essentialist approach, see Elizabeth L'Estrange, *Holy Motherhood: Gender, Dynasty and Visual Culture in the Later Middle Ages* (Manchester: Manchester University Press, 2008).

24. *Gendered Voices: Medieval Saints and their Interpreters*, ed. Catherine M. Mooney (Philadelphia: University of Pennsylvania Press, 1999); *Gendering the Master Narrative: Women and Power in the Middle Ages*, ed. Mary C. Erler and Maryanne Kowaleski (Ithaca: Cornell University Press, 2003). See also, John Coakley, *Women, Men and Spiritual Power: Female Saints and Their Male Interpreters* (New York: Columbia University Press, 2006).

25. On reification see Aers and Staley, *The Powers of the Holy*, pp. 18–19.

26. On the way this approach has characterized feminist approaches to history in general, see Ludmilla Jordanova, *History in Practice* (London: Edwards Arnold, 2000).

27. *Women and Power in the Middle Ages*, ed. Mary C. Erler and Maryanne Kowaleski (Georgia: University of Georgia Press, 1994); *Aristocratic Women in Medieval France*, ed. Theodore Evergates (Philadelphia: University of Pennsylvania Press, 1999); Judith Bennett and Amy Froide, *Singlewomen in the European Past, 1250–1800* (Philadelphia: University of Pennsylvania Press, 1999). See also Sheppard and Walker, 'Gender, Change and Periodisation', p. 454.

28. The special issue of the *Journal of Medieval History*, 34 (2008), edited by Monica Green, looks at the interaction between Jewish, Christian and Muslim women in a number of different areas, including healthcare, money lending and slavery, in medieval Europe. For an examination of the ways in which women's secular leadership could become entwined with religious practice, see Erin Jordan, *Women, Power, and Religious Patronage in the Middle Ages* (New York: Palgrave Macmillan, 2006), pp. 61–110.

29. R.W. Connell, *Masculinities* (Cambridge: Polity Press, 1995), pp. 76–81. Cf. R.W. Connell, 'The Social Organization of Masculinity', in *The Masculinities Reader*, ed. Stephen M. Whitehall and Frank J. Barrett (Cambridge: Polity, 2001), pp. 30–51 (pp. 31–32). As Alexandra Sheppard has demonstrated, 'hegemonic masculinity' is dependent on relations between groups of men as between men and women. See, Sheppard, *Meanings of Manhood in Early Modern England* (Oxford: Oxford University Press, 2006), pp. 1–13.

30. Cf. Anthony Synnott, *Re-thinking Men: Heroes, Villains and Victims* (Farnham: Ashgate, 2009), pp. 11–54; Sheppard, *Meanings of Manhood*, pp. 21–92.

31. Ruth Mazo Karras, *From Boys to Men: Formations of Masculinity in Late Medieval Europe* (Pennsylvania: University of Pennsylvania Press, 2003); Kuefler, *The Manly Eunuch*.

32. Sheppard, *Meanings of Manhood*; Rosalind Brown-Grant, *French Romance of the Later Middle Ages: Gender, Morality, and Desire* (Oxford: Oxford University Press, 2008); Andrea Pearson, *Envisioning Gender in Burgundian Devotional Art, 1350–1530: Experience, Authority, Resistance* (Aldershot: Ashgate, 2005).

33. Gabrielle Spiegel, 'Introduction', in *Practising History: New Directions in Historical Writing After the Linguistic Turn* (London and New York: Routledge, 2005). Cf. Maria Polinsky and Ezra van Everbroeck, 'Development of Gender Classifications: Modelling the Historical Change from Latin to French', *Language*, 79 (2003), 356–90 (p. 358).

34. John Toews, 'Intellectual History after the Linguistic Turn: The Autonomy of Meaning and the Irreducibility of Experience', *American Historical Review*, 92 (1987), 879–907 (p. 882).

35. For a critical analysis of the use of images as historical evidence, see Martha W. Driver, 'Mirrors of a Collective Past: Re-Considering Images of Medieval Women', in *Women and the Book: Assessing the Visual Evidence*, ed. Lesley Smith and Jane H.M. Taylor (London: The British Library and Toronto University Press, 1997), pp. 75–93.

36. Laura Mulvey, 'Visual Pleasure and Narrative Cinema', in her *Visual and Other Pleasures* (Basingstoke: Macmillan, 1989), pp. 14–26. Studies influenced by Mulvey include Patricia Simons, 'Women in Frames: The Gaze, the Eye, the Profile in Renaissance Portraiture', *History Workshop*, 25 (1988), 4–30, and Madeleine H. Caviness, 'Patron or Matron? A Capetian Bride and a *Vade Mecum* for her Marriage Bed', *Speculum*, 68 (1993), 333–62.

37. *Patronnes et mécènes en France à la Renaissance*, ed. Kathleen Wilson-Chevalier (St-Etienne: Presse universitaire St-Etienne, 2007); Adrian W.B. Randolph, 'Renaissance Household Goddesses: Fertility, Politics, and the Gendering of Spectatorship', in *The Material Culture of Sex, Marriage and Procreation in Premodern Europe*, ed. Anne L. McClaren and Karen Rosoff Encarnación (New York: Palgrave, 2001), pp. 163–89; and 'Gendering the Period Eye: *Deschi Da Parto* and Renaissance Visual Culture', *Art History*, 27 (2004), 538–62; Jeffrey Hamburger, *Nuns as Artists: The Visual Culture of a Medieval Convent* (Berkeley: University of California Press, 1997); and *The Visual and the Visionary: Art and Female Spirituality in Late Medieval Germany* (New York: Zone Books, 1998); see also the special edition of *Medieval Feminist Forum*, 44 (2008), on feminist approaches to medieval visual culture, ed. Marian Bleeke.

2

'What, after all, is a male virgin?'[1] Multiple Performances of Male Virginity in Anglo-Saxon Saints' Lives

Cassandra Rhodes

Hagiographic texts from Anglo-Saxon England depict a variety of models of male sanctity. Regardless of their differences in content and date, the majority of these narratives make some reference to these male spiritual figureheads as chaste or virginal. Scholars of later medieval masculine virginity have identified male saints who were tested with carnal temptations, who used virginity to legitimize a break in royal succession, or who became virgins through a semantic association with tropes familiar from female virgin *passiones*. However, despite growing interest in this area of study, Anglo-Saxon writings about saints have received comparatively little attention.[2] This essay examines the representations of male virginity in two Anglo-Saxon prose hagiographic works, Aldhelm's late seventh-century Latin *De Virginitate* and the late tenth-century vernacular works of Ælfric. Scholars working on the later medieval period have convincingly argued that virginity is performed and, employing Judith Butler's theoretical stance, posit that virginity actually constitutes a third gender, where virginal behaviours 'can be categorized as neither masculine nor feminine but proper to virgins'.[3] This essay will assess whether this is the case in representations of male saintly virginity in these Anglo-Saxon *Lives*.

There is a three-century gap in the production of Aldhelm's and Ælfric's manuscripts, and it is not the aim here to conflate the two texts in meaning or purpose, but rather to explore the multiplicity of Anglo-Saxon male saintly virginities across this period. Aldhelm, writing during the period of conversion when double monasteries were relatively common, had a very different audience to Ælfric, who is thought to have composed his *Lives of Saints* for the royal military advisor Æthelweard and his son Æthelmær.[4] While Ælfric's intended audience largely appears to have been lay men who are likely not to have followed the path of virginal devotion, Aldhelm wrote specifically for the religious, unprecedentedly creating a list of both female and male saints as virginal exemplars. He dedicated his work to Abbess Hildelith of Barking among others, seeking to replace a family model of biological ties with one based on the avoidance of carnal activity, and focused instead on the family of the Church.[5] By pairing these two texts, this discussion will evidence an under-examined preoccupation with male, as well as female, virginity in Anglo-Saxon texts and will propose an answer to Maud Burnett McInerney's question posed in the title of this essay: 'What, after all, is a male virgin?'

Whereas female saints in the Anglo-Saxon corpus are almost always virgin martyrs or virgin abbesses, whose virginity is always discussed with reference to their bodies, their male counterparts represent a variety of religious and secular aristocratic spheres, and their virgin sexuality is intertwined with multiple aspects of their lives.[6] This essay identifies five ways in which male virginity is presented in the works of Aldhelm and Ælfric: a nominal or minimal feature of a life; a locus of sanctity enabling the performance of miracles; a source of strength in physical battle; a factor contributing to torturous martyrdom, on one occasion specifically resulting from the refusal to relinquish virginity and, finally, as a signifier demonstrating Christian identity through victory in the battle with carnal temptation. It will be argued that the often perceived binary division of female Anglo-Saxon saints *Lives* as purely concerned with the performance of virginity, and the converse absence of this preoccupation in male saints' *Lives*, is illusory and has led to an underestimation of the significance of virginity for male saints.[7] Although there is not the space here to examine all of the saints from the two works at length, a table at the end of the essay lists the relevant saints and page references for all male virgin saints in Aldhelm's and Ælfric's texts (see pp. 31–32).

The potential for re-evaluating binary gender divisions in Anglo-Saxon hagiographic texts does not appear immediately promising. Some of the *Lives* only briefly state that these men are virgins. Others centralize virginity in the saint's sanctity, but present it as static, not portraying the behaviour as necessary to achieve this ideal and thus not centralizing the motif as the primary route to sanctity.[8] Aldhelm's entries of this type are often obscurely metaphorical. He describes Ambrose's virginity through the metaphor of bees; his 'pure virginity' is prefigured when, as a baby, a swarm flies into his mouth leaving him unharmed.[9] Taking authority from the *Physiologus*, a second-century Greek text of uncertain authorship, the bee was frequently used as a symbol of virginity in the Middle Ages, due to its apparent ability to procreate without sexual intercourse. Worker bees in particular were thought of as chaste creatures, and so 'signify a type of virginity and the likeness of the Church'.[10] The asexual bees enter Ambrose's body and fertilize him with Christian faith which he in turn reproduces in his writings.

Aldhelm describes no subsequent episodes testifying to Ambrose's virginity as signifier of sanctity. Similarly, while claiming that Gregory conserves his 'undefiled purity with tireless energy in every way', Aldhelm does not elaborate on how he succeeds in this quest.[11] Gregory's virginal performance therefore occurs out of the audience's gaze. Similarly, Ælfric reports that Basil claimed 'that he never in his life came near a woman by cohabitation but he kept his virginity' ('þæt he næfre on his life ne come neah wife þurh hæmed-þing ac heold his clænnysse'),[12] but makes no further reference to this aspect of his sanctity. Aldhelm's description of the Old Testament prophet Jeremiah perhaps most explicitly demonstrates this particular narrative trope, since the prophet is described as born for virginity, '"before thou camest forth out of the womb, I sanctified thee" (Jeremiah 1:5), that is, by the beautiful prophecy of virginity'.[13] The *Lives* of male saints are less singularly located in virginity than their female counterparts. Ælfric's Basil is benevolent and charitable. He heals and converts pagans and Jews and successfully prays for the forgiveness of sinners. His virginity constitutes only once sentence of a *vita* that fills twenty pages of Old English in an edition edited by Walter Skeat.[14] These brief examples of male virginity uphold rather than destabilize binary gender divisions – while women generally enact their virginity by dramatically resisting a physical assault on their chastity, for these men, virginity is automatically assumed and does not have to be proved.

Elsewhere in *De Virginitate*, Aldhelm states that virginity is not merely a biological state. Instead, he describes it as one which evolves 'in the manner of happy youth, [which] continually flourishes and is constantly growing'.[15] His comment that 'carnal integrity is in no way approved of unless spiritual purity is associated with it as companion' implies that it is not enough simply to be a virgin in the biological sense.[16] This must be accompanied by virginal behaviour in a social context. Such theorizing is evident elsewhere in patristic and Anglo-Saxon theological thought, particularly in Augustine's claim (later used by Ælfric), that raped women can remain virgins if they resist in both body and mind.[17] Virginity as an identity which evolves and is strengthened through performed behaviour, is however, in the *Lives* of the men examined thus far, nullified. So far, the portrayals have been of complete stasis but this is not the case in all of the *Lives*.

Aldhelm, unlike Ælfric, presents virginity as the locus of sanctity from which miracles occur.[18] In the cases of these saints, their virginity is expressed through the miracles that they perform. Aldhelm pinpoints virginity as the virtue which facilitates sanctity and prioritizes it in his narrative before listing the ensuing miracles. Because of this structure the men, to some extent, demonstrate their virginity through a method of performance which Aldhelm seems to gender as male. In Aldhelm, miracles as 'essential qualifiers of sanctity, are overwhelmingly a male activity', with far more miracles occurring in the *Lives* of male saints than those of female saints.[19] For instance, the Old Testament prophets Elisha and Elijah perform miracles entirely because of their virginity. Elisha, 'because of the distinction of his virginal modesty', divides the River Jordan, makes a bear eat some children mocking the Christian word and brings a corpse back to life.[20] Elijah triumphs over nature making it rain, due to 'the favour of virginity'.[21] In contrast, Aldhelm's female virgins are less active in the working of miracles, being more likely to invoke God's power than influence natural phenomena themselves.[22]

Aldhelm also allies virginity with miracles which overcome the punishments God placed on post-lapsarian society. Jerome links Adam and Eve's virginity before the Fall with their prompt matrimony afterwards, when they became 'joined together', with all of the connotations of the conjugal bond.[23] Thus, virginity is connected with the paradisal state, and carnality with the temporal. In Aldhelm's depiction of Elijah, the prophet remains 'aloof from the general destiny of death which all people [...] fettered by the bonds of the first transgression, are compelled to pay'.[24] Similarly, in Aldhelm's description of John, 'dust bubbles up from the vault of his sepulchre [...] as if with alternating inhalations of someone breathing'.[25] The removal of these male virgins from the constraints of sinful humanity is manifested in Aldhelm's portrayal of virginal miracles, where male saints such as Martin of Tours and Apollonius are both linked with angelic forces.[26]

However, miracles are not a distinctive indicator or quality of the virginal state, and many saints not described as virgins also perform miracles. It therefore seems pertinent to consider why Aldhelm's *De Virginitate* only focuses on the performance of miracles as an indicator of virginity. Aldhelm writes specifically on virginity rather than collating and authoring a collection of texts designed to encourage the reader in all aspects of religious devotion and promote the Benedictine coenobitic ideal, as Ælfric does.[27] Most of these miracle virgins are not even included by Ælfric. Holy male virgins who perform miracles project the sanctity of their virginity onto other people and external natural phenomena. Though virginal, they are productive, generative and fertile forces – like the bees that figure so widely in Aldhelm's work – who spread and enact the Christian word through their miraculous behaviour.[28] Aldhelm's depictions of miraculous male virgins show virginity to be considered as a dynamic trait. Emma Pettit argues that Aldhelm aligns these men, through their miracles, with an 'active spiritual potency' which resonates with secular models of medieval masculinity and authority.[29] However, while miracles verify the spiritual potency of these male virgins, they do not bear witness to the evolution of their virginal identity. Unlike the *vitae* of female virgins, these men's virginity does not develop during the narrative as a signifier of spiritual integrity; it simply goes unquestioned.

Scholars have frequently noted that the female virgin martyr legends display a pervasive concern with the body as spectacle, where tortures are watched by both torturer and public.[30] In these legends, the displays and exploits of the women's bodies, through their symbolic stances and eloquent reactions to bodily violations, signify the truth of their spiritual devotion. The bodies of the male virgins examined thus far did not act as discursive canvases upon which to write virginal identifiers. Kathleen Coyne Kelly argues that male literary virginity is less definable than that of their female counterparts. She considers that the male body is not objectified in the same way as the female, but may be feminized.[31] However, in Aldhelm's depiction of the chastely married martyr Julian, the spectacle of his immersion into a vat of burning sulphurous bitumen in front of a bawdy crowd undeniably objectifies his body.[32]

The virginal identity of some of these saints is inherently attached to their physicality. Narratives of male saintly virginity from both the seventh and tenth centuries appropriate motifs of battle in promoting the sanctity of male virgins, providing the saints with superhuman physical prowess in a typically masculine sphere. As is evident from Alison More's essay in this volume, such motifs continued to be present in the *Lives* of holy men from the high Middle Ages. In her study of twelfth-century monastic life, Jacqueline Murray examines how many men who entered the Church came from the military aristocracy, noting that 'the tensions that resulted from leaving one world and entering another reveal how men sought to reconcile their masculinity within two coexistent but contradictory belief systems: secular virility military power and the opposing spiritual chastity.[33] Patricia Cullum notes that 'aspects of the religious life required the setting aside of emblems of masculine authority or autonomy which might have implications for the subject's sense of his own masculinity and others' views of it'. In Cullum's view, this has lead to a situation in which, in some constructions of religious chastity, men are modelled as warriors.[34] Such imagery is appropriate in an Anglo-Saxon context, particularly given Ælfric's Christian warrior audience of military advisor Æthelweard and his son Æthelmær, and serves to create a Christian masculine elite in harmony with approved secular models.[35]

Before cataloguing his saintly ideals of virginity, Aldhelm describes how Christ's virgins of both sexes 'must fight with muscular energy against the horrendous monster of Pride' and other vices, urging them to violently destroy those who are spiritually 'unarmed and despoiled of the breastplate of virginity'.[36] He urges the virgins away from effeminacy, calling them to arms as 'combatants in the monastic armies'.[37] Described in the concrete lexicon of battle, this is mental or spiritual, not physical, warfare. Sinéad O'Sullivan argues that the equation of virginity with masculine warrior ethics in Aldhelm largely refers to female virginity, finding that he follows the model found in the *Psychomachia* of personifying vices and virtues as female.[38] However, if, as Scott Gwara convincingly argues, the audience of *De Virginitate* incorporated male and female monastics, then references to warrior virgins can equally apply to the male religious.[39] Aldhelm clearly aligns his male virgins, members of the chaste religious rather than heterosexual lay family units, with powerful masculine structures through military lexis. Both Pettit and George Dempsey examine Aldhelm's work, and argue that the virgin in battle is relevant to early Anglo-Saxon society. Dempsey contends that Aldhelm aims to create a version of virginity as heroic ideal, concomitant with the Germanic code and understood by an Anglo-Saxon society permeated by bloody internecine battle.[40] Pettit makes her argument gender specific, locating this depiction in the context of changeable notions of holiness and masculinity in medieval culture. She considers that the transmission from secular to religious life posed more cultural difficulties for men than women, deeming Aldhelm's warrior model to enable the redirection of martial energy into 'a new type of service for Christ'.[41] Some of the Anglo-Saxon *Lives* take this mental battle further, to actual military victory against enemies of the Christian faith.

One particularly prominent motif linking virginity and strength is the slaying of dragons, illustrated in Aldhelm's depictions of the virgin saints Silvester and Hilarion. Silvester, 'relying on [the] uncontaminated chastity of [the] body and endowed with the abstemiousness of continual abstinence' punishes a dragon by collaring him.[42] Similarly, Hilarion slays a dragon which has been terrorizing a Dalmatian community, by compelling it to ascend a pyre, and then burning it.[43] The reader is told 'Oh how great is the force of virginity, which curbed the insanity of a raging monster with a humble prayer'.[44] Perhaps, as Pettit argues, the slaying of dragons, symbolic of a lack of civility and sin, allows these virginal men access to secular models of masculine warriorhood through displays of physical strength.[45] If so, Aldhelm succeeds in synthesizing accepted models of authoritative masculinity with devotion to religious virginity.

The motif of battle is also apparent in Ælfric's *Life* of Martin of Tours where Martin's virginity is not unequivocally explicit. However, he is described in lexis similar to that which Ælfric uses to describe female virgins as being undefiled by worldly pollution.[46] Martin also advocates virginity to his monks, has heavenly visions of the Blessed Virgin Mary as well as the holy virgins Thecla and Agnes, and is received into heaven by a company of virgins.[47] Ælfric's employment of martial imagery varies significantly from other vernacular versions.[48] Aldhelm does not mention Martin's military credentials, whereas Ælfric manipulates his sources, making this the focus of the early part of the *Life*.[49] Ælfric relates how Martin was born into the soldier's life and fought in the Roman army in his youth.[50] Martin goes to battle unarmed, under God's spiritual protection, presenting the perfect opportunity for his corporeal body to be threatened violently, yet this spectacle does not occur.

Ælfric proclaims that while the omnipotent God could protect Martin in this way due to the strength of his faith, he prefers to shield Martin's eyes from death by preventing the battle completely.[51]

Martin's corporeal body is not ignored by Ælfric. However, while he recounts that Martin is scourged with whips by pagan soldiers, leaving him with bleeding limbs and beaten body ('blodigum limum and to-beatenum lichaman'), his injuries bear no relation to the grotesque manner in which some of the female virgin martyrs are killed.[52] Martin is dignified under torture, but, unlike the women, has to be rescued by his companions. His tortures are not inflicted because he refuses to relinquish his virginity, but because of his general Christian conviction. In Aldhelm's depictions of Silvester and Hilarion, their bodies are not even mentioned. Their battles are utterly one-sided victories. While Martin in particular displays the eloquence and steadfast determination that are some of the pervasive distinctions of the virgin, his body is not presented as immutable in the same way as those of the women.[53]

The apex of the performance of virginity in the *Lives* of female virgins is normally their torturous martyrdom since it reveals the truth of their virginal identity and Christian conviction. Robert Mills discusses pain and torture in later hagiography concerning male saints, and aspects of his analysis resonate with these earlier male *Lives*. Employing Freudian and post-Freudian theory to examine the relationship between 'representation' and 'desire', he convincingly argues that pain is not just a physiological fact, but is imbued with cultural significance. He comments that in martyrdom narratives 'corporeal agony becomes [...] positively sought after as a mnemonic tool and ultimately as a means of triumph'.[54] Torture is useful in the saintly construction of virginal identity, since the saints' behaviour under torture, and the representation of their bodies as corporeal sights, help to locate their victory as virgins of Christ.[55] Such an interpretation has been widely explored in *Lives* of female saints, but less fully examined in those of their male contemporaries. Yet, various male virgin saints from Anglo-Saxon texts are presented as using torture and bodily pain with exactly this level of self-awareness.

In Ælfric's depiction of the martyr Edmund, the king refuses to surrender to the Vikings, and declares that he would rather die than turn from Christianity. The reader is left more acutely aware of the theological implications through an inversion of the heroic motif of a warrior dressing for battle. Edmund's performance of disarming purposefully renders his body vulnerable to physical attack, an enactment of belief resulting in the willing sacrifice of his earthly life. His eloquent passivity in the face of torture does not represent powerlessness, but power.[56] He seeks to protect the inheritance of his people and in imagery of cleanliness often associated with the chaste existence, refuses to 'defile my clean hands with thy foul blood' ('afylan on þinum fulum blode mine clænan handa'). Edmund chooses to harness the usefulness of torture, but there is a tension between whether this is due to his virginity or nationalistic desire to set an example of Christian resistance to his country. Perhaps he does both. Edmund represents multiple models of sanctity in different versions of his *Life*.[57] This fluidity is apparent in Ælfric's version of his martyrdom, since it attests to both the nationalistic and virginal features of his saintliness.

Edmund's virginity is only explicit at the climax of the *passio*: the translation of his incorrupt body. The audience is told that his body which remains undecayed shows us that he lived in this world without fornication.[58] His incorrupt body, like that of female royal Anglo-Saxon virgin saint Æthelthryth, provides a central feature of his sanctity and is inextricably linked with his virginity. In her analysis of the hagiographic construction of Edward the Confessor who was canonized in the 1160s, Joanne Huntingdon notes that similar attention to the male virginal corpse occurs in Osbert of Clare's *Life of Edward*. She asserts that 'the incorruption of Edward's corpse – linked with his virginity – is stressed, and he is placed in the context of English kings who were holy by virtue of virginity, as opposed to martyrdom'.[59] Edmund's sanctity is a fusion of both his virginity and martyrdom, with his martyrdom acting as a prelude which performatively establishes the theme of rejecting pagan sin, specifically carnality. The fact that his sanctity is linked to his bodily acts is further emphasized by the description of a widow cutting the hair and nails from his corpse and keeping them enshrined as powerful relics to help others.[60]

In the accounts of posthumous miracles which form the closing episodes to Ælfric's *passio*, the incorrupt virginal body of Edmund becomes a site and sight of spectacle and spiritual power. We are informed that Leofstan arrives at the shrine of Edmund and arrogantly commands the monks guarding him to reveal the saint to him, to enable him to see Edmund's alleged, famed incorruption.[61] The monks oblige and 'as soon as he saw the saint's body, then he straightaway raved and roared horribly, and miserably ended by an evil death' ('swa hraðe swa he geseah þæs sanctes lichaman þa awedde he sona and wæl-hreowlice grymetede and earmlice geendode yfelum deaðe').[62]

Leofstan's wish to see Edmund is voyeuristic. Edmund's virginal body has become a site of spiritual power and Leofstan desires to control the image, wanting to find the tale of his incorruption false. However, 'vision can have an unsettling effect on subjective boundaries'.[63] His gaze aims to objectify Edmund and nullify his spiritual potency, yet its result is the opposite. Slavoj Žižek's reading of the Lacanian gaze is here useful in an analysis of vision in Ælfric's narrative. Žižek argues that the gaze is a disturbing force; it does not allow a binary division between object and subject, but rather 'marks the point in the object (in the picture) from which the subject viewing it is already gazed at, i.e., it is the object that is gazing at me'.[64] Edmund has become a source of corporeal spectacle; an object for consumption. However, Edmund is not presented simply as an object. Rather, his corpse looks back at Leofstan, countering his gaze and overpowering it in a defiant message of virginal faith, a message which drives Leofstan mad and ultimately kills him. Leofstan does not understand the Christian narrative which Edmund's corpse symbolizes, and is rendered helpless. For this male virgin, being a corporeal sight is part of a spiritual contest and one which becomes more potent and more effective the more that he is seen.

The economy of sight is exploited in the martyrdom of several male virgins in Anglo-Saxon hagiography. In both Aldhelm and Ælfric's *passiones* of Julian and Chrysanthus, the sight of the tortured male saint is central to imagery of Christian power.[65] The tortures are performed in the sight of many people, but part of the spectacle emanates from the covering of their bodies in grotesque and degrading manners, rather than in visibly exposing them. The torturers seek to shroud the men's anatomy and God, through the men, seeks to reveal aspects of their bodies again. The male virgin body here is a symbol of defiance, signifying the saints' concern with their Christian identity rather than the secular world. As Mills remarks, male martyrs indulge in 'demonstrative exhibitionism'.[66] Both Aldhelm and Ælfric relate how Julian walks out of the burning pyre and from his bitumen-filled vat after God has quelled the fire, glittering as if gold, in full view of the spectators.[67] Particularly in Aldhelm, this potent sight further angers the torturer implying the torturer's failure while Julian's power grows. These virgin men actively court the apparently objectifying gaze of their pagan torturers. Julian, while being flogged, symbolically heals his blind torturer by marking the tormentor's eye with the sign of the cross.[68] He replaces the man's pagan blindness with Christian clarity of vision and consequently his adversary converts to a belief in God. For these virgins, being a corporeal sight is part of a spiritual contest, where they achieve more the more they are seen.

In Karen A. Winstead's examination of Middle English virgin martyrs, she posits binary distinctions between men and women, arguing that the *vitae* of female martyrs emphasize gender, sexuality and virginity, while those of male martyrs do not.[69] This theory, however, needs to be qualified further. In Aldhelm's anomalous *passio* of Malchus, the saint is martyred specifically because he refuses to relinquish his virginity. His parents want him to marry and, to avoid this, he becomes a monk. He is later captured by pirates and we are told that 'he was forced at the point of a sword into abandoning the glories of the chastity he longed for [...] he preferred to die transfixed cruelly by the sword rather than to defend his life by profaning the laws of chastity'.[70] The text certainly operates on a binary dichotomy between virginity and idolatrous lust, and Malchus's oppressors explicitly seek to coerce him into carnality before killing him with a penetrative weapon. This feature of Aldhelm's *passio* of Malchus differs to Jerome's *Vita Malchi*, the original source of this text.[71] In Jerome's *Life* and in an anonymous Old English version probably dating from the tenth century, Malchus *is* forced into marriage and persuades his wife to live chastely, before escaping when both separately enter the coenobitic life.[72] Aldhelm focuses instead entirely on Malchus's resistance to physical threats to his virginity. Here, the depiction of torture and martyrdom is intrinsically concerned with the protection of virginity.[73]

The final trope of male virginity identified here applies to men who are forced to undergo a test of their virginity.[74] Like their female counterparts, several male saints are forced into marriage by their parents or are tempted into carnality.[75] In both Aldhelm and Ælfric, the *passio* of Chrysanthus most dramatically provides evidence for the resistance of temptation as a performative enactment of virginity. Chrysanthus, a well-educated and eloquent young man, converts to Christianity and preaches the Christian word. This angers his father, who tries various strategies to make him renounce his faith, primarily tempting Chrysanthus with sexually alluring women. Chrysanthus is taken to an elaborate banquet, where a harem of women awaits him. Whilst Ælfric describes the women as 'fair and blooming' ('wlitige and rance'), he does not focus as greatly on their physical appeal as Aldhelm.[76] In both versions Chrysanthus passes the test, not succumbing to these sexual and sensual temptations by asserting the power of his will. While in Aldhelm's *De Virginitate* this seems to be wholly an internal power, in Ælfric's version it is a combination of the individual power of will and divine intervention.[77] Here Chrysanthus not only refused their kisses ('forbeah heora cossas'), but also prays for the preservation of his virginity. As a result, God intervenes by causing the women to fall asleep, rendering them powerless to awaken lust in him.[78] By refusing any sensual awareness of the women, Chrysanthus avoids temptation. He is just as defiant of carnal pressure as his female virgin counterparts in a victory against temptation which concurs with patristic interpretations of virginity. Jerome comments that 'through the five senses, as through open windows, vice has access to the soul'.[79] Chrysanthus's conscious avoidance of all sensual contact with both women and food is therefore a physical enactment of his virginity.

A prevalent Christian perception of virginity proposed that it was a coherent fusion of body and mind, which could potentially be undermined even by lustful thoughts.[80] Augustine and Jerome for example both consider that virginity can be negated if a virgin intends to yield to carnal advances, even if s/he never actually does so.[81] Foucault examines this tenet of thought in an investigation of Cassian's account of the battle for chastity, where one variety of fornication is identified as 'libido', which develops in 'the dark corners of the soul' without 'physical passion'.[82] Foucault notes that this implies a 'subjectivisation [...] linked with a process of self-knowledge which makes the obligation to seek and state the truth about oneself an indispensable and permanent condition of this asceticism'.[83] It is a process of wilfully denying all sexual thoughts, overcoming temptation through one's own will and self-knowledge.[84] This is then furthered and complicated in the *Life* by the presence of the temptress Daria. Daria enters the life of Chrysanthus, not just as a physical temptation adorned with gemstones and gold, but also as an educated woman with the potential to persuade the saint to abandon his Christian path. In Ælfric's *passio*, Chrysanthus's successful conversion of Daria is described in detail.[85] The pair then co-habit in a chaste marriage, converting others. Although it is usually the woman who initiates conversion and agreement upon chastity, here, and in the other cases of chaste marriage in the Anglo-Saxon *Lives*, it is the man who does so.[86] Their carnally innocent relationship, consummated not in coitus, but in joint love of God, is made eternal through their burial in the same grave. Ælfric's depiction of the climactic torture finds the pair buried together alive.[87]

Kelly argues that the titillating details of the female temptresses in these seduction scenes constitute a 'shifting of attention away from the male virgin' which is 'very different from what we find in tales of near-rape of the female virgin'.[88] This is true in that Chrysanthus is not presented as carnally desirable, whereas the women are. The predators in female virgin *Lives* desire to enact their carnal urges on the women, while these tempting women are usually enacting the wishes of a family concerned with inheritance; their reasons are social, not sexual. These narratives consistently display females as alluring temptresses, yet they are not simplistically misogynistic. As John Arnold argues, it is the men who have to resist their own failings of lust, commenting that 'in opposition to the common claim that women are the bearers of uncontrolled desire in medieval discourse, it is quite clear that men are similarly afflicted', going on to note that 'desire becomes most dangerous when it meets an exterior element with which it can resonate'.[89]

Male and female saints arrive at their virginal identity in different ways. Women can be physically raped through penetration but, unless we are talking about homosexual rape, which is avoided at least overtly in Anglo-Saxon *Lives*, men must be physically aroused to have sex. However, the spectacle of male and female virginity is in this instance more similar than many studies allow for. It is consent which confirms the presence or loss of virginity, and here the male's struggle to reject female advances forms a spectacle in many ways similar to the female's refusal to consent to sex in the face of grotesque torture. This is particularly true in Ælfric's version, where the physicality of the temptresses is glossed over.

The spectacle and performance of virginity in these narratives illustrates the men's constant battle to attain and maintain true virginity, which is then validated by God. In his analysis of Middle English representations of male virginity, Arnold argues that saints who overcome a test of seduction through the power of will are merely chaste, while those whose virginity is protected divinely are true virgins. He proposes that willpower can only control lust, leaving the potential for it to return, whereas divine intervention has the ability to remove lust entirely and therefore cannot fail.[90] However, this analysis of the seduction motif in Anglo-Saxon *Lives* has revealed that equal weight is placed on divine intervention and the assertion of personal will. In this category of male virginal experience, virginity is a social and personal construction, residing in the mind just as much as the body. These men refuse to bow to the wishes of their sexual tormentors through a combination of individual and holy strength.

From the few saints' *Lives* analyzed here, it is clear that the presentations of male virginity in Anglo-Saxon prose *Lives* are multiple. The scholarly preoccupation with the virginity of female saints does of course reflect a historical truth. Throughout the Middle Ages, virginity formed a legal category for women but not for men. Similarly, while 'virgin' was the nominal category in Anglo-Saxon liturgy for nearly all female saints, including reformed harlots and abbesses known to have biological children, it was never applied to men.[91] However, this should not detract from the potential wealth of research into Anglo-Saxon male hagiographic virginity. Binary divisions in Anglo-Saxon representations of male and female virginity and the pre- and post-conquest chronology of virginity need to be qualified and stereotypes readdressed. So, perhaps as an answer to Maud Burnett McInerney's question, 'what, after all, is a male virgin?', it seems that in Anglo-Saxon hagiography, he is just as varied, multiple, complex and unstable as his female counterpart; perhaps even more so.

Notes

1. Maud Burnett McInerney, 'Rhetoric, Power and Integrity in the Passion of the Virgin Martyr', in *Menacing Virgins: Representing Virginity in the Middle Ages and Renaissance*, ed. Kathleen Coyne Kelly and Marina Leslie (London: Associated University Presses, 1999), pp. 50–70 (p. 57).

2. For examinations of later medieval male virginity see the essays in *Gender and Holiness: Men, Women and Saints in Late Medieval Europe*, ed. Samantha J.E. Riches and Sarah Salih (London: Routledge, 2002). See also Jacqueline Murray, 'Masculinizing Religious Life: Sexual Prowess, the Battle for Chastity and Monastic Identity', in *Holiness and Masculinity in the Middle Ages*, ed. Patricia H. Cullum and Katherine J. Lewis (Cardiff: University of Wales Press, 2004), pp. 24–42; the essays in *Medieval Virginities*, ed. Anke Bernau, Ruth Evans and Sarah Salih (Cardiff: University of Wales Press, 2003); and Kathleen Coyne Kelly, *Performing Virginity and Testing Chastity in the Middle Ages* (London: Routledge, 1999), pp. 91–118.

3. See, Jo Ann McNamara, 'An Unresolved Syllogism: The Search for a Christian Gender System', in *Conflicted Identities and Multiple Masculinities: Men in the Medieval West*, ed. Jacqueline Murray (New York: Garland Publishing, 1999), pp. 1–24 (p. 7); Sarah Salih, *Versions of Virginity in Late Medieval England* (Cambridge: D.S. Brewer, 2001). Cf. Judith Butler, *Gender Trouble: Feminism and the Subversion of Identity* (London: Routledge, 1990; repr. 1999).

4. For Ælfric's audience see Robert K. Upchurch, 'The Legend of Chrysanthus and Daria in Ælfric's *Lives of Saints*', *Studies in Philology*, 101 (2004), 250–69 (p. 251) and idem, 'Virgin Spouses as Model Christians: The Legend of Julian and Basilissa in Ælfric's *Lives of Saints*', *Anglo-Saxon England*, 34 (2005), 197–217 (p. 197).

5. It has long been considered that *De Virginitate* was written for Abbess Hildelith and her nuns at the double monastery at Barking. See *Aldhelm: The Prose Works* (Ipswich: D.S. Brewer, 1979), trans.

Michael Lapidge and Michael Herren (Ipswich: D.S. Brewer, 1979), p. 51; Carol Braun Pasternack, 'The Sexual Practices of Virginity and Chastity in Aldhelm's *De Virginitate*', in *Sex and Sexuality in Anglo-Saxon England: Essays in Memory of Daniel Gillmore Calder*, ed. Carol Braun Pasternack and Lisa M.C. Weston (Tempe, AZ: Arizona Center for Medieval and Renaissance Studies, 2004), pp. 93–120 (p. 94). However, Scott Gwara argues that the prose *De Virginitate* was written 'for the abbesses of double monasteries throughout Wessex'; see *Aldhelmi Malmesbiriensis Prosa De Virginitate: Cum Glosa Latina Atque Anglosaxonica*, ed. Scott Gwara, 2 vols (Turnhout: Brepols Publishers, 2001), I, p. 51 (hereafter *Aldhelmi*). This argument is particularly persuasive when one considers that, as Emma Pettit notes, 'at times he specifically counsels "ecclesiastics", "brothers" and "individuals" of either sex', see Emma Pettit, 'Holiness and Masculinity in Aldhelm's *Opus Geminatum De Virginitate*', in *Holiness and Masculinity*, pp. 8–23 (p. 10). Lapidge and Herren note how atypical Aldhelm's male catalogue is, having 'no antecedent in earlier patristic treatises on virginity' (Lapidge and Herren, *Aldhelm: The Prose Works*, p. 56).

6.   For discussion of the various routes through which men could access sanctity see Janet L. Nelson, 'Monks, Secular Men and Masculinity c. 900', in *Masculinity in Medieval Europe*, ed. Dawn M. Hadley (London: Longman, 1999), pp. 121–42.

7.   It should be noted that the division of male virginity into five tropes somewhat simplifies these heteroglossic narratives. Some saints who are martyred or who are seduced also perform miracles. In outlining these five narrative versions, this analysis takes the most significant element when thematically categorizing the texts.

8.   For the Latin, see *Aldhelmi*, II, pp. 233–35, 283–87, 293–95, 297–301, 321–25, 335–47, 349–53, 379–87.

9.   *Aldhelmi*, II, p. 321. For an English translation see Aldhelm, 'De Virginitate' (hereafter 'Aldhelm, ET'), in Lapidge and Herren, *Aldhelm: The Prose Works*, pp. 59–132 (pp. 84–85).

10.   Rudolf Ehwald, quoted in Pasternack, 'Sexual Practices', p. 101.

11.   'illaesae puritatis coronam usque ad metam sortis supremae indiffessis uiribus usquequaque custodisse. Aldhelmi' (*Aldhelmi*, II, p. 339). Cf. Aldhelm, ET, p. 86.

12.   *Ælfric's Lives of Saints*, ed. Walter W. Skeat, EETS, o.s., 2 vols (London: Oxford University Press, 1866–1900, repr. 1966), I, pp. 62–64. For Anglo-Saxon cults of Basil, see Gabriella Corona, 'Saint Basil in Anglo-Saxon Exeter', *Notes and Queries*, 49 (2002), 316–20.

13.   *Aldhelmi*, II, p. 285; Aldhelm, ET, p. 77.

14.   *Ælfric's Lives of Saints*, I, pp. 50–91.

15.   'in modum iocundae pubertatis usquequaque uirescit et iugiter adolescit!' (*Aldhelmi*, II, p. 209). Cf. Aldhelm, ET, p. 74.

16.   'ergo nequaquam carnalis integritas comprobatur, nisi consors spiritalis castimonia comitetur' (*Aldhelmi*, II, p. 191). Cf. Aldhelm, ET p. 72.

17.   Augustine, 'City of God', in *A Select Library of Nicene and Post-Nicene Fathers of the Christian Church*, ed. Philip Schaff and Henry Wace, 14 vols (Buffalo: The Christian Literature Company, 1887), II, pp. 1–511 (p. 12) and *Ælfric's Lives of Saints*, I, p. 215.

18.   *Aldhelmi*, II, pp. 225–33, 235–55, 273–83, 287–93, 325–35, 399–413, 547–73. For Ælfric's ambivalence regarding miracle stories see Malcolm R. Godden, 'Ælfric's Saints' Lives and the Problem of Miracles', *Leeds Studies in English*, 16 (1985), 83–100.

19.   Pettit, 'Holiness and Masculinity', p. 13. Pettit notes that in *De Virginitate*, only thirty-eight miracles occur in female *lives*, while 114 occur in those of their male counterparts.

20.   *Aldhelmi*, II, pp. 231–33.

21.   *Aldhelmi*, II, pp. 225–29.

22.   See Pettit, 'Holiness and Masculinity', p. 14.

23.   'Before the Fall, Adam and Eve were virgins in Paradise, but after they had sinned, and were cast out of Paradise, they were immediately married' (Jerome, 'Against Jovinian', in *A Select Library*, VI, pp. 346–416 (p. 359)).

24.   'degens hactenus generali mortis debito caruisse denoscitur, quam cuncti uiolentis naturae legibus addicti et primae praeuaricationis nexibus adstricti […] pendere coguntur' (*Aldhelmi*, II, pp. 227–29). Cf. Aldhelm, ET, p. 76.

25. 'cum de sepulcri tumba puluis ebulliat et quasi reciproco spirantis flatu in superficie antri sensim scaturiat' (*Aldhelmi*, II, pp. 282–83). Cf. Aldhelm, ET, p. 81.

26. *Aldhelmi*, II, pp. 327 and 559–61; Aldhelm, ET, pp. 85 and 104.

27. For Ælfric's intentions, see his preface to *Lives of Saints*, where he comments that he desires to write the book '*mannum to getrymminge and to munde us sylfum*' (for the encouragement of men and for our own protection): *Aldhelmi*, I, p. 6.

28. Similar observations can be found in Pasternack, 'Sexual Practices', p. 102.

29. Pettit, 'Holiness and Masculinity', p. 14.

30. See Elizabeth Robertson, 'The Corporeality of Female Sanctity in the Life of Saint Margaret', in *Images of Sainthood in Medieval Europe*, ed. Renate Blumenfeld-Kosinski and Timea Szell (Ithaca: Cornell University Press, 1991), pp. 268–87; Shari Horner, 'The Violence of Exegesis: Reading the Bodies of Ælfric's Female Saints', in *Violence Against Women in Medieval Texts*, ed. Anna Roberts (Gainesville: University Press of Florida, 1998), pp. 22–43; Sarah Kay, 'The Sublime Body of the Martyr: Violence in Early Romance Saints' Lives', in *Violence in Medieval Society*, ed. Richard W. Kaeuper (Woodbridge: Boydell Press, 2000), pp. 3–20; Salih, *Versions of Virginity*. See also Jennifer Borland's contribution in this volume.

31. Kelly, *Performing Virginity*, pp. 91–118.

32. *Aldhelmi*, II, p. 519.

33. Murray, 'Masculinizing Religious Life', p. 25.

34. Patricia H. Cullum, 'Introduction: Holiness and Masculinity in Medieval Europe', pp. 1–7 (p. 4). For crises in medieval masculinity, see Nelson, 'Monks, Secular Men and Masculinity'.

35. This usage of the imagery of battle in relation to virginity has not gone unnoticed by scholars. See Catherine Cubitt, 'Virginity and Misogyny in Tenth- and Eleventh-Century England', *Gender and History*, 12 (2000), 1–32 (p. 19).

36. 'contra horrendam superbiae bestiam simulque contra has uirulentorum septenas uitiorum biluas, and uirginitatis lorica spoliatos pudicitiaeque'(*Aldhelmi*, II, p. 129, cf. pp, 129–31). Cf. Aldhelm, ET, p. 68.

37. '…coenubialis militiae pugiles…' (*Aldhelmi*, II, p. 133). Cf. Aldhelm, ET, p. 68.

38. See Sinéad O'Sullivan, 'Aldhelm's De Virginitate – Patristic Pastiche or Innovative Exposition?', *Peritia*, 12 (1998), 271–95 (p. 277).

39. *Aldhelmi*, I, p. 48.

40. George T. Dempsey, 'Aldhelm of Malmesbury's Social Theology: The Barbaric Heroic Ideal Christianised', *Peritia*, 15 (2001), 58–80 (pp. 77–78).

41. Pettit, 'Holiness and Masculinity', p. 9.

42. *Aldhelmi*, II, pp. 303 and 305; Aldhelm, ET, pp. 82–83.

43. *Aldhelmi*, II, p. 309; Aldhelm, ET, p. 88.

44. 'O quanta est pudicitiae uirtus, quae bachantis beluae rabiem humillima prece compescuit' (*Aldhelmi*, II, p. 369). Cf. Aldhelm, ET, p. 89.

45. Pettit, 'Holiness and Masculinity', p. 16.

46. 'ungewemmed […] fram woruldlicre besmitennysse' (*Ælfric's Lives of Saints*, II, p. 222). The translation is my own.

47. See, *Ælfric's Lives of Saints*, II, pp. 264–65, 286–87 and 312–23.

48. These are the Blickling Homilies, the Vercelli Homilies, Ælfric's Catholic Homilies, and as a fragmentary homily in Junius 86. For a detailed discussion, see Marcia A. Dalby, 'The Good Shepherd and the Soldier of God: Old English Homilies on St. Martin of Tours', *Neuphilologische Mitteilungen*, 85 (1984), 422–34.

49. Judith Gaites examines Ælfric's manipulation of sources through abridging, omissions and reordering of events from those in Sulpicius Severus's *Vita Sancti Martini* and its supplementary epistles (Judith Gaites, 'Ælfric's Longer *Life of Saint Martin* and its Latin Sources: A Study in Narrative Technique', *Leeds Studies in English*, 13 (1982), 23–41). See also Frederick M. Biggs, 'Ælfric

as Historian: His Use of Alcuin's *Laudationes* and Sulpicius' *Dialogues* in his Two Lives of Martin', in *Holy Men and Holy Women: Old English Prose Saints' Lives and their Contexts*, ed. Paul E. Szarmach (Albany NY: State of New York University Press, 1996), pp. 289–316.

50. *Ælfric's Lives of Saints*, ii, pp. 220–21.

51. *Ælfric's Lives of Saints*, ii, pp. 226–29.

52. *Ælfric's Lives of Saints*, ii, pp. 280–81.

53. For common tropes of virgin martyrdom, see Riches, 'St George', pp. 66–67.

54. Robert Mills, 'A Man is Being Beaten', *New Medieval Literatures*, 5 (2002), 115–53 (p. 117).

55. For Aldhelm, Felix, Malchus, Babilas and Cosmas and Damianus, see Aldhelm, ET, pp. 87, 91 and 94–96; *Aldhelmi*, ii, pp. 347–49, 393–99, 433–53. For Protus and Hyacinthus (mentioned in *passio* of Saint Eugenia) and Edmund, see *Ælfric's Lives of Saints*, i, pp. 24–51, ii, pp. 314–35. Other male virgin martyr saints, such as Chrysanthus and Julian, are included in the final category. See the table at the end of this essay.

56. Salih claims these to be qualities, 'proper to virgins'. See Salih, 'Performing Virginity', p. 99.

57. Emma Cownie claims that 'St Edmund was a fluid symbol with a chameleon-like capacity for periodic reappraisal and renewal, in many media and many languages'; see 'The Cult of St Edmund in the Eleventh and Twelfth Centuries: The Language and Communication of a Medieval Saint's Cult', *Neuphilologische Mitteilungen*, 99 (1998), 177–97.

58. '…lichama us cyð þe lið un-formolsnod þæt he butan forligre her on worulde leofode' (Ælfric's *Lives of Saints*, ii, p. 328).

59. Joanna Huntington, 'Edward the Celibate, Edward the Saint: Virginity in the Construction of Edward the Confessor', in Bernau, Evans and Salih, ed., *Medieval Virginities*, pp. 119–39 (pp. 120–21). For a translation of the Life of Edward, see *The Life of King Edward who Rests at Westminster*, ed. and trans. Frank Barlow, 2nd edn (Oxford: Clarendon, 1992).

60. *Ælfric's Lives of Saints*, ii, pp. 328–29. For the place of relics in Anglo-Saxon society, see David W. Rollason, 'Lists of Saints' Resting Places in Anglo-Saxon England', *Anglo-Saxon England*, 7 (1978), 61–94, and idem, *Saints and Relics in Anglo-Saxon England* (Oxford: Blackwell, 1989).

61. *Ælfric's Lives of Saints*, ii, pp. 330–31.

62. *Ælfric's Lives of Saints*, ii, pp. 330–31. Ælfric provides a precedent for men dying from looking at the body of a saint without Christian conviction by mentioning Gregory's account of Saint Lawrence in his *vita* of Edmund. In Gregory's account, seven disbelieving men die while looking at Saint Lawrence (*Ælfric's Lives of Saints*, ii, pp. 332–33).

63. Emma Campbell, and Robert Mills, 'Introduction: Troubled Vision', in *Troubled Vision: Gender, Sexuality and Sight in Medieval Text and Image*, ed. Emma Campbell and Robert Mills (Basingstoke: Macmillan Palgrave, 2004), pp. 1–14 (p. 5).

64. Slavoj Žižek, *Looking Awry: An Introduction to Jacques Lacan through Popular Culture* (Cambridge, MA: MIT Press, 1992), p. 126.

65. Both of these saints are discussed further in the final section of this essay.

66. Robert Mills, '"Whatever you do is a delight to me!" Masculinity, Masochism, and Queer Play in Representations of Male Martyrdom', *Exemplaria*, 13 (2001), 1–37 (p. 9).

67. *Aldhelmi*, ii, p. 521; Aldhelm, ET, p. 101; and *Ælfric's Lives of Saints*, i, p. 110.

68. *Aldhelmi*, ii, p. 511; Aldhelm, ET, pp. 100–101; and *Ælfric's Lives of Saints*, i, p. 101.

69. Karen A. Winstead, *Virgin Martyrs: Legends of Sainthood in Late Medieval England* (Ithaca: Cornell University Press, 1997), p. 56.

70. 'cumque ibidem optatae castitatis insignibus, quae in genitali solo seruauerat, carere stricta machera extorqueretur, malluit mucrone transfossus crudeliter occumbere quam pudicitiae iura profanando uitam defendere, nequanquam animae periculum pertimescens, si integer uirginitatis status effusione sanguinis seruaretur' (*Aldhelmi*, ii, pp. 397–99). Cf. Aldhelm, ET, p. 91.

71. Jerome, '*Vita Malchi monachi cativi*', *PL* 23, 55–62 (col. 55–60).

72. See, *Angelsachische Homilien und Heiligenleben*, ed. Bruno Assmann (Kassel: G.H. Wigand, 1889; repr. Darmstadt: G.H. Wigand, 1964), pp. 199–207. The Old English version is extant in ff.

139v–143v of a mid-eleventh-century manuscript from Worcester, London, BL, Cotton Otho C.i, part II. For a synopsis of the Old English text and a linguistic analysis, see Michael S. Armstrong and Peter Jackson, 'Job and Jacob in the Old English *Life of Malchus*', *Notes and Queries*, 49 (2002), 10–12.

73. In relation to the determining criteria for the torture of female saints, Mills argues that the Anglo-Saxon life of Saint Vincent contains a male parallel to the mammary mutilation of Agatha. Perhaps here, such tortures are testament to a virginal identity (Mills, 'Whatever you do is a delight to me!').

74. *Aldhelmi*, ii, pp. 371–78, 413–31, 455–547.

75. Alison More's essay in this volume explores the role of sexuality in the *vitae* of male saints from the diocese of Liège during the thirteenth century.

76. *Ælfric's Lives of Saints*, ii, p. 380. Cf. Aldhelm, ET, pp. 125–32.

77. Aldhelm, ET, p. 97.

78. *Ælfric's Lives of Saints*, ii, pp. 380–83.

79. Ambrose, 'Letter No. 25', in *Saint Ambrose: Letters*, trans. M.M. Beyenke (New York: Fathers of the Church, 1954), p. 132; Jerome, 'Against Jovinian', p. 394.

80. Ambrose highlights the Virgin Mary as the epitome of this ideal, remarking 'videte quod meritum non sola carnis virginitas facit, sed etiam mentis integritas' ('She [Mary] was a virgin not only in body but also in mind', Ambrose, *De Virginitate*, PL 16, 279–316 (col. 284)).

81. See Augustine, 'City of God', p. 13; Jerome, 'Letter XII, To Eustochium', in *A Select Library*, vi, pp. 22–41 (p. 24).

82. Michel Foucault, 'The Battle for Chastity', in *Western Sexuality: Practice and Precept in Past and Present Times*, ed. Philippe Ariès and André Béjin, trans. Anthony Forster (Oxford: Basil Blackwell, 1985), pp. 14–25 (p. 17).

83. Foucault, 'Battle For Chastity', p. 25.

84. This was perhaps deemed more relevant to men, particularly in the context of the medieval preoccupation with nocturnal emissions in a post-conquest context. Dyan Elliott, *Fallen Bodies: Pollution, Sexuality and Demonology in the Middle Ages* (Philadelphia: University of Pennsylvania Press, 1999), especially pp. 14–34, and Jacqueline Murray, '"The law of sin that is in my members": The Problem of Male Embodiment', in *Gender and Holiness*, pp. 9–22. See also Foucault, 'Battle for Chastity', pp. 22–24.

85. See *Ælfric's Lives of Saints*, ii, pp. 384–85.

86. Elliott, *Spiritual Marriage*, p. 67. See also Jo Ann McNamara, 'Chaste Marriage and Clerical Celibacy', in *Sexual Practices and the Medieval Church*, ed. Vern L. Bullough and James Brundage (New York: Prometheus Books, 1982), pp. 22–33.

87. *Aldhelmi*, ii, p. 491; Aldhelm, ET, p. 99; *Ælfric's Lives of Saints*, ii, pp. 396–97.

88. Kelly, *Performing Virginity*, pp. 96–97.

89. Arnold, 'The Labour of Continence', pp. 110, 113.

90. Arnold, 'The Labour of Continence', pp. 110–11.

91. For virginity in medieval law, see Sarah Salih, Anke Bernau and Ruth Evans, 'Introduction', in *Medieval Virginities*, pp. 1–13 (p. 4) and Mary P. Richards and B. Jane Stanfield, 'Concepts of Anglo-Saxon Women in the Laws', in *New Readings on Women in Old English Literature*, ed. Helen Damico and Alexandra H. Olsen (Bloomington, IN: Indiana University Press, 1990), pp. 89–99 (p. 93). Magdalene is listed as 'virgin' in all twenty-three litanies referencing her, as is repentant harlot Pelagia in the one litany mentioning her. See *Anglo-Saxon Litanies of the Saints*, ed. Michael Lapidge, Henry Bradshaw Society, cvi (London: Boydell Press, 1991), pp. 95, 117, 124, 126, 130, 134, 145, 150, 169, 175, 179, 184, 190, 199, 216, 237, 241, 245, 252, 267, 278, 285, 301 (for Mary Magdalene); p. 199 (for Pelagia). Similarly, Sexburg, abbess of Ely from 679 to c. 700, who was apparently married with a daughter, always appears in the list of virgins in litanies and is identified as a virgin in eleven of sixteen calendar entries. See *Bede's Historia Ecclesiastica*, ed. and trans. Bertram Colgrave and Roger A.B. Mynors (Oxford: Oxford University Press, 1969), pp. 238–39. Lapidge, *Anglo-Saxon Litanies*, pp. 96, 127, 135, 145, 169, 190, 208, 238, 252, 271, 298.

Table of Male Virgin Saints

The following table splits male virgin saints in Anglo-Saxon texts into the five tropes that I have discussed. It records page references of their commemoration in translations and editions of the Anglo-Saxon prose hagiographic texts examined in the course of this essay. I have also included references in *The Old English Martyrology* as it is a useful point of comparison in various cases. The full reference to each text is listed at the beginning of the table. The saints are listed vertically in the second column and are alphabetical within each trope. If a cell is blank, then the saint is not commemorated in the text in question.

		Aldhelm	Ælfric	Old English Martyrology
Tropes of male virginity	Virgin saint	Aldhelm, 'De Virginitate', in M. Lapidge and M. Herren, trans., *Aldhelm: The Prose Works* (Ipswich, D.S. Brewer, 1979), pp. 59–132.	W.W. Skeat, ed. and trans., *Ælfric's Lives of Saints* EETS. o.s. 76 and 82 (London, Oxford University Press, 1966).	G. Herzfeld, ed. and trans., *An Old English Martyrology*, EETS o.s. 116 (London, Oxford University Press, 1900).
Trope 1 Virginity is a nominal or minimal feature of the *Life*	Ambrose	84–85		
	Anthony	87		20–23
	Basil	86–87	I, 50–91	
	Benedict	89–91		
	Clement	82		
	Didymus (Thomas)	81		
	Gregory of Nazianzus	85–86		
	Jeremiah	77		
	Luke	82		186–87
	Paul	81	I, 364–69 (in On Augeries)	
Trope 2 Virginity is a locus of sanctity enabling the performance of miracles	Apollonius	103–106		

		Aldhelm	Ælfric	Old English Martyrology
	Daniel	77–9		
	Elijah	76		
	Elisha	76		
	John Evangelist	63–4 and 80–81		
	Narcissus	91–92		
	Paul hermit	87–88		
Trope 3 Virginity is source of strength in physical battle	Hilarion (M)	88–89		192–95
	Matin of Tours (M)	85	II, 218–313	
	Silvester (M)	82–84		
Trope 4 Virgin martyrs	Babilas (M)	94–95		30–31
	Cosmas (M)	95–96		
	Daminanus (M)	95–96		
	Edmund (M)		II, 314–35	
	Felix (M)	87		
	Hyacinthus (M)			166–67
	Malchus (M)	91		
	Protus (M)			166–67
Trope 5 Virginity is identifier of Christian identity through battle with temptation	Amos (M) – chaste marriage	102–103		
	Athanasius (M)	92–94		
	Chrysanthus	96–99	II, 378–99	212–15
	John hermit (M)	89		
	Julian (M) – chaste marriage	99–102	I, 90–115	14–17

3

Convergence, Conversion, and Transformation: Gender and Sanctity in Thirteenth-Century Liège

Alison More

Medieval literature often depicts manly strength, or *virtus*, as an ideal to which both male and female saints aspired. However, a comparison of thirteenth-century *vitae* of Liégeois(e) *sancti* and *sanctae* reveals a far more complex picture than this simple goal.[1] This essay explores the use of gendered imagery in illustrating the journey towards holiness as it was perceived by hagiographers in thirteenth-century Liège. A close examination of these texts reveals that Liégeois holy men are frequently portrayed moving away from masculine ideals and Liégeoise holy women towards them as they progress in holiness. As the imagery is fluid, rather than fixed, these texts not only question the binary association between masculinity and virtue, but also the idea of fixed gender associations. The instability of gendered imagery facilitates the portrayal of the saint as an individual who has moved to a place beyond gender and sexuality.

Gender transformation was closely connected to the medieval ideal of conversion. Medieval conversion is somewhat different from its modern counterpart in that it was understood as a journey or life-long process rather than a singular event. Its focus was not the adoption of new beliefs, but the universal Christian call to sainthood by moving towards union with the divine. Variations of this path have existed since patristic times, and the journey of conversion was still prevalent in the writings of theologians from the high Middle Ages.[2] The first occurrence of contrition in a saint's life, such as Paul's experience on the road to Damascus or the Magdalene in tears at Christ's feet, should be understood simply as a *call* to conversion.[3] Answering that call was the beginning of a journey towards holiness and ultimately towards God.[4] The traditional model for understanding this journey was threefold: the stages through which one would pass were purgation and illumination, finally ending in union with the Godhead.

Scholars have already noted the correlation between gendered language and conversion; however, discussion has generally focused on the movement from femininity to masculinity. Early Christian writers, from Paul to the Church Fathers, applied masculine imagery to holy women, whose journey towards holiness was also seen as a journey towards 'becoming male'.[5] Patristic texts describe such women as acting 'manfully' (*viriliter*) or even as 'having become male'.[6] As is clear from the essays by Helen Swift and Jennifer Cavalli in this volume, the same trope became popular in secular texts from the later medieval period.

This scholarly focus on achieving masculinity is not without justification: Christian literature has traditionally portrayed women as being weaker and less virtuous than their male contemporaries. The Latin word 'man' (*vir*) was intrinsically linked to the word virtue (*virtus*), while the word 'woman' (*mulier*) was linked to softness or decadence (*mollia*).[7] There is considerable evidence to support Christianity's view of femininity as immoral: patristic writers held a negative view of women, and Tertullian even referred to women as 'the devil's gateway'.[8] Moreover, medieval men who transgressed the societal norm – those who were non-Christian, criminal, uneducated or otherwise immoral – were portrayed as being in some ways analogous to women.[9]

Although masculinity was considered the ideal state, both marginalized men and the concept of masculinity are relatively new topics in medieval studies. The Liégeois men who are examined in this article come from three different Cistercian vocations, the abbot, the monk and the lay brother or *conversus*. This study has drawn from: one *vita abbatis*, the *life* of Walter of Birbech (+ c.1222); three *vitae* of choir monks, Gobertus of Aspremont (+1263), Werricus of Aulne (+1217) and Abundus of Villers (+1239) and three *vitae* of lay brothers or *conversi*, Arnulfus of Villers (+1228), Petrus of Villers and Nicholaos of Villers, whose precise dates are uncertain, but who died in the early thirteenth century.[10] These men, with the possible exception of Arnulfus, are unfamiliar to scholars;[11] however, it would seem that their obscurity is modern. Manuscript evidence suggests that these *vitae* and the associated book of the illustrious deeds of the Villers brothers, the *Chronica Villariensis*, were both known and influential throughout Western Europe in the later medieval and early modern period.[12] Like their female contemporaries, these men underwent an internal change throughout their journey towards sanctity which is explored and expressed through gendered imagery. However, their transformation is expressed through feminization rather than the acquisition of manly characteristics. In a break with the traditional moral binary, the feminization of these men does not signify corruption or weakness, but demonstrates their inner transformation.

The female contemporaries of the above-mentioned men have, by contrast, received considerable scholarly attention in the past twenty years.[13] Social and devotional changes in the high Middle Ages, including increased emphasis on enclosure and greater emphasis on institutionalized *cura monialium*, created a world which was no longer suited to the existing canonically recognized forms of religious life.[14] Instead of effecting institutional change, religiously inclined women in the diocese of Liège – and throughout Europe – chose to dedicate their lives to the Lord without leaving the secular world.[15] In order to compare gendered behaviour and explore the validity of existing scholarly paradigms, this essay examines the gendered imagery in the *vitae* of the holy men of Liège in conjunction with five of their female contemporaries: Marie d'Oignies (+1213), Christina of St Trond (+1224), Juette of Huy (+1228), Ida of Nivelles (+1232) and Lutgard of Aywières (+1246).[16] As the *vitae* of the Liégeoise holy women reflected the spiritual climate of the period, they have been regarded as textual witnesses to developing forms of feminine devotional expression.[17]

Feminine spirituality from the high Middle Ages has been characterized as affective, sensual and, particularly, linked to the physical body.[18] Of course, one must be careful not to take this too literally. Not only do hagiographic topoi play a role in dictating the norms of feminine religiosity, but also, and perhaps more importantly, texts which emphasize these forms of devotion were generally written by men who did not have access to the daily lives of their subjects. For this reason, scholars such as Michel Lauwers have argued that the behaviour depicted in the *vitae* of female saints represented an ideal rather than a reality.[19]

While, as is discussed below, the hagiographers of the *mulieres sanctae* often portray their spirituality in masculine imagery, their religious behaviour is generally characterized as feminine. Similarly, the hagiographers of their aforementioned male contemporaries often use feminine imagery or portray their subjects as 'brides of Christ', yet never diminish the inherent masculinity of their subjects. The curious juxtaposition of masculine and feminine imagery in the *vitae* of both groups suggests that their focus is illustrating that these women have gone through a transformation rather than that they have overcome their gender.

The perceived connection between women and the physical is not unfounded. As is discussed in Jennifer Borland's essay in this volume, female saints of the high Middle Ages typically carry out acts of penitence which are connected with the physical body. In the *vita* of Christina of St Trond, her initial call to conversion began with her first bodily death, which occurs in the first chapter of her *vita*. Following her dramatic resurrection during her funeral mass, Christina recounts her otherworldly experience,

When I died angels of God […] immediately took my soul and led me into a dark and terrible spot which was filled with human souls. The torments which I saw in that place were so many and so cruel that no tongue is adequate to tell of them

[...] my guides said to me that this place is purgatory and it is here that penitent sinners atone for the sins they committed in their life [...] After these events, I was taken into Paradise. [...] The Lord [said to] me [...] "I now offer you two choices, either to remain with me now or to return to the body and to suffer there the sufferings of an immortal soul in a mortal body[...] and by your sufferings deliver those souls on whom you had compassion in purgatory".[20]

Christina chose to return to earth and, for the remainder of her life, she effected the satisfaction necessary for suffering souls through enduring a type of purgatory. The acts that Christina carried out on behalf of the souls experiencing post-mortem purgation were as dreadful as anything that could await sinners in the afterlife.[21] Her self-inflicted penances included torturing herself in fire and water and being hanged on the gallows by her own hand.[22] Though unusual in her extremes, Christina was not exceptional in using physical asceticism to make satisfaction for sin. One of her contemporaries, Marie d'Oignies cut the skin off her feet when walking in a city which she perceived as sinful, and Lutgard of Aywières endured long fasts in atonement for the sins of heretics.[23]

The physical body also plays a central role in the devotional practices of holy men from the same period. In particular, the *vitae* of the lay brothers from Liège read as veritable litanies of horrors. In these texts we are told that Nicholaos scourged his flesh until it turned black;[24] Petrus restricted himself to a diet of bread and water during Lent;[25] Arnulfus mortified his flesh with ropes, tortured himself with chains, spent nights without sleep and wore a vest that he fashioned from the pelts of hedgehogs.[26] At least in the case of Arnulfus, the salvific intent of such actions was recognized by his contemporaries. A certain monk came to Mellemont seeking Arnulfus, only to be told that he was 'in his purgatory'. The monk eventually met Arnulfus and found his tunic 'muddied with blood' and 'blood still trickling from his beaten body'.[27]

The precise function of asceticism and of the body in devotional practice becomes clearer when its position in the saint's *vita* is observed. In the *vitae* of both male and female saints, ascetic behaviour is almost entirely confined to the earlier sections, or at least the first two thirds, of the text. As the hagiographer portrays the saints' progression towards holiness, fasting, flagellation or torments in fire are replaced by accounts of contemplation, visions and ecstasy. At the beginning of the *vita* of Werricus of Aulne, his hagiographer portrays extreme asceticism and contempt for the body.[28] Both this portrayal of the flesh and Werricus's dramatic acts of asceticism become less of a focus towards the end of the text. Following his description of Werricus's secret torments such as self-flagellation and the wearing of a hair shirt, his hagiographer describes a vision, in which Werricus saw a sevenfold light and heard a voice saying,

The body that you have now is cumbersome and bitter. After this life, you will see clearly with a sevenfold light, and through that light, you will see that the same body has shone for you.[29]

As the *vita* progresses, Werricus's self-inflicted torments allow him to reach new heights in his journey towards God.[30]

For both male and female saints, the initial call to conversion was usually portrayed as physical. In the *vitae* of female saints illness, or death in the case of Christina of St Trond, was not an uncommon depiction. For male saints, it was often depicted as resisting sexual temptation. Scholars of medieval religious history are familiar with the images of the Dominican Thomas Aquinas (+1274) attacking his would-be seductress with a firebrand, or the Cistercian Bernard of Clairvaux (+1153) avoiding similar temptation by rousing his household with cries of 'thief'.[31] It should come as no surprise to discover that the same pattern is found in the *vitae* of less eminent religious men.[32] For instance, the *vita* of Arnulfus of Villers relates that while he was still discerning his path, a demon in the guise of a comely woman appeared in his bed and attempted, unsuccessfully, to arouse his lust. Arnulfus immediately went to Villers and resolved to dedicate himself to the Lord according to the Cistercian custom as a *conversus*.[33]

Similarly, the second stage, the stage of purgation, is portrayed through penitential physical asceticism or service. In scholarship of the past twenty years the ascetic practices of women have received a disproportionate amount of attention compared to those of men: Christina of St Trond is more familiar for her wild asceticism than her advisory role to Count Louis of Looz, while Bernard of Clairvaux is more notable for revitalizing the Cistercians or supporting the disastrous Second Crusade than his practice of immersing himself in icy water at the first stirring of lust.[34] The explanation for this may be simpler than the gendered paradigm suggested by modern scholarship: in the case of prominent churchmen, sanctity is already shown by education, holy orders or a combination thereof and there is no need for their hagiographers to emphasize pious behaviour. At the same time, male saints were often public figures. In these cases, it is no surprise that their hagiographers devoted more time to their public actions than their devotional practices. Although studies, including the essays in this volume by Aislinn Loconte and Francesca Sautman, have shown that women often held positions of power, these same studies have emphasized that this was an exception to the norm. In cases where women held power, it was necessary to re-configure the parameters of existing gendered and social paradigms. Public acts by women, whether secular or religious, had to be justified.[35]

Although fewer opportunities for public expression were available to women, the state of being powerless was not unique to the female sex. Clerics and most persons of secular influence were male, yet being born a man guaranteed neither authority nor sacramental orders. The *vitae virorum* which make significant use of devotional practices generally discussed as feminine are those of the *conversi* or lay brothers.[36] The Cistercian lay brotherhood was more socially diverse than is traditionally believed, yet it appears that lay brothers usually held positions of lower status than monks or abbots.[37] The duties of the lay brothers were usually menial, and detailed descriptions of their public roles would not have made fascinating hagiography. In some ways, lay brothers are, as Martha Newman has argued, feminized.[38]

Close examination of *vitae* from thirteenth-century Liège would suggest that the body also played a significant role in the *vitae* of other holy men. As is discussed below, holy men with a military background, such as Gobertus of Aspremont, are portrayed using their bodies in defence of Christ's earthly kingdom. Like their female contemporaries, their physical devotion was not portrayed as an ideal, but merely a stage of the journey of ongoing conversion that is described above. In this way, the physical service, or battle asceticism of the *milites Christi* – knights of Christ – is a direct parallel to the physical service through purgatorial asceticism carried out by the *mulieres sanctae* and the *conversi*.

This form of devotion was perfectly suited to its time. From the late eleventh century onwards, crusading or defending the Holy Land from the 'infidel' had been seen as a social necessity. For this reason, it is no surprise that literal expressions of Christian military imagery became common. In Clermont during the year 1095, Pope Urban II issued a dramatic proclamation, *De expeditione Hierosolymitana*, declaring that it was the duty of all Christian faithful to defend Christendom, their Christian brethren and, most importantly, the name of Christ.[39] In a period where crusading devotion was considered vital, it stands to reason that a number of *milites Christi* would make their way into the hagiographic record.[40]

In keeping with this vocation of chivalry came an increase in devotion to the quintessential *miles Christi*, Martin of Tours, who is frequently named in Liégeoise hagiography.[41] The future bishop of Tours was born in the mid-fourth century to a military family, and was therefore required by Roman law to serve as a soldier. He was baptized while still in the army and despite Christian prohibitions on military service remained a soldier for some time. Martin's hagiographer, Sulpicius Severus, does not provide a detailed account of Martin's time in the military, but simply states that Martin lived in such a way that he seemed more a monk than he did a soldier. As evidence of his Christian inclinations, Sulpicius recounts incidents which emphasize Martin's charity – notably the occasion he divided his cloak in two so that he might give half to a poor man on the road.[42] In Sulpicius's telling, Martin's military career came to an abrupt end when he confronted the emperor Julian and stated that he could not, as a Christian, participate in a forthcoming battle. Martin was then dismissed from military service and fulfilled a life-long dream of founding a community of desert-hermits before forcibly being made bishop of Tours.[43] As a soldier and saint, Martin provided an ideal model for saintly knights who, given the aforementioned emphasis on crusading, became more prevalent in the high Middle Ages. The hagiographers of the knights from Liège used Martin as a model when drawing attention to the military prowess of their subjects; however, they, like Sulpicius, placed more emphasis on their subjects' charity and compassion than skill on the battlefield.[44]

Jacqueline Murray has observed that when a monk left the world, he renounced sexuality, riches and military prowess, or the trappings of secular masculinity.[45] Her research indicates that spiritual battle imagery is emphasized in writings associated with male saints primarily to relieve the tension between moving away from worldly masculinity and achieving the *virtus* associated with the manly Christian. In Murray's estimation, the saintly knight is depicted as being *able* to use his physical skills to defend Christendom, his fellow Christians and the name of Christ, but having made sufficient progress in virtue to *choose* a spiritual interpretation of this duty over a physical one. Saintly knights used their masculine bodies to defend the heavenly kingdom in the physical realm before achieving the virtue necessary to battle sin in the spiritual realm through devotional practices.

The *vita* of Gobertus of Aspremont serves as a fitting demonstration of Murray's model. From his earliest days, Gobertus had enjoyed the privileges and hardships associated with nobility. Though he was the younger son, his physical strength and skill at arms had convinced his father to name him heir to the family estate.[46] In the year 1228, like many of his contemporaries, Gobertus 'took the Cross' and left Flanders to protect the Holy Land under the leadership of Frederick II.[47]

Gobertus's time on crusade began the process of inner transformation. His *vita* recounts that although Gobertus earned great renown for his military skill and chivalrous demeanour, he began to worry that these things would not bring him comfort in the next life.[48] Rather than immediately renouncing the secular world, Gobertus began to incorporate acts of charity into his daily routine: he gave his worldly possessions to the poor, protected widows and orphans, and began to show a great reverence for Church officials.[49] Gobertus's desire for a new life remained with him when he returned to Flanders. Seeking guidance, Gobertus approached the beguine Emmeloth, who counselled him to ask the advice of Abundus in the house of Villers of which he was a patron.[50] After speaking with Abundus, Gobertus sold his remaining belongings and entered the novitiate.

The second book of Gobertus's *vita* begins by highlighting the transformation that choosing to enter religious life caused in him. Although he had been a powerful knight – 'not merely a simple soldier, but a lord from the most noble lineage' – he 'put his hand to the ploughshare for the sake of the kingdom'. At the same time, his attitude towards worldly power and success changed: 'the riches which he had once used, he now, for the Lord's sake, condemned not only as inane but also loathsome filth'.[51] Significantly, Gobertus's entry to monastic life caused him to leave his wife and family, or the masculine realms of sexuality and responsibility. When Gobertus entered the monastic life, his hagiographer cited Christ's words, 'if any man come to me without hating his mother, father, children, wife, and possessions, he cannot be my disciple' (cf. Luke 14:16).The remainder of the *vita Goberti* focuses on the blessings achieved during this new phase of Gobertus's spiritual journey. The emphasis in the text is not on what was lost, but what was gained. It does not emphasize Gobertus renouncing the trappings of secular masculinity – power, wealth, military prowess and sexuality – so much as allowing them to be transformed: he did not give up his riches, so much as come to consider them worthless; he did not anguish over being separated from his wife, but rejoiced that he had become part of a new family with a new spouse.[52] Gobertus achieved worldly honours, but realized that there was something else that he had to attain. After leaving the world, he was still portrayed as battling for Christ; however, his battlefield was spiritual rather than physical. Though Gobertus renounced much of what comprised conventional masculinity, he became anything but effeminate. Instead, it was turning away from one accepted ideal of manliness which freed him to pursue a second: in renouncing his 'manly' secular authority, Gobertus freed himself to attend to the 'manly' task of protecting Christ's kingdom. Like Sulpicius, Gobertus's hagiographer does not recount a single explicit instance of shedding blood in his *vita*.

While physical knighthood was praised in the *Lives* of the *milites Christi*, it was obviously spiritual knighthood that hagiographers held as ideal. The model used was still Martin of Tours, yet subjects of *vitae* were modelled more closely on the Martinian topos of charity than on military experience. Gobertus's hagiographer is typical in that he describes the charitable activities his subject undertook while on crusade.[53] In countering need, Gobertus endeavoured to bring about the justice of the heavenly kingdom. In particular, the *vita Goberti* recounts that Gobertus gave his worldly possessions to the poor, and protected widows and orphans.[54]

The use of charity in bringing about Christ's kingdom is also associated with Werricus, also from a knightly background and master of the *conversi* in the Cistercian house of Aulne. Werricus was once approached by a *conversus* in obvious distress. The *conversus* confided in Werricus that he had learned that his mother had become so poor that she was unable to provide herself with a cloak. The distraught man went on to say that he was considering leaving the religious life temporarily so that he might provide for his mother until her death. Werricus listened sympathetically to the man's plight, but refused to release him from his vows. He then ordered that a cloak from the monastery storeroom be given to the woman.[55] On another occasion, Werricus was travelling in the middle of winter when he encountered a poor woman on the road. The poor woman looked up at Werricus, and cried, 'Lord, protect me for I am unable to clothe myself'.[56] In what can only be seen as a direct imitation of St Martin, Werricus immediately descended from his horse, and gave her the better of the two cloaks that he was wearing.

Charitable activity, purgatorial asceticism and other forms of devotion were often cast as spiritual warfare in the *vitae* of both male and female saints from thirteenth-century Liège. Images of warfare that could not be meant as literal are also used in the *vitae* of the *mulieres sanctae*.[57] In his prologue to the *Life* of the semi-religious married virgin, Marie d'Oignies, Jacques de Vitry describes the many holy women who were 'soldiering' (*militantium*) for Christ.[58] The usury committed by Juette of Huy, a Liégeoise widow who repented her marriage and interest in secular affairs, is compared to the foundations of a church being shaken in battle;[59] the beguine who became a Cistercian abbess, Lutgard of Aywières, is described as battling against her flesh[60] and the Cistercian Ida of Nivelles is referred to as a 'victorious warrior-maid'.[61] As Borland's essay in this volume demonstrates with respect to St Margaret of Antioch, on each occasion, the transformed and transforming female *miles Christi* used the 'weapons' of her flesh to gain victory over Satan.[62] This portrayal seems more in keeping with the *virago* of the *vitae mulierum* from the early Church than the sensual or somatic holiness often associated with the female saints of the high Middle Ages. However, it is important to keep in mind that when such images are used, the subjects of the *vitae* have already advanced on the journey of transformation.

Military imagery was easily adapted to spiritual life; however sexual prowess, another characteristic of secular masculinity, was more problematic. Men were compelled both to fight the often uncomfortably visible signs of their inner longings, and to struggle with the knowledge that the body could find its own way to be satisfied while its unwary owner slept. Despite a long-standing association between femininity and the physical, medieval society could not help but acknowledge the fact that one of the greatest potential barriers to a man's salvation was his body's desire for sexual release. It was generally acknowledged that even a man with the purest intentions could be tempted by a mere glimpse of any part of a woman's body. For example, the *vita* of Marie d'Oignies recounts the tale of a knight who becomes sexually aroused after brushing Marie's arm and glimpsing her wrist.[63] Sexual arousal was considered both a strong and integral part of the secular masculine ideal but was not compatible with religious masculinity.

Nevertheless, the lustful aspects of sexuality were seldom emphasized in the *vitae* of holy men from Liège. Instead, sexual expression was used to indicate the depth of their relationship to the divine. After showing that they had overcome the constraints of their physical bodies through spiritual warfare, on the physical battlefield or through physical asceticism, the hagiographers were free to portray them as 'brides of Christ', in a topos generally considered feminine.[64] Despite the use of feminine imagery in the *vitae* and writings of male saints, the idea of men having achieved 'femininity' is conspicuously absent from modern scholarship.[65] However, in the *vitae* themselves the move away from masculinity is symbolized by the use of feminine imagery in their *vitae* or writings. The juxtaposition of masculine and feminine imagery emphasizes that these individuals had reached a place beyond sex and gender: instead of men and women they had become genderless saints, though they still lived in male and female bodies.[66]

Nevertheless, this femininity was not considered a sign of weakness, but celebrated as a sign of strength. The *Chronica Villariensis* recounts the tale of monks preparing a saintly abbot for burial. While washing his body, they discovered that his genitalia had disappeared. Rather than depicting this as a loss of masculine power, the chronicler portrays this as a sign that the abbot's manly virtue (*virtus*) had triumphed over the sexual urges considered indicative of secular masculinity.[67] As is the case for this abbot, masculine metaphors of strength are typically used when talking about the journey away from masculine sexuality. In more typical cases, men were given divine help in their fight to conquer their manly bodies, or in more rare cases, such as the aforementioned abbot, appeared to gain sexual control either effortlessly or through miraculous means.[68] When freed from their masculine physicality, such men were free to cultivate a new masculinity: one divorced from male physiology, but which involved both their masculine intellect (through study of theology, writing and preaching) and their grammatically and allegorically feminine souls (*animae*) which sought, and often achieved, union with the divine.[69]

The strikingly bodily, yet wholly mystical, topos of overcoming sexual urges adds a curious dimension to the discussion of gendered transformation. During the high Middle Ages, it was increasingly common for clerics to have regular interaction with both lay and religious women.[70] At the same time, an emphasis on clerical celibacy, combined with the emphasis on sexual purity for both genders, rendered any contact between men and women suspicious. Naturally, this situation increased the potential for sexual misconduct, which resulted in clerics who managed to control their sexual urges being increasingly valued.[71] Although sexual prowess was perceived as an essential component of secular masculinity, it prevented the virtuous cleric from behaving in a manner which was in accordance with manly strength, or *virtus*. Here, the ideal of Christian virtuous masculinity was wholly incompatible with the secular ideal of masculine sexual prowess. Again, as Murray points out, this difficulty can be resolved by one conquering the other: men who possessed the grace necessary to conquer their sexual urges exerted such strength, or virility, that they merited the ability to control their bodies.[72] The 'manly' Christian, even the manly cleric, was an individual who had gained control over his masculine physiology.[73] In this instance, the physiology remained the same, but the interpretation of it in creating normative gender identity changes. In keeping with what Judith Butler's work has repeatedly shown, this demonstrates that interpretations of physiology are as fluid as other aspects of gender identity.[74]

The hagiographers' use of inverted gender imagery enhances their discussions about the unitive aspects of the final stage of the journey of conversion. The saints have passed through their earthly struggles and made reparation for their own transgressions and those of others. When they reached this stage, the saints were as close as possible in the earthly realm to achieving the beatific vision, or union with God. The nature of mystical experience, particularly one involving the divine, necessitated some form of symbolic description.[75] When the beatific vision occurred, the human soul was being taken out of the realm of ordinary experience, and was being united with an ineffable being.

The spiritual or theological language of eros has traditionally been used to discuss or depict mystical union in the Christian tradition. The psalmist describes the soul as 'yearning' for God in the same manner that the deer yearns for running streams (Psalm 41: 1–2), and 'thirsting' for God as desert land thirsts for water (Psalm 142: 6); the Song of Songs is often interpreted as depicting the erotic longing between two lovers on their wedding night (cf. Song of Songs 1–8).[76] Such images would have had a profound effect on the audience, and such images occur frequently in the *Lives* of the Liégeois *sancti*. When hearing the communion antiphon, Abundus felt that 'his heart grew warm within him', and was overcome by a blazing passion. On another occasion, a chance hearing of the same antiphon instigated an irresistible urge to roll on the floor and rejoice as if in the arms of his bridegroom.[77] Similarly, upon seeing, experiencing and understanding the mystery of the triune God, Arnulfus is overcome by an ecstatic bliss. As was typical of the period, his hagiographer described this incident in words from the Song of Songs, 'my beloved to me and I to him' (Song of Songs 2:16), and 'I have found the one my soul loves: I shall hold him fast and not let go' (Song of Songs 3:4).[78] Some *vitae* even made direct parallels between the saints and Solomon's bride, referring to the men as 'black but beautiful', or 'the loveliest of the daughters of Jerusalem'[79] (Song of Songs 1:5).

Caroline Walker Bynum has pointed out that Cistercian writers often portrayed authority, particularly religious authority, as being connected with motherly nurturing. Cistercian abbots were often described as 'mothers', and were seen as having a formative, or maternal, responsibility for caring for the souls of the monks in their monastery.[80] The fact that abbots could be referred to as both 'father' and 'mother' is a further indicator that gendered imagery is not necessarily connected with biological sex. As both male and female saints progress on their journeys towards holiness their gendered attributes change from feminine to masculine or masculine to feminine. A cursory glance would suggest that near the end of their *vitae*, Liégeois(e) saints have become either manly women or womanly men; however, the process which is being illustrated is not simple inversion but transformation. The women who 'achieve' masculinity and the men who are discussed as brides of Christ are simply individuals who have undergone an inner transformation so complete that their hagiographers wish to convey it being shown in their outer countenance. Ironically, the transformation, which is revealed through a reversal of gendered imagery, shows the individual's journey *away from* sexual identity.

Despite views of masculinity and femininity that had their roots in classical thought, the Christian notion that Christ would eventually reconcile all opposites seems to have prevailed. Christian scriptures included the Pauline injunction: '…you have clothed yourselves in Christ, and there are no more distinctions between Jew and Greek, slave and free, man and woman, but all of you are one in Christ Jesus' (Galatians 3: 27–28).This passage provides a refreshing contrast to the misogyny of other early Christian texts; however, at the same time, it reinforces the paradox present in Christian ideals about gender: although masculinity was considered more virtuous than femininity, it also had to be transcended before it was possible to reach the heavenly kingdom. As masculinity and femininity were and are socially constructed and largely understood in relation to one another, transcending either meant re-arranging, or re-gendering what remained – in these instances, a journey away from sexual identity and towards sanctity.[81]

Liégeois(e) *vitae* use both traditional masculine imagery and more feminine, affective, bridal or sensual forms of devotional expression to represent the stages of a saint's journey to holiness. When the two sets of gendered images are viewed in conjunction with one another, it becomes apparent that the imagery has very little to do with biological sex. For the saints, biological sex is simply an innate part of human nature, which is to be transcended on the spiritual journey. For this reason these texts use gendered imagery as a symbolic language which is closely connected with the journey of conversion. Specifically, they are used to illustrate the stages of inner transformation rather than the end result of that change. The transforming and converging gendered imagery used in the *vitae* illustrates that both male and female saints had moved beyond their physical bodies. It was only then that they were free to pursue union with God. The disembodied portrayal of the physical indicates that the language of gender must be read as a demonstration of an internal transformation illustrated on the canvas of a saint's body. The outcome is neither achieving masculinity nor femininity, but moving through gender to a place beyond both gender and sexuality where it is possible to become one with God.

Notes

1. Mathew Kuefler, *The Manly Eunuch: Masculinity, Gender Ambiguity and Christian Ideology in Late Antiquity* (Chicago and London: University of Chicago Press, 2001), passim; Steven F. Kruger, 'Becoming Christian, Becoming Male', in *Becoming Male in the Middle Ages*, ed. Jeffrey Jerome Cohen and Bonnie Wheeler (London: Garland Publishing, 1997), pp. 21–41 (pp. 21–34).

2. An example of the way in which it was understood in the high Middle Ages is found in the writings of Bonaventure (Bonaventure, *De triplici via incendium amoris*, Fontes Christiani, no. 14 (Freiburg: Herder, 1993), Prologus, p. 94). Bonaventure's writings on the threefold path to conversion were influenced by earlier sources, significantly Pseudo-Dionysius (see, Aimé Solignac, 'Voies', in *Dictionnaire de Spiritualité, ascétique et mystique, doctrine et histoire*, ed. M. Viller et al., 16 vols (Paris: Beachesne, 1932–95), xvi, cc. 1204–206). Pseudo-Dionysius's writings on the ascent of the soul and the celestial hierarchy were included in the 1309 catalogue of the Villers library (Thomas Falmagne, *Un Texte en contexte: 'Les Flores Paradisi' et le milieu culturel de Villers en Brabant dans la première moitié du 13e* (Turnhout: Brepols, 2001), pp. 373, 375).

3. Martha Newman, *The Boundaries of Charity* (Stanford: Stanford University Press, 1996), pp. 28–29; Jean Leclercq, 'Conversion to the Monastic Life: Who, Why and How?', in *Studiosorum Speculum: Studies in Honour of Louis J. Lekai O. Cist.*, ed. Francis R. Swietek and John R. Sommerfeldt (Kalamazoo: Cistercian Publications, 1993), pp. 201–32 (pp. 209–11).

4. Philip Schmitz, 'Conversatio Morum', in *Dictionnaire de Spiritualité*, ii, cc. 2206–12.

5. Elizabeth Castelli, '"I Will Make Mary Male": Pieties of the Body and Gender Transformation of Christian Women in Late Antiquity', in *Body Guards: The Cultural Politics of Gender Ambiguity*, ed. Julia Epstein and Krista Straub (New York: Routledge, 1991), pp. 29–49. Cf. Kuefler, *The Manly Eunuch*, pp. 226–38.

6. Dyan Elliott, 'Tertullian, the Angelic Life, and the Bride of Christ', in *Gender and Difference in the Middle Ages*, ed. Sharon Farmer and Carol Braun Pasternack (Minneapolis and London: University of Minnesota Press, 2003), pp. 16–33. Cf. Caroline Walker Bynum, *Holy Feast and Holy Fast: The Religious Significance of Food to Medieval Women* (Berkeley: University of California Press, 1987), pp. 237–44; Kerstin Aspegren, *The Male Woman: A Feminine Ideal in the Early Church* (Stockholm: Almqvist and Wiksell International, 1990), pp. 133–43.

7. Isidore of Seville, "Etymologiarum," c. 11, par. 17–18, *PL* 82, col. 417.

8. Tertullian, *On the Apparel of Women*, 1.1, in *The Ante-Nicene Fathers*, ed. Alexander Roberts and James Donaldson, 10 vols (Peabody, MA: Hendrickson Publishers, 1994), iv, p. 14.

9. Mathew Kuefler, 'Male Friendship and the Suspicion of Sodomy in Twelfth-Century France', in *Gender and Difference*, pp. 145–81 (pp. 165–67); idem, *The Manly Eunuch*, pp. 21–30.

10. *Vita Walterus de Birbaco, mon. Hemmenrodensis*, *AASS*, Ian. ii, pp. 447–50 (hereafter *Vita Walterii*; *De b. Goberti Confessor*, *AASS*, Aug. iv, pp. 370–95 (hereafter *Vita Goberti*); *Vita domini Werrici, prioris de Alna*, in *Catalogus Codicum Hagiographicorum Bibliothecae Regiae Bruxellensis*, 2 vols (Brussels: Typis Polleunis, Ceuterick an Lefébure, 1886), i, pp. 445–63 (hereafter *Vita Werrici*); Goswin of Bossut, 'De vita Abundus van Hoei', ed. A.M. Frenken, *Cîteaux*, 10 (1959), 5–33 (hereafter '*Vita Abundi*'); 'Petrus conv. Villariensis in Belgio', Brussels, Royal Library, MS 7776-7781, ff. 86r–90v (hereafter '*Vita Petri*'); 'De b. Nicolao fratre converso Ordinis Cisterciensis Villarii in Brabantia', *AASS*, Nov. iv, pp. 277–79 (hereafter '*Vita Nicolai*'); Goswin of Bossut, 'De b. Arnulfo, monacho Ordinis Cisterciensis Villarii in Brabantia', in *AASS*, Iun. v, pp. 606–31 (hereafter '*Vita Arnulfi*'). The word *conversi* is used to describe members of the lay brotherhood. For a detailed discussion of Cistercian *conversi* see Brian Noell, 'Expectation and Unrest Among Cistercian Lay Brothers in the Twelfth and Thirteenth Centuries', *Journal of Medieval History*, 32 (2006), 253–74 (pp. 255–58).

11. Brian Patrick McGuire, 'Self-Denial and Self-Assertion in Arnulf of Villers', *Cistercian Studies Quarterly*, 28 (1993), 241–59. For a more comprehensive examination of the Villers *vitae conversorum* see Martha Newman, '"Crucified by the Virtues": Monks, Lay Brothers and Women in Thirteenth-Century Cistercian Saints' Lives', in *Gender and Difference*, pp. 182–209. Some work has been done with the manuscripts of the *vitae*, see Falmagne, *Un Texte en contexte*.

12. Falmagne, *Un Texte en contexte*, pp. 37–49.

13. Bynum, *Holy Feast and Holy Fast*; Barbara Newman, *From Virile Woman to WomanChrist* (Philadelphia: University of Pennsylvania Press, 1995). A collection of essays is devoted to discerning the voices of medieval holy women, *Gendered Voices: Medieval Saints and their Interpreters*, ed. Catherine M. Mooney (Philadelphia: University of Pennsylvania Press, 1999).

14. Herbert Grundmann, *Religious Movements in the Middle Ages*, trans. Steven Rowan (Notre Dame: Notre Dame University Press, 1995).

15. Walter Simons, *Cities of Ladies: Beguine Communities in the Medieval Low Countries 1200–1565* (Philadelphia: University of Pennsylvania Press, 2001).

16. Jacques de Vitry, 'De b. Maria', *AASS*, Iun. iv, bk. 1, c. 1, par. 12, pp. 639–40 (hereafter '*Vita Mariae*'); Thomas de Cantimpré, 'De sancta Christina mirabili virgine vita', *AASS*, Iul. v, 637–60 (hereafter '*Vita Christinae*'; Hugh de Floreffe, 'De b. Ivetta, sive Iutta, vidua reclusa, Hui in Belgio', *AASS*, Ian. i, pp. 863–87 (hereafter '*Vita Juettae*'); Goswin of Bossut, *The Life of Ida of Nivelles*, trans. Martin Cawley (Lafayette, OR: Guadalupe Abbey, 1987) (hereafter '*Vitae Idae*'); Thomas de Cantimpré, 'De s. Lutgarde virgine, sanctimoniali Ordinis Cisterciensis, Aquiriae in Brabantia', *AASS*, Iun. iii, 231–63 (hereafter '*Vita Lutgardis*').

17. See the essays included in, *New Trends in Feminine Spirituality: The Holy Women of Liège and Their Impact*, ed. Juliette Dor, Lesley Johnson and Jocelyn Wogan-Browne (Turnhout: Brepols, 1999).

18. Bynum, *Holy Feast and Holy Fast*, p. 105.

19. There is some question as to whether these themes represented the reality of women's religious experience or the ideal their hagiographers held for holy women (see Michel Lauwers, 'L'Expérience béguinale et récit hagiographique: à propos de la *Vita Mariae Oigniacensis* de Jacques de Vitry', *Journal des savants*, 11 (1989), 61–103).

20. 'Statim, inquit, ut defuncta sum, susceperunt meam animam ministri lucis, angeli Dei, et deduxerunt me in locum quemdam tenebrosum et horridum, animabus hominum plenum. Tormenta, quae in ipso loco videbam, tanta et tam crudelia erant, ut nulla lingua haec loqui sufficeret. [...] Et responderunt mihi ductores mei: Quia hic locus purgatorius est, in quo poenitentes peccatores in vita poenas luunt [...]Post haec delata sum in paradisum [...] nunc tibi duorum optionem propono: aut nunc scilicet permanere mecum; aut ad corpus reverti, ibique agere poenas immortalis animae per mortale corpus sine detrimento sui, omnesque illas animas, quas in illo purgatorii loco miserata es ...'(*Vita Christinae*, bk. 1, c. 1, par. 11, pp. 651–52).

21. For a complete discussion of the connections between the *vita Christinae* and Thomas de Cantimpré's purgatorial piety see, Robert Sweetman, 'Christine of St Trond's Preaching Apostolate: Thomas de Cantimpré's Hagiographical Method Revisited', in *On Pilgrimage*, ed. Margot King (Toronto: Peregrina Press, 1994), pp. 411–31 (pp. 415–23).

22. *Vita Christinae*, bk. 1, c. 1, par. 11, p. 652 (fire); bk. 1, c. 1, par. 13, p. 652 (gallows).

23. *Vita Mariae*, bk. 1, c. 1, par. 12, pp. 639–40; *Vita Lutgardis*, bk. 2, c. 1, par. 2, p. 243.

24. *Vita Nicolai*, par. 5, p. 279.

25. *Vita Petri*, f. 87v.

26. *Vita Arnulfi*, bk. 1, c. 2, par. 14–16, pp. 611–12.

27. *Vita Arnulfi*, bk. 1, c. 2, par. 13, p. 611.

28. *Vita Arnulfi*, bk. 1, c. 2, par. 14, p. 611.

29. 'Corpus erit quod habes onerosum nunc et amarum, / Post istam vitam septemplice lumine clarum, / Ultra quam lux sit quam respicis et tibi luxit' (*Vita Werrici*, pp. 454–55).

30. Cf. *Vita Arnulfi*, bk. 1, c. 2, par. 12, p. 611, bk. 1, c. 3, par. 22, p. 613.

31. William of St Thierry, et al., 'Vita prima sancti Bernardi', *PL* 185, cc. 225–368 (bk. 1, c. 3, par. 12–16, cc. 230–31). For a discussion of this tradition in relation to Thomas, see, Ruth Mazo Karras, 'Thomas Aquinas's Chastity Belt', in *Gender & Christianity in Medieval Europe*, pp. 52–67 (pp. 62–63).

32. Simone Roisin, *L'Hagiographie cistercienne dans le diocèse de Liège au XIIIe siècle* (Louvain: Bibliothèque de l'Université, 1947), pp. 32–34.

33. *Vita Arnulfi*, bk. 1, c. 1, par. 7, pp. 609–10; Cf. *Vita Abundi*, c. 9, pp. 20–21. Donald Weinstein and Rudolph Bell remind us that, 'concupiscence was [...] much more than lust; it was the desire for any part of the world, any need of the self that stood in the way of loving God' (Donald Weinstein and Rudolph Bell, *Saints and Society: The Two Worlds of Western Christianity* (Chicago: University of Chicago Press, 1982), pp. 73–99).

34. Cf. Jacqueline Murray, '"The law of sin that is in my members": The problems of male embodiment', in *Gender and Holiness: Men, Women and Saints in Late Medieval Europe*, ed. Sarah Salih and Samantha J.E. Riches (New York: Routledge, 2002), pp. 9–22 (p. 15).

35. Cf. Mary C. Erler and Maryanne Kowalski, 'A New Economy of Power Relations: Female Agency in the Middle Ages', in *Gendering the Master Narrative: Women and Power in the Middle Ages* (Ithaca: Cornell University Press, 2003), pp. 1–16 (pp. 14–16).

36. Newman, '"Crucified by the Virtues"', pp. 182–209.

37. Noell, 'Expectation and Unrest', pp. 262–63.

38. Newman, '"Crucified by the Virtues"', pp. 182–209. Cf. Katrien Heene, 'Deliberate Self-Harm and Gender in Medieval Saints' Lives', *Hagiographica*, 6 (1999), 213–33 (p. 228).

39. Alan Forey, 'The Military Orders and the Conversion of Muslims in the Twelfth and Thirteenth Centuries', *Journal of Medieval History*, 28 (2002), 1–22 (pp. 13–18).

40. Katherine Allen Smith, 'Saints in Shining Armor: Martial Asceticism and Masculine Models of Sanctity, ca. 1050–1250', *Speculum*, 83 (2008), 572–602.

41. Cf. Jean Leclercq, 'Saint Martin dans l'hagiographie monastique du moyen âge', in *Saint Martin et son temps* (Rome: Studia Anselmiana, 1961), pp. 180–85.

42. Sulpicius Severus, *Vie de saint Martin*, ed. and trans. Jacques Fontaine. Sources Chrétiennes 133 (Paris: Les Editions du Cerf, 1967), p. 256.

43. Sulpicius, *Vie de saint Martin*, pp. 248–345.

44. Like the men discussed in this article, Martin is used as a model for the monk Werricus of Aulne and Charles of Villers, a thirteenth-century abbot of Villers (*Vita Werrici*, pp. 447–50; 'De Carolo VIII Villariensi abbate in Brabantia', *AASS*, Ian. ii, pp. 976–80). Even Arnulfus of Villers is described as another Martin (*Vita Arnulfi*, bk. 2, c. 1, par. 3, p. 617).

45. Jacqueline Murray, 'Masculinizing Religious Life: Sexual Prowess, the Battle for Chastity and Monastic Identity', in *Holiness and Masculinity*, ed. Katherine J. Lewis and Patricia Cullum (Cardiff: University of Wales Press, 2004), pp. 24–42 (p. 30).

46. Jean-Baptiste Lefèvre, 'Gobert, seigneur d'Aspremont et moine de Villers (v. 1187–1263)', *Villers*, 8 (1998), 5–13 (pp. 5–6); Roisin, *L'Hagiographie*, pp. 38–40.

47. Cf. M. Michaud, *Histoire des Croisades* (Paris: Furne et Cie, 1854), bk. 3, pp. 1–50, esp. pp. 20–21.

48. 'Sic dum praefatus miles, pius scilicet Gobertus, mundanae militiae adhuc vacaret, et prae cunctis coaetaneis nomen famosum usurparet; coepit in corde praeponderare, quod fama mundanae gloriae non poterat in caelo perennare' (*Vita Goberti*, bk. 1, c. 1, par. 13, p. 379).

49. *Vita Goberti*, bk. 1, c. 2, par. 22–23, p. 381.

50. *Vita Goberti*, bk. 2, c. 1, par. 38. Evidence of Gobertus's patronage is preserved in the Archives of Villers (Brussels, Archives écclesiastique du Brabant, 10967, f. 30r).

51. 'Divitias multas, quibus utebatur, [fuit] postponens, non eas tantum quasi nihilum et inane vilipendens, sed quasi vilia stercora propter Deum contemnens' (*Vita Goberti*, bk. 2, c. 1, par. 38).

52. *Vita Goberti*, bk. 2, c. 1, par. 38.

53. Barbara H. Rosenwein and Lester K. Little, 'Social Meaning in the Monastic and Mendicant Spiritualities', *Past and Present*, 63 (1974), 4–32.

54. *Vita Goberti*, bk. 1, c. 2, par. 22–23, p. 381.

55. *Vita Werrici*, p. 451.

56. 'Protege me domine, quia nil queo vestis habere' (*Vita Werrici*, p. 452). The word 'protego –ere' has the meanings of both 'to protect' and 'to cover' (*Lewis and Short* s. v. *protego –ere*, p. 1478, col. A).

57. Cf. Newman, *From Virile Woman to WomanChrist*, pp. 137–67.

58. *Vita Mariae*, prologue, par. 2, p. 636; bk. 1, c. 3, par. 31, p. 644.

59. *Vita Juettae*, c. 9, par. 21, p. 867; c. 10, par. 34, p. 870; c. 14, par. 43, pp. 871–72.

60. *Vita Lutgardis*, bk. 2, c. 3, par. 43, p. 253.

61. *Vita Idae*, c. 13, p. 50; c. 14, p. 51.

62. Cf. *Vita Mariae*, bk. 1, c. 3, par. 31, p. 644; bk. 2, c. 6, par. 61, pp. 651–52.

63. *Vita Mariae*, bk. 2, c. 8, par. 75, p. 656. Cf. Murray, '"The law of sin"', pp. 14–18.

64. E. Ann Matter has explored the theme of mystical marriages in the *vitae* of female saints. See Matter, 'Mystical Marriage', in *Women and Faith: Catholic Religious Life in Italy from Late Antiquity to the Present* (Boston: Harvard University Press, 1993), pp. 31–41. Bridal imagery in the *vitae* of holy men has been addressed, but remains a promising area for further study. Cf. Carolyn Diskant Muir, 'Bride or Bridegroom? Masculine Identity in Mystic Marriage', in *Holiness and Masculinity*, pp. 58–78.

65. Ruth Mazo Karras makes a compelling case for celibate clerics not renouncing masculinity. Similar arguments apply here, see Karras, 'Thomas Aquinas' Chastity Belt', pp. 53–58.

66. Catherine Mooney has shown how masculine and feminine imagery complement each other in the portrayal of Francis of Assisi. See Catherine M. Mooney, 'Francis of Assisi as Father, Mother and Androgynous Figure', in *The Boswell Thesis: Essays on Christianity, Social Tolerance and Homosexuality*, ed. Mathew Kuefler (Chicago: University of Chicago Press, 2006), pp. 301–32.

67. 'Nec apparuit in loco dicto aliquod vestigium genitalium nisi sola planities plana, clara et mundo, reverberans oculos intuentium claritate nimia' (*Chronica Villariensis monasterii*, ed. Georg Waitz, *Monumenta Germaniae Historica, Scriptores*, 29 vols (Hanover: Hahn, 1826–94), xxv, pp. 192–235 (bk. 1, c. 25, p. 202).

68. Jacqueline Murray, 'Mystical Castration: Some Reflections on Peter Abelard, Hugh of Lincoln and Sexual Purity', in *Conflicted Identities and Multiple Masculinities*, ed. Jacqueline Murray (New York: Garland Publishing, 1999), pp. 73–110.

69. On the process of cultivating another form of manliness see Martin Irvine, 'Abelard and (Re) Writing the Male Body: Castration, Identity, and Remasculinization', in *Becoming Male in the Middle Ages*, pp. 87–106. On the masculinization of women see Castelli, '"I Will Make Mary Male"', pp. 29–49.

70. For a discussion of the interdependence of male and female religious communities see Jean-Baptiste Lefèvre, 'L'Abbaye de Villers et le monde des moniales et des béguines au XIIIe Siècle', *Villers: Une Abbaye revisitée* (Villers-la-Ville: APTCV, Actes du colloque 10–12 avril 1996), pp. 183–230.

71. For observations on the difficulties of clerical celibacy in the changing devotional climate of the high Middle Ages, see Murray, 'Mystical Castration', pp. 73–74, 86–87, n. 2.

72. Murray, '"The law of sin"', pp. 9–22; idem, 'Masculinizing Religious Life', pp. 24–42.

73. Murray, '"The law of sin"', pp. 9–22.

74. Judith Butler, *Gender Trouble: Feminism and the Subversion of Identity* (New York: Routledge, 1990; repr. 1999), pp. 181–90.

75. Bernard McGinn, *The Flowering of Mysticism* (New York: The Crossroad Publishing Company, 1998), pp. 18–24.

76. Denys Turner, *Eros and Allegory* (Kalamazoo: Cistercian Publications, 1995), pp. 47–49.

77. *Vita Abundi*, c. 7, p. 18. Cf. Luke 12: 49 and Psalm 38: 3–4.

78. *Vita Arnulfi*, bk. 2, c. 3, par. 20, p. 621.

79. *Vita Arnulfi*, bk. 1, c. 5, par. 37, p. 616; *Vita Nicolai*, par. 5, p. 279.

80. Caroline Walker Bynum, *Jesus as Mother: Studies in the Spirituality of the High Middle Ages* (Berkeley: University of California Press, 1982), pp. 154–62.

81. Butler, *Gender Trouble*, pp. 73–83.

4

Constructing Political Rule, Transforming Gender Scripts: Revisiting the Thirteenth-Century Rule of Joan and Margaret, Countesses of Flanders

Francesca Canadé Sautman

The Exception and the Rule

Aristocratic women, who ruled on their own, or as consorts, widows, mothers and sisters, have been documented all over Europe.[1] Yet, as Kimberly LoPrete has argued, the leadership of high-born women in the Middle Ages is less akin to an unfurling of startling gender transgressions than to an extension of their domestic roles in the realms of organization and politics.[2] Indeed, it appears that in the thirteenth century, the weakness assigned to the female sex by a patriarchal ideology could be superseded by lineage and direct blood lines, and could confer to high-born women the prestige and sacred aura normally reserved for the male ruler.

This essay considers the rule of two countesses of Flanders: Joan (b. 1200, r. 1214–44) and her sister Margaret (b. 1202, r. 1244–78). These women were the rightful heirs to the comital throne and, following the Flemish disaster at Bouvines in 1214, they ruled successfully for over sixty years. During this time, social and political upheavals frequently threatened their rule and most modern historians have linked these events to gender constraints. However, I will argue here that it was the general political context, rather than sex and gender, which, at times, hampered the countesses' rule. I suggest that the countesses were able to affirm themselves at once as 'rightful lords' (*droit seigneur*) and as ruling princes through inheritance and prestigious lineage. For instance, they used force, and applied policies and managerial skills that benefited the economy of their counties, making use of the 'commercial revolution' of the thirteenth century.[3] Thus the rule of the countesses at once overlaps with and diverges from the model proposed by LoPrete. Their leadership and managerial roles did not extend effortlessly from a primarily domestic sphere as LoPrete has argued for other women: Joan was effectively alone for much of her life, contending directly with the world of male power, and Margaret was accused of deviating from the proper roles of wife and mother to maintain her own rule, and engaged in military conflict with her first sons over territory and for political power. This perceived deviation was more disturbing to later and modern commentators than to Joan and Margaret's contemporaries, for whom waging war against neighbours over territorial integrity was the duty of a ruler, meaning that Margaret was judged according to local and regional allegiances.[4]

The countesses have elicited the attention of chroniclers since the thirteenth century, although most accounts were written much later than the events narrated.[5] Most recently, Erin Jordan has focused on the ways the countesses shaped their rule through monastic donations and other received practices of piety. They aimed towards both spiritual and secular gains, and towards the articulation and reinforcement of political power under otherwise difficult conditions.[6] Jordan's interpretation of the countesses' rule postulates a clear distinction between authority and power. She sees authority, not infrequently given to women, as resulting from hereditary claims; however, she defines power, or the ability to actually exercise rule, as the province of men. According to Jordan, only a warrior-count physically able to lead his troops and do battle for his lands could hold both authority and power. She remarks that Joan and Margaret brokered arrangements that obtained them power through the careful and extensive management of piety, an area not contested to women. Nevertheless, Jordan maintains that, to a large extent, their reigns were made possible and durable only because having a militarily weak female ruler on the comital throne was to the advantage of the French kings.[7]

This stark contrast requires further nuance. Neither gendered prejudice nor the fact that women did not traditionally bear arms prevented many power-sharing instances where women ruled, nor, conversely, did force of arms guarantee the stable exercise of power by men. Rather, both countesses maintained their rule in spite of the way specific gender scripts – submissive daughter, loyal and obedient wife, protective and self-effacing mother – were invoked against them within broader social and political movements. Their durability reflected the major changes in the way regional power was being exercised from the thirteenth century, as lineage and social position played an increasingly decisive role along with gender, and 'managerial' skills countered the absence of military ones. Furthermore, in the period in question, 'power' itself could be broken down into many forms, including those of 'coercion' and those of 'persuasion'.[8] 'Power' was not limited to 'being able to command and to punish, both functions of the sword,' as Georges Duby proposed; instead, as Karen Nicholas argues, '[...] there is also power in leadership, family connections, administration, property, and money, and women might wield these'.[9] As many complex layers of power are examined, it becomes increasingly apparent that the assumption that women could not defend their realms is a major obstacle to understanding how exactly women *were* able to govern successfully. Furthermore, since women, including the countesses, often fulfilled their potential during times of peace, when they could be apt administrators and managers, war should not be taken as the yardstick by which to measure the success of the countesses' reigns.

Joan and Margaret were not the first female rulers of Flanders. From Richildis of Hainaut (r. 1067–70) to their mother Marie of Champagne (r. 1194–1204), women had ruled or had claimed the right to rule the country.[10] Some acted as regents, some as direct heirs to whom their husbands conceded authority on many state affairs, and some ruled because their strong personalities enabled them to exert influence. A number of noteworthy aspects of the reign of Joan and Margaret have attracted the attention of chroniclers and historians. First, the daughters of Baldwin IX acceded to the throne of Flanders in the absence of male heirs and ruled fully in their own right and largely alone.[11] It was extremely rare for sisters to succeed each other. Joan, who died childless, was survived by her second husband, Thomas of Savoy. Although Thomas had been recognized as count by the Flemish, he made no claims to the Flemish throne and returned to Savoy after Joan's death. The accession of Margaret therefore appears to indicate a preference for the direct bloodline. In addition, several other events to be examined here generated commentary on the reigns of Joan and Margaret. These are the False Baldwin's claim to being their returned father, and the consequences of Margaret's two marriages.

In 1225, the minstrel Bertrand de Rains claimed to be the real Baldwin IX, Joan and Margaret's father, who had finally returned alive and incognito from the Crusades. Bertrand's fanciful claims became the rallying point, first of resentful noblemen, and then of a vast popular movement, leading to uprisings against an increasingly isolated Joan. She was accused of being a denatured daughter and had to seek help from King Louis VIII to end this rebellion.[12] As for Margaret, she was married in 1212 to the knight Burchard of Avesnes (c. 1172/1182–1244), her tutor and a trusted retainer of the counts. The marriage took place in the absence of Joan and her first husband Ferrand of Portugal (+1233) or any of their representatives, in front of Burchard's allies and relatives at the comital castle of Le Quesnoy.[13] Within a few years, it was revealed that Burchard had been ordained, and was thus ineligible to marry. The union was finally dissolved after several papal decrees and ten years of acrimonious disputes spearheaded by Joan.[14] In 1223, Margaret married William of Dampierre, and her children by Burchard were withheld from their father. Joan died in 1244 without direct heirs, and the inheritance of the counties, especially of the larger and more prosperous Flanders, incited lasting dissent between Margaret's Avesnes and Dampierre sons.[15] Claims and counter-claims of illegitimate birth and of who was to rule the counties were settled by two royal decrees, one in 1246 and one in 1256, which bypassed the vexed legitimacy issue. These decrees permanently separated Hainaut, which was allocated to the Avesnes, and Flanders, allocated to the Dampierres.[16] Conflict between half-brothers was not unusual: customary law in lands under French sovereignty (including Flanders), by stating that no man could be claimed bastard by the mother, implied that mothers were in fact expected to disfavour their first issue, as Margaret did.[17] Yet, while Margaret did not support John of Avesnes's relentless pursuit of legitimation and thus primogeniture and the lordship of Flanders, she herself did not officially speak against legitimation until her appeal to the pope in 1253.[18] This petition was mostly about financial hardship, and came years after the Avesnes had betrayed and attacked her in an alliance with William of Holland and other enemies of Flanders that, by then, had orchestrated a full-scale rebellion against her in Hainaut. The traditional view that Margaret harried her first sons was largely due to later commentary such as Jacques de Guyse's irate reaction to that petition, in which she had invoked procedure and the need for peace.[19] In effect, it was Margaret's separation from Burchard that was held against her by contemporaries in particular. In 1242, she remarked that she had been deceived and would never have stayed with Burchard had she known he was a subdeacon.[20] This was considered proof of her good faith at the time, a key element in the arguments for the validity of the marriage invoked by the Avesnes, and upheld by accommodations to canon law (putative marriage).[21] By contesting the validity of her marriage – or allowing her Dampierre sons to make that public statement, as they did repeatedly in disputing their brothers' legitimacy – Margaret assumed the dishonourable status of concubine. Despite the irregularities of the marriage, leaving Burchard elicited widespread condemnation. This is evident not only, predictably, from the Avesnes, who sternly remarked that the 'real scandal was that she left him of her own authority',[22] but also in a passage from Mouskes.[23] Finally, in depositions in the 1249 legitimacy proceedings (concluded in the Avesnes' favour by papal decree in 1252), Avesnes witnesses to the 1212 wedding swore not only to Margaret's consent, but to her marriage proposal to Burchard, and joyful mood and amorous behaviour towards him, so public and sexually aggressive that guests were 'averting their eyes'.[24] Thus, in all its forms, the legitimacy quarrel could only reflect poorly on the dignity of Margaret's person, yet it appears that she had reasons of her own for agreeing to endure these stains on her honour.[25]

Despite these ordeals, the countesses survived and prevailed. They acted in secular and religious matters, on behalf of trades, towns, and of churches, abbeys and particularly women's monasteries and religious houses. Contrary to what has been affirmed, they were not unable to conduct war when major political crises offered no other solution, as had been the case for many ruling women before them. Yet war was not the defining feature of their reigns, during which protecting the economic interests of Flanders by 'managing peace' was of the greatest importance. The role of rank in the countesses' ability to withstand these challenges and to continue to rule cannot be underestimated.[26] Joan and Margaret were first cousins to King Louis VIII.[27] They carried royal blood through their mother, Marie of Champagne, and they were related to the kings of England through their paternal grandmother.[28] Nevertheless, rank was not everything, and the volatile fusion of the public and the private compelled them to face intense public displays of their domestic and even intimate lives. At the same time, in Flanders, the limitations imposed on medieval women by the gender order were mitigated by a number of favourable legal provisions.[29] Joan and Margaret's reigns show the complex relations of gender to power, the delicate balance between the constraints of gender and the ability not only of women to handle it, but of contemporaries, male in the first instance, to look beyond it.

Women and the Rule of War

It is necessary to readdress two fallacies regarding medieval women's role in military conflicts due to their perceived significance for the difficulties the countesses faced. First, the fact that women were not trained in fighting skills does not mean that they were unable to lead troops in the face of danger. Second, the fact that men did bear arms did not guarantee that they would successfully protect their lands. The historical record both includes precedents for the military involvement of aristocratic women in medieval Flanders, and evidence that it was not uncommon for such women to lead their troops. Both the dangers and the acceptance of this are illustrated by the example of Richildis, countess of Hainaut and, briefly, of Flanders, who lost her claim to that county in a battle with Robert the Frisian in 1071.[30] Later, in an Hennuyer assault on Douai in 1147, Count Baldwin IV was repelled by forces led by the Countess Sibyl. Interestingly, Gislebertus of Mons, loyal to the Hainaut counts, only vaguely alludes to this embarrassing event in his chronicle, simply noting that Baldwin fought '…especially with Count Thierry of Flanders and his wife, Sibyl, daughter of the count of Anjou'.[31] Even reluctant aristocratic women, like Johanna, the pregnant wife of Raymond of Toulouse, could be ordered to battlefield duty.[32] Thus, even though there is no indication that women rulers were actual combatants, their presence at the head of troops ranged from accepted to expected, or even required.

Indeed, 'virile' women – those who displayed courage by acting, as the hagiographers and early Church fathers would have it, not '*mulieriter*' but '*viriliter*'[33] – performed combativeness in contexts of which their society approved, and these could be extensive during wars.[34] Margaret did not shock commentators as a woman waging war with neighbouring rulers over territorial rights and homage due – on the contrary. After the disastrous Walcheren expedition of 4 July 1253, her son-in-law Thibaut of Bar, imprisoned by the Avesnes, penned a plaintive couplet reminding her that he had obeyed her every wish since a young age and was now in dire straits on her account, and calling on her to retaliate, underscoring her legitimacy as lord and war leader, as is consistent with accounts of Flemish operations during that episode.[35] Thus, women's socially prescribed roles as daughters, wives and mothers somehow coexisted with the approved gender deviance of temporary virility. The conduct of warfare underlines how much the workings of gender are not only historically determined, but also a reflection of the local and the particular. Here, an aspect of Judith Butler's understanding of gender is helpful. The situation reflects what Butler terms 'dissonant gendered features', which lose their significance if one regards masculinity and femininity, or by extension the gendered expectations of the roles of 'man' and 'woman', as performances rather than substantial categories. In other words, attributes (such as virility or virile qualities) might signify most effectively without being forced into a 'coherence' that is neither intrinsic nor essential, but 'created by the regulation of attributes'.[36] As feminine rule necessitates a flexible construction of gender that does not adhere to a single script it is not surprising that the varied factors that shaped rule or military action by medieval women formulate a set of dissonant gendered features.

Once entrusted with hereditary rule, women acted as sovereigns who were to be obeyed; familial and societal roles could complicate women's management of power, as well as enhance their access to it. This was hardest for unmarried daughters, as in the case of Joan, who was only released from the king's authority after her marriage to Ferrand. For women such as Joan, only a break in standardized gender coherence allows the masculine political and military functions of the prince to be inscribed and enacted on the sexed body of a woman. The presence of non-combatant aristocratic women at the head of troops was unrelated to military prowess but akin to a galvanizing symbolic force that transcended both sex and gender roles. It effectuated the displacement to the front lines of the sacred efficiency of a ruler embodied in the person itself. We see some of these types of complex relations operating in the struggles of the countesses against rebellion and territorial loss.

Joan resorted to force early in her reign. The object of that local war was none other than her sister. How Burchard's marriage to the sister of the countess of Flanders and Hainaut was allowed to take place remains a mystery, but Joan's opposition to the union became most evident once she ruled alone. Immediately after the marriage, Burchard began to stake serious claims to Flemish lands as part of his wife's share of Baldwin IX's inheritance, and reaffirmed them after the battle of Bouvines. Joan adamantly refused his demands and, beginning in 1214, took every step to have the marriage annulled, Burchard excommunicated and her sister returned to her. Physical warfare ensued between the Countess Joan and Burchard over these matters.[37] People faithful to the countess found and killed Burchard's younger brother Guy during skirmishes in Hainaut in 1219 and Burchard himself was taken prisoner by Joan and held for two years, while she kept her sister with her at her court, a situation which led to Margaret's prompt remarriage.[38]

The next incident in Joan's reign that required the use of force was the crisis brought about by the appearance of the False Baldwin in 1225. The minstrel Bertrand, claiming to be Baldwin IX, long presumed dead, returned from the Crusades, exacerbating existing social unrest. At the time of his appearance, Flanders was suffering from famine. Furthermore, the lower guilds, increasingly disenfranchised by the wealthy burghers who were consistently favoured by the counts in administrative arrangements, were growing ever more indignant and angry. Actions by powerful aldermen worsened stark class divisions and the revolt against Joan was one of the first among many social uprisings in Flanders based on deep class oppositions among the masses.[39] Foremost among these opponents were a vengeful Burchard (also desirous of retrieving his children) and his allies, who actively campaigned against Joan. Their actions influenced many of the nobility who then deserted Joan.[40] Flemish cities rose against the countess, communes rallied to the impostor's cause and only a few remained loyal to Joan who had to flee one stronghold after another and was almost seized by rebels.[41] Henry III of England, eager to keep a hand on Flemish affairs, recognized the False Baldwin as count, which benefited the pro-English stance of many of the towns.[42]

Joan had little choice but to call for back-up from her liege and cousin, King Louis VIII, who used a ploy to unmask the impostor, something only outside, regal, authority (deemed impartial) could achieve. Bertrand fled to the borderlands of Burgundy. He was eventually caught by the French and handed over to the countess, who exacted fierce retribution, hanging the man after a carefully crafted spectacle of public shaming.[43] The French monarch extracted considerable sums from Flanders as a result of the incident and, once again, historians blamed Joan, or Joan's gendered status, for Flanders' new debt. The suggestion in modern interpretations that Joan's husband Ferrand or another male would have fared better assumes that fear or repression could undo the impact of such explosive social conditions.[44]

In response to this, Joan resorted to as much force as she could muster, choosing a military course of action and rallying those faithful to her: in fact, contrary to what is repeated in most commentary on the events, some of the most significant men of the realm stood by her.[45] She campaigned successfully against the rebel cities, Valenciennes, Lille and Le Quesnoy and between November 1225 and May 1226 Joan re-established her authority over Flanders. Yet Joan appeared to prefer entreaty and persuasion to outright repression while besieging Valenciennes. It was during this siege, related in an extensive passage of Mouskes' chronicle, that Joan tried to balance 'powers of coercion' with 'powers of persuasion', negotiating with the besieged citizens who would not renounce Bertrand as Baldwin. The *jurati* had been deposed, and the 'little people' had taken over, refusing to bow to the countess unless the wildcat commune they had set up was recognized. At this point Joan rejected their demands and intimated that the rebels would have to throw themselves on her mercies, or 'never enjoy her love again', and that they had, 'by their folly', heaped shame on both Hainaut and Flanders. The stalemate ended in words of 'mortal defiance', but the town soon gave in.[46] Mouskes' description is remarkable in its subtle gendered coding of words of beseeching and aggression, and in the rare defining of 'honour' in a woman's voice.

Margaret's relation to war was embedded in a long history of regional struggles over territory. The rivalry of Margaret's sons dramatized these military situations, but the larger picture was the centuries-old battle with the rulers of Holland over control of the Zeeland islands, ancient hostilities and competition for control between Flanders and Hainaut,[47] and competition between the German empire and the French king. These were all serious territorial disputes rooted neither in gender nor in motherhood.[48] An expedition led by Margaret herself in 1247 against the Zeeland islands, in affirmation of Flemish claims, had to be abandoned because, she later charged, her support on the ground from her Avesnes sons, allies of Holland, was tantamount to sabotage.[49] Then her son John of Avesnes attacked her directly by taking over her castle of Rupelmonde, an important strategic position. In response, Margaret mobilized her troops and took it back.[50] To hold on to Hainaut, where, as its first *pairie*, the Avesnes had a strong footing and nobles supported John as its rightful lord over his mother, she engaged in large-scale military operations and made drastic decisions, not all of them successful or wise. Finally, however, she triumphed over all her enemies, combining might with a powerful alliance with the French king.

Similar events with all-male casts are not unknown but it is unlikely that a male ruler would have been blamed, whether by contemporaries or by later historians, for trying to maintain the territories under his governance; keeping Hainaut and Flanders together was no easy task in view of the tensions between the two neighbouring counties.[51] While rebellion against Joan was easily imputed to her 'weak sex', the fact is that after Margaret, no ruler of Flanders, from her son Guy of Dampierre to the powerful dukes of Burgundy in the fifteenth century, was spared major rebellion and unrest emanating from Flemish cities and their warring factions. Joan and Margaret's rule was not, therefore, the watershed of disaster for Flanders that some have claimed. Rather, in late medieval Flanders, several male rulers had to contend with a much higher level of social and political unrest than either Joan or Margaret.[52]

Ruling Peace

Facing crises with much broader implications than their personal fates, both countesses adopted complex strategies to navigate a delicate political situation between the French and English monarchs. More specifically, both countesses supported the needs of the Flemish economy and its place in an international trade largely based on wines and textiles. This economy created an intricate web of obligations and competing interests. For instance, wool was essential for the Flemish textile industry, and obtaining it readily and at the most advantageous costs was a fundamental motor of the connection between England and Flanders. Trade and accumulation of wealth thus meant very high stakes for all involved, from the burgers to the contending monarchs, and success could be increasingly evaluated, not in counts of gender transgression, but in bags of wool. As Theo Luykx has suggested, this kind of peaceful management, in which their administrative skills found a favourable terrain, was a more effective theatre of operations for the countesses than waging constant war.[53] This was especially true for Margaret, who came to the throne with greater experience of life and power than Joan had possessed.

Over the years, Joan was able to make important administrative and economic decisions. In 1219, in what appears to have been a response to a constant financial worry among rulers at this time, she substituted a yearly gift of eighty *hoeds* of oats, to be paid in three terms, for the yearly gift of eighty Flemish pounds that her father had instituted for the church of Notre-Dame at Courtrai.[54] In 1225, she ordered fact-finding missions to ascertain the attribution of certain privileges, like the *grute*, a fee collected on the grain used to make beer.[55] In 1237, she negotiated indemnities directly with the king of England in the trade war that was brewing over the damage sustained by her merchants from Ypres and her men from Bruges.[56] After Ferrand's return from captivity, when he was ransomed by her, and through her later marriage to Thomas of Savoy, Joan was no longer left out or marginalized in official documents, which were signed and sealed by the countess.[57] Her policies regarding urban government included typical collaboration with the patrician classes but they were also intended to reduce and eliminate various servitudes imposed on the poorest people.[58] Thus, Ferrand and Joan conferred a charter certifying that the inhabitants of the Franc of Bruges and of Ursele were freed from the servitude of the *meilleur catel* ('highest asset'),[59] and in another, with her second husband, Thomas of Savoy, she abolished the tax known as the 'Balfard', 'understanding that only the poor suffered in the imposition of the Balfard'.[60]

Joan's marriage to Thomas of Savoy in 1237 was conducive to this form of economic management. They appear to have worked as efficacious rulers, pursuing the reduction of privileges, delivering more *keures* to lands and towns.[61] Joan bequeathed Thomas a hefty yearly revenue, which Margaret later tried to eschew paying on the pretext that Thomas was then in the service of the excommunicated emperor, Frederic II.[62]

Widowed in 1233, Margaret did not remarry. Once she inherited the throne from Joan, she never entirely relinquished comital power and remained actively involved in it even when one of her sons became the titular count.[63] Contrary to frequently negative depictions of her by later chroniclers and historians, Margaret was a savvy administrator who sought to develop the wealth of her lands. Debt reduction was a pressing problem and figured high on her list, as witnessed by her decision in February 1245 concerning Joan's will, in which she divided up yearly payment for charitable gifts and debts into twenty-nine separate individual and municipal holdings.[64] Around 1250, she produced a protectionist ordinance with very detailed regulations for the yearly trade fairs of Flanders, which became the standard for subsequent such legislation in the region.[65] Combining protection of Flemish trade with incentives for foreign merchants, it limited sales of wool cloth right before and after the fair, closed down all the covered markets before the fair and during merchant travel and stipulated allowances for overseas and foreign merchants. It also limited sales of items such as wax, furs and leather and strictly regulated the price of wine during the fairs. The countess reserved the right to clarify and interpret this already complex ordinance, reflecting a comprehensive outlook towards commerce ranging from profit to access and distribution.[66] Margaret encouraged canal-building in her county which led to the development and wealth of the town and port of Gravelines through franchises to the mayors and communes of St-Jean d'Angelys and Niort in the west of France, and to the merchants of Poitou and Gascogne who came there to do business.[67] She also increased state revenues by investment, purchasing unused lands and leasing them, while efficiently and consistently reducing Flanders' debt, so that it was much lower when she died than when she began her reign.[68]

The shift in the concept of nobility, which Fiona Dunlop illustrates later in this volume for the early sixteenth century, was already apparent in the rise of the Flemish patricians in the late fourteenth century.[69] It was also foreshadowed by thirteenth-century changes in aristocratic women's exercise of power, as seen in the countesses' rule. While many of its components were present in earlier reigns by women (the combination of prestige, rank, power, the use of both offensive and defensive force, even attention to social and economic policies), the balance of these elements was different. The intensity of economic concerns within it reflected that great economic leap of the second half of the thirteenth century in Flanders, referred to by Marc Boone as 'the "Indian Summer" of medieval economic growth'.[70] At this time it appears that talents such as policy-making and administration increasingly paralleled or even replaced military competence as the basic requirement of secular leadership, perhaps more so even at a juncture when Flanders' independence was being chipped away. This may have been particularly the case for women rulers who were expected to behave *'viriliter'*, but not to be warriors, and more so later when infantry became the decisive factor over noble cavalries in the success of battles. The advent of an organized, professionalized, bureaucratic class did not lead to women losing their tiny foothold on power; rather the rise of that class provided a number of high-ranking women with a niche to occupy – a trend which continued through the fifteenth and sixteenth centuries. These possibilities expanded as power became less invested in the person and more enacted through a state, organized with a vast and carefully structured bureaucracy. As Jordan has astutely suggested, 'the count's authority did not derive from his person, but rather from the office he inherited and occupied'.[71] Not only could women benefit from this type of situation, but women at many levels of society had a role in public affairs. Ellen Kittell has shown that in Flanders, particularly before the fifteenth century, noblewomen of all ranks and even middle-class women were fully involved in business, commerce and financial matters, and were present as officials and creditors, not just as debtors, at routine financial accounting sessions.[72] It is no coincidence that Margaret waged a protracted battle to establish her rule against an increasingly hostile Hainaut, where the rules of the empire for inheriting fiefs through the male line only were marshalled against her in 1245 by the bishop of Liège and his allies.[73] Thus, while wielding power in their own right and in the context of their time, Joan and Margaret also seem to announce these changes on the horizons for women rulers, due to the alacrity of rising economic needs that counterbalanced the demands of fierce performance on the battlefield. This is evident in the region in the fourteenth century with Mahaut of Artois, Margaret of Flanders, duchess of Burgundy, and Margaret of Bavaria.[74] In the fifteenth century, Isabel of Portugal (1397–1471), consort of Philip the Good, brought to the duchy her competence and constant interest in civil and economic affairs. She negotiated contracts and diplomatic treatises, and vied for optimal trade agreements with England at the very moment when her husband was falling increasingly under the sway of France.

Conclusion

This essay has revisited the negative or limiting assessments of the rule of Joan and Margaret by viewing gender roles as contextual, morphing and transformative, rather than fixed and constraining. Through the fluctuations of gender, the now-axiomatic theory of the 'king's two bodies' can also be applied to the histories of women rulers as a symbolic division of comital power into a contingent aspect, incarnated in an individual who might be a woman, and an essential, revered aspect, that of political representation. Furthermore, a woman's femininity could be affirmed or attacked through an array of potentials that included both conformist and, often temporary, unconventional interpretations of the feminine role.

These processes were at work in the rule of the countesses. Joan was able to maintain, against a powerful and effective gender script directed at her as a wayward daughter, the notion of 'rightful lord'. She did this by making use of bloodlines, inheritance, rank and regional authority. She also found ways to circumvent various forms of male overlordship and in particular to weld power to marriage, especially in her second union, as she matured as a woman and a ruler. Her sister Margaret survived hatred, humiliation and ridicule imparted by marital and familial conflicts. Her sons' legitimacy proceedings implicated the integrity of her person and made very public a part of herself, the socially and intimately marked body of the married woman, over which they sought rhetorical and narrative control. By rejecting the legitimacy of her first marriage and, thus, first sons, she took the risk of casting doubt on the moral legitimacy of her own body. She handled the risk by welding the integrity of her person to a familiar script: the battles of a prince sparing no effort to maintain legitimate lordship and territorial integrity.

The vulnerabilities in the countesses' reigns were due neither to an essential category of sex, nor to proscriptive articulations of gender identifications, but mostly to larger societal factors, in which they were both free agents and collective participants. Of course, war did not cease to be a major element in the European political landscape, but at the time of their rule, the needs of economic administration conferred new weight to the organizational, accounting and diplomatic skills possessed by many high-ranking women. Expectations placed on a ruler shifted from the exclusive focus on the qualities of a male-defined warrior-prince to include those of a managerial ruler in step with the economic needs of a complex trade and production society such as Flanders. Yet, Joan and Margaret operated fully in the thick of power relations, gender constraints and presumptions of female inferiority notwithstanding, forcefully ruling as 'rightful lords' and as princes who 'managed peace' through the economic, rather than the domestic sphere. The countesses of Flanders thus performed a delicate balancing of the contradictions of gender and the imperatives of politics at a turning point in Flemish history.

Notes

1. See for example Erin Jordan, *Women, Power, and Religious Patronage in the Middle Ages* (New York: Palgrave Macmillan, 2006); the essays in *Medieval Queenship*, ed. John Carmi Parsons (New York: St. Martins Press, 1993); *Queens, Regents and Potentates*, ed. Theresa M. Vann (Dallas: Academia, 1993); *Aristocratic Women in Medieval France*, ed. Theodore Evergates (Philadelphia: University of Pennsylvania Press, 1999); Michelle Bubenicek, *Quand les femmes gouvernent: droit et politique au XIVe siècle, Yolande de France* (Paris: Ecole des Chartes, 2002); *Capetian Women*, ed. Kathleen Nolan

(New York: Palgrave, 2003); *Queenship and Political Power in Medieval and Early Modern Spain*, ed. Theresa Earenfight (Aldershot: Ashgate, 2005).

2.   Kimberly A. LoPrete, 'The Gender of Lordly Women: The Case of Adela of Blois', in *Pawns or Players? Studies on Medieval and Early Modern Women*, ed. Christine Meek and Catherine Lawless (Dublin: Four Courts Press, 2003), pp. 90–110.

3.   Mark Angelos, 'Urban Women, Investment, and the Commercial Revolution of the Middle Ages', in *Women in Medieval Western European Culture*, ed. Linda E. Mitchell (New York: Garland Publishing, 1999), pp. 257–72; on Flanders specifically, see pp. 259–61.

4.   Charles Albert Duvivier, *La Querelle des Avesnes et des Dampierre, jusqu'à la mort de Jean d'Avesnes, 1257*, 2 vols (Brussels: C. Muquardt, Paris: Alphonse Picard, 1894), lists pertinent texts of the thirteenth century and later, both favourable to Countess Margaret, such as the *Récits d'un Ménestrel de Reims*, c. 1260, and Flemish chronicles written later under the Dampierres, or supportive of the Avesnes cause, such as Matthew Paris, in the service of the English king, whose chronicle goes to 1259, and Jacques de Guyse's fourteenth-century compilation, *Histoire de Hainaut par Jacques de Guyse, traduite en français [moderne] avec le texte latin en regard, et accompagné de notes*, 2 vols (Paris: A. Sautelet; Brussels: Arnold Lacrosse, 1826–38), I, pp. 5–12.

5.   Despite his avowedly pro-French stance, Philippe Mouskes (also written Mousket), bishop of Tournai in the thirteenth century and a witness to some of these events, provides one of the most useful narratives. See *Chronique rimée de Philippe Mouskes, évêque de Tournai au 13e siècle. Publiée pour la première fois avec des préliminaires, un commentaire, et des appendices*, ed. Baron de Reiffenberg, 2 vols (Brussels: M. Hayez, 1836). For a precise review of all available sources and their respective flaws, see Jordan, *Women, Power, and Religious Patronage*, pp. 6–9.

6.   Jordan, *Women, Power, and Religious Patronage*, pp. 112–15.

7.   Jordan, *Women, Power, and Religious Patronage*, pp. 39, 46–47.

8.   See Anneke B. Mulder-Bakker, 'Jeanne of Valois: The Power of a Consort', in *Capetian Women*, pp. 255–69.

9.   Karen S. Nicholas, 'Women as Rulers: Countesses Jeanne and Marguerite of Flanders (1212–1278)', in *Queens, Regents and Potentates*, pp. 73–89 (p. 76). Here, Nicholas discusses George Duby's conference paper, 'Les femmes et le pouvoir', given at 'Power and Society in the Twelfth Century (1050–1225)' (Harvard University, 1991).

10.   Others include Clemence of Burgundy (1093–1119), Sybil of Anjou (1134–57), Margaret of Flanders (1191–94) and the Portuguese Mathilda of Flanders (1183–91).

11.   Joan ruled alone from 1214 to the end of 1226 while her husband Ferrand of Portugal was jailed in France, and again after Ferrand's death from 1233 to 1237, before she remarried; Margaret ruled alone for most of the thirty-four years of her reign.

12.   For the full narrative of the Bertrand de Rains episode, see Mouskes, *Chronique*, II, pp. 452–85, vss. 24465–25324. Mouskes alludes to the 'bad daughter' theme; in upholding her double status as rightful lord and heir to the land, he notes that she was unfairly 'renoiiee' (disowned, denied, p. 464, v. 24797) for, had she recognized the lost count for certain, she would have been the first to rejoice. Mouskes denounces those 'que lor dame del sien gietoient / Cil ki si home et sierf estoient / Et si l' avoient doublement / Asseuree voirement' (who were ejecting their lady from her own lands / those who were her (liege) men and her serfs / and who had doubly given their / oath and assurance to her), II, pp. 464–65, vss. 24800–24817. In this essay, all translations from Old French are my own.

13.   See Jordan, *Women, Power, and Religious Patronage*, pp. 39–41, on lack of consent from Joan and Ferrand. Duvivier, partial to the Avesnes, claims that they did consent to the marriage, on the basis of documents signed by Ferrand and that it was public, not secretive – a cause for invalidation – as asserted by Avesnes supporters in the 1249 proceedings (Duvivier, *La Querelle des Avesnes*, I, pp. 62–63 and II, #144, pp. 228–51). Duvivier also takes Margaret's consent at face value, dismissing her pre-nubile age, although he admits such a marriage was normally at age twelve (Duvivier, *La Querelle des Avesnes*, I, pp. 57–61 and I, p. 110, II, #43). However, a passage in Mouskes (*Chronique*, pp. 412, vss. 23275–23278) suggests that the wedding was indeed unofficial: 'Et mesire Boucars ot prise, / Al mious k' il pot et a sa guise, / Serour Jehane, la contesse, / Sans don, sans tiere et sans promesse' (and Sir Burchard took / as best he could and to his fancy / the sister of Joan, the countess, / without gift, without land and without her being promised).

14.   Joan invoked Burchard's ordained status, the absence of comital authorization and prohibited consanguinity. The papal decrees (Duvivier, *La Querelle des Avesnes*, I, pp. 67–71, 76–80, II, #s 14–18, pp. 22–31) endorsed these points. The decree of 20 February 1215 highlighted Margaret's

excessively young age ('sororem suam parvulam', her child sister), and Innocent III's Bull of 24 April 1219, threatening Margaret with excommunication if she did not leave, suggested that her sexual honour (*pudor*) was at great risk. See Duvivier, *La Querelle des Avesnes*, II, #13, p. 20 and II, 18, p. 30.

15.   See William Te Brake, *A Plague of Insurrection: Popular Politics and Peasant Revolt in Flanders, 1323–1328* (Philadelphia: University of Pennsylvania Press, 1993), p. 48.

16.   Duvivier, *La Querelle des Avesnes*, I, pp. 138–53, II, #s 81–84, 86–94, pp. 122–43; 97, pp. 165–68; 122, pp. 203–204; 240, pp. 414–21.

17.   In his commentary on this law, Beaumanoir explicitly stated as much; see Duvivier, *La Querelle des Avesnes*, I, pp. 148, 150.

18.   Duvivier, *La Querelle des Avesnes*, II, #187 (Feb. Ma. 1253), pp. 306–12.

19.   Quoted in Duvivier, *La Querelle des Avesnes*, I, p. 221, note 3.

20.   Duvivier, *La Querelle des Avesnes*, I, pp. 117–18.

21.   The legal, gender and political intricacies of these competing views of marriage and these events are beyond the scope of this essay and will be discussed in a study planned on violence and gender in Flanders and the French North, which will consider, in particular, the conflicts around Margaret's two marriages and the competing points of view they generated.

22.   Memorandum of March–July 1246, to the king by John of Avesnes, Duvivier, *La Querelle des Avesnes*, II, #96, pp. 144–65 (p. 161).

23.   Mouskes, *Chronique*, p. 412, vss. 23287–23292, says that while Burchard was in Rome seeking dispensation to stay married to her, Margaret just changed her mind: 'Fu la dame d'autre maniere / Si prist Guillaume de Dampiere / Mais ele en fust partot blasmee / Quars Boucars l'avoit moult amee' (and the lady was of different mind / and took William of Dampierre [as husband] / but she was reproached everywhere for this / For Burchard had loved her greatly). Contemporary Matthew Paris was frankly injurious, spuriously attributing to her a scornful retort to Burchard that he should now stay in the orders, while she enjoyed the heated embrace she had long craved; quoted in Duvivier, *La Querelle des Avesnes*, I, p. 90. Duvivier echoes the grievances of the Avesnes camp, which simply ignored Burchard's poorly concealed journey through the lower orders (esp. I, pp. 277–323).

24.   Depositions, Duvivier, *La Querelle des Avesnes*, II, #144, pp. 234, 236–37, 242.

25.   The matter was assessed by chroniclers according to political position – the Menestrel de Reims condemning the marriage as unlawful, Matthew Paris deriding Margaret as another Helen of Troy – but later writers did circulate stories, from cavalier to outrageous, of rape or seduction and children born out of wedlock, although the wedding was in 1212 and the children born between 1217 and 1219; see Duvivier, *La Querelle des Avesnes*, I, pp. 297–301.

26.   For a discussion of the impact of rank, see LoPrete, 'Adela of Blois: Familial Alliances and Female Lordship', in *Aristocratic Women*, pp. 7–43.

27.   Their paternal aunt, Isabel of Hainaut, married King Philip Augustus.

28.   On these connections, see Karen S. Nicholas, 'Countesses as Rulers in Flanders', in *Aristocratic Women*, pp. 111–37 (pp. 121, 130). On the alliance of Baldwin with England, Duvivier, *La Querelle des Avesnes*, I, p. 15.

29.   On customs favourable to women see Ellen E. Kittell, 'Guardianship over Women in Medieval Flanders: A Reappraisal', *Journal of Social History*, 31 (1998), 897–930; Ellen E. Kittell and Kurt Queller, 'Whether Man or Woman': Gender Inclusivity in the Town Ordinances of Medieval Douai', *Journal of Medieval and Early Modern Studies*, 30 (2000), 63–100; and John Glissen, 'Le privilège de masculinité dans le droit coutumier de la Belgique et du nord de la France', *Revue du Nord*, 43 (1961), 201–16.

30.   Gislebertus of Mons, *Chronicon Hanoniense. Chronicle of Hainaut*, ed. and trans. Laura Napran (Woodbridge: Boydell, 2005), [3–5] pp. 4–6, [10–11] pp. 10–11, [20] p. 21; on Richildis, see also [8] pp. 8–9, [12] pp. 11–12, [28] p. 31, and n. 118 p. 30.

31.   Gislebertus of Mons, *Chronicon Hanoniense*, [33] p. 37 and n. 67 p. 21; Nicholas, 'Countesses as Rulers in Flanders', p. 123.

32.   Raymond of Toulouse dispatched Johanna, former queen of Sicily, to lead his beleaguered troops against rebellious vassals while he was occupied elsewhere. See Edmond-René Labande, 'Les filles

d'Aliénor d'Aquitaine: étude comparative', *Cahiers de civilisation médiévale Xe–XIIe siècles*, 29 (1986), 101–12 (p. 110).

33.　Claire Thiellet, *Femmes, reines et saintes (Ve–XIe siècles)* (Paris: Presses de l'Université Paris–Sorbonne, 2004), p. 48.

34.　Mouskes seems to present Joan in this manner on several occasions: during the Baldwin crisis, as she flees, she feels at once "duel, ire et honte' (sorrow, anger and shame), *Chronique*, II, p. 464, v. 24800, not necessarily 'womanly emotions', and, during the siege of Valenciennes, she acts like any other offended liege lord, as discussed below.

35.　Duvivier, *La Querelle des Avesnes*, II, #206, pp. 356–57. On Walcheren events and West-Capelle battle, see Duvivier, I, pp. 226–31.

36.　Judith Butler, *Gender Trouble: Feminism and the Subversion of Identity* (New York, London: Routledge, 1990; repr. 1999), p. 32.

37.　Both Burchard and Joan seemed to commingle the matter of the disputed land share with holding Margaret against the countess's will, inserting Joan in a 'male' register, as suggested by this passage in Mouskes: 'A Mons estoit od ses mescines / Sa suer, et il l'en ot portee / Et si l'ot a feme espousee / S'ot entre lui et la contesse / Une guierre moult felenesse / Pour tière qu' il en demandoit' (she, her sister, was in Mons with her ladies / and he took her away / and he married her as wife / so there was between him and the countess / a very ferocious war/for the land he demanded from [his wife's side]), *Chronique*, II, p. 410, vss. 23214–23219.

38.　Mouskes, *Chronique*, II, pp. 409–12, vss. 23207–292.

39.　Geneviève De Cant, *Jeanne et Marguerite de Constantinople: Comtesses de Flandre et de Hainaut au XIIIe siècle* (Brussels: Editions Racine, 1995), pp. 128–29.

40.　Duvivier, *La Querelle des Avesnes*, I, pp. 90–93.

41.　For accounts and variants, see Mouskes, *Chronique*, II, pp. 456–66, vss. 24490–24607; *Istore et croniques de Flandres d'après les textes de divers manuscrits*, ed. Baron Kervyn de Lettenhove, 2 vols (Brussels: F Hayez, 1879), I, 130–32, and 150–52 (hereafter *Chronique de Flandres*).

42.　See De Cant, *Jeanne et Marguerite*, p. 123, who reproduces a letter from Henry III dated 11 April 1225, thus from the onset of the crisis.

43.　Mouskes, *Chronique*, II, pp. 482–84, vss. 25245–25310.

44.　Jordan, *Women, Power, and Religious Patronage*, p. 46.

45.　On Joan's side, Mouskes lists a large and varied group of noblemen: Arnoul, Michel de Harnes and Radous, Rasse de Gavre, son of the one killed at Bouvines, the Grinbierghes brothers, Gilles of Brabant, Gautier de Ghistelle, Gilbert de Sotengien, Philip de Soubrengine, castellan of Ghent, Sohier of Bornhem, Walter of Fontaines, Fastre and Gautier de Ligne, the bishop Godefroy of Cambrai, the count of Blois, Gauthier II of Avesnes, and the new count of Namur Philip II of Courtenay (Mouskes, *Chronique*, II, pp. 466–68, vss. 24869–24894).

46.　Mouskes, on the siege of Valenciennes, *Chronique*, II, pp. 473–82. The rebels pressed her to meet their new demands, but she 'Respondi tot briement a aus / Qu'a sa mierci entirement / Seroient, u ja autrement / N'auraient pas a li nul jour / Ne concordance ne amour / Qu'il avoient Flandres honnie, / Et tout Hainaut, par leur folie' (responded curtly to them / that they would be entirely at her mercy / or in no other manner / would they ever enjoy either her agreement or love / that they had shamed Flanders / and all of Hainaut, by their folly), *Chronique*, II, p. 479, vss. 25163–25170.

47.　In the eleventh century, Countess Richildis had safeguarded it from Flanders by placing it under homage to the bishop of Liège and through him to the German emperor. Baldwin V had renewed his homage for Hainaut to the bishop and the German emperor; Gislebertus, *Chronicon Hanoniense*, [8–9] pp. 8–10, [255] p. 182. Joan and Margaret both failed to renew that homage, which fed into the armed conflicts of the 1250s.

48.　On clauses of the Treatise of 1167 to the disadvantage of the counts of Holland, renewed by Count Louis of Holland in 1206, see Octave Delepierre, *Précis analytique des documents que renferme le Dépôt des Archives de la Flandre-occidentale à Bruges. Premier volume. Inventaire des pièces concernant la ville de Bruges, qui reposent aux archives générales du département du Nord à Lille. Année 1089 a 1359* (Bruges: Vandecasteele-Werbrouck, 1840), x–xv, anno 1206, confirmed in 1206 and 1246. In this work, the first section of the volume is numbered in Roman numerals, the second part in Arabic numerals. This distinction is maintained here.

49.   Duvivier, *La Querelle des Avesnes*, I, pp. 167–68; 1253 petition to the pope, II, 187, pp. 309–10: 'confederati cum comite Hollandie qui in regem Allemanie postmodum est electus, qui inimicus noster erat' (allied with the count of Holland, who was subsequently elected king of Germany, who has been our enemy […]).

50.   Duvivier, *La Querelle des Avesnes*, I, pp. 168–69.

51.   Gislebertus, *Chronicon Hanoniens*, [175] pp. 142–43, and [81] p. 69, [122–123] pp. 104–105, [126] p. 106, [128] pp. 106–107.

52.   Delepierre, *Précis analytique*, LXXXIV–LXXXV, text of 27 May 1281, spelling out fines owed to Count Guy by aldermen and communes of Bruges for rebellion during riots.

53.   Theo Luykx, *De Grafelijke Financiële Bestuursinstellingen en het Grafelijk Patrimonium in Vlaanderen tijdens de Regering van Margareta Van Constantinopel (1244–1278)* (Brussels: Paleis der Academiën, 1961).

54.   Delepierre, *Précis analytique*, XXIX–XXX, anno 1219, 25 September.

55.   Jules Ludger Dominique Ghislain Baron de Saint-Génois, *Inventaire analytique des chartes des comtes de Flandre avant l'avènement des princes de la Maison de Bourgogne* (Ghent: Vanryckegem-Hovaere, 1843–46), *Inventaire des chartes déposées au château de Rupelmonde, commence ca. 1086*. Hereafter, indicated as: SG p. number/item number/date (e.g. SG 4/8/1212): SG 9/22/1225 (5 March 1226) Bruges.

56.   SG 18/51/1237.

57.   Jordan, *Women, Power, and Religious Patronage*, pp. 30–32, discusses the silence of charters between 1212 and 1214 regarding Joan's role in the government of Flanders, as her name appears rarely or only jointly with that of Ferrand; see also the diverging view in Nicholas, 'Countesses as Rulers', p. 130. Both names appear on charters and other documents, but in keeping with male privilege, the count's name usually appears first.

58.   In 1240, Thomas and Joan define the process for choosing Bruges aldermen, with exclusions favourable to wealthy burgers; see Delepierre, *Précis analytique*, XXXVIII–XL.

59.   The Old French term *catel-chatel* refers generally to assets except movable objects – including lands, homes, vineyards, rents, benefits from owning something, value of an asset used against a loan, interest, etc., but has many complicated legal and economic meanings. Frédéric Godefroy, *Dictionnaire de l'ancienne langue française et de tous ses dialectes du Ixe au XVe siècle* (Paris: Vieweg, 1881–1902) tome II, pp. 89–90.

60.   'intelligentes quod paupers solum in solutione Balfardi gravabantur' (Delepierre, *Précis analytique*, partie 2, carton 2, n. 32, Doc of 1232. p. 11; and Jan. 1240, p. 13 carton 3 n. 1).

61.   De Cant, *Jeanne et Marguerite*, pp. 177–80. *Keures* are the customary laws of a community, by-laws or collected statutes or ordinances governing various legal and social procedures accorded Flemish towns by their local rulers or by the counts.

62.   Duvivier, *La Querelle des Avesnes*, I, p. 128 n. 1. The pope originally approved Margaret's refusal to pay, but once Thomas reconciled with him, received absolution and married his niece, he insisted that Margaret pay the pension, which was completed between 1252 and 1257. Her dealings with Thomas regarding paying off the debt accumulated by Joan are also an interesting glimpse into her money management efforts; see Luykx, *De Grafelijke Financiële Bestuursinstellingen*, pp. 319–21, docs 2, 4 and 9.

63.   Jordan, *Women, Power, and Religious Patronage*, pp. 49–59.

64.   Delepierre, *Précis analytique*, XLII, Feb. 1244. Margaret tried to sway her main creditor, the French king, by exposing her deficit to the pope in 1253; see Duvivier, *La Querelle des Avesnes*, I, p. 288 and p. 314. She paid off most of her debts between 1257 and 1271; see also Luykx, *De Grafelijke Financiële Bestuursinstellingen*, p. 333, doc. 17.

65.   Simone Poignant, *La Foire de Lille. Contribution à l'étude des foires flamandes au moyen age* (Lille: Chez Emile Raoust, 1932), p. 9. See also Henri Dubois, *Les Foires de Chalons et le commerce dans la vallée de la Saône à la fin du Moyen Âge: vers 1280–vers 1430* (Paris: Publications de la Sorbonne, 1976). A surge in markets and fairs derives from the increased monetary economy after the first half of the eleventh century, and becomes a general movement during the thirteenth century; see Judicaël Petrowiste, *A la foire d'empoigne. Foires et marchés en Aunis et Saintonge au Moyen Âge (vers 1000–vers 1500)* (Toulouse: CNRS-Université de Toulouse-Le Mirail, 2004), pp. 87–89, 94.

66.   Delepierre, *Précis analytique*, XLIV, ca. 1250, confirmed by Gui on 30 June 1290.

67. On the canal building, see the letter of 30 Sept. 1251 in L.A. Warnkoenig, *Histoire de la Flandre et de ses institutions civiles et politiques jusqu à l'année 1309*, 5 vols (Brussels: M. Hayez, 1835), III: Gand, xxv, p. 279, and the documents of 30 Sept. 1251 and 20 Oct. 1251, xxvi, pp. 280–82. On the impact on communes and merchants, see Delepierre, *Précis analytique*, LI–LII, June 1262, and Petrowiste, *A la foire d'empoigne*, p. 105.

68. Luykx, *De Grafelijke Financiële Bestuursinstellingen*, pp. 307–16.

69. Jan Dumolyn, 'Nobles, Patricians and Officers: The Making of a Regional Political Elite in Late Medieval Flanders', *Journal of Social History*, 40 (2006), 431–52.

70. Marc Boone, 'Urban Space and Political Conflict in Late Medieval Flanders', *Journal of Interdisciplinary History*, 32 (2002), 621–40 (p. 625).

71. Jordan, *Women, Power, and Religious Patronage*, p. 55, and discussion pp. 55–58.

72. Ellen E. Kittell, 'Women, Audience, and Public Acts in Medieval Flanders', *Journal of Women's History*, 10 (1998), 74–96 (p. 76).

73. Duvivier, *La Querelle des Avesnes*, I, pp. 130–31, II, #s 68–69, pp. 105–106, #71, pp. 107–109, clergy from the diocese of Liège complain against Margaret for taking over Hainaut by force; #s107–108, pp. 184–85, peers and towns are ordered to accept John of Avesnes as their liege lord; #177 (Nov. 1252); pp. 294–99, threats against Margaret's agents in Hainaut.

74. On Margaret of Flanders, duchess of Burgundy, see Dubois, *Les Foires de Chalons*, pp. 135, 431.

5

Violence on Vellum: St Margaret's Transgressive Body and its Audience

Jennifer Borland

Among the collection of Passions and other texts in a twelfth-century manuscript probably produced in southern Bavaria and now in Munich (Bayerische Staatsbibliothek Clm. 1133), *The Passion of St Margaret* stands out. As the only illustrated text within this book, Margaret's story is emphasized as having special significance (figs 5.1–5.4). Through a variety of formal components and pictorial choices made by the manuscript's designer(s), Margaret's position within her story of martyrdom is depicted as uncontained, oscillating and ultimately transformed. In this essay, I begin my discussion with a detailed account of Margaret's story and its images, which highlights how the saint's body is treated within the illustrations. It will become apparent that the audience of this manuscript has become heavily implicated in the existing presence of Margaret on these pages. The viewers' unambiguous handling of these representations directly supports Margaret's noteworthy corporeal integrity. Margaret represents both victim and hero, masculine and feminine, body and soul, thus straddling binary categories as martyr saints are often depicted doing in their *vitae*.[1] Moreover, given the manuscript's visual and textual indicators for a mixed audience, it is beneficial to read these ambiguities in light of a broad group of viewers and those for whom they might have prayed. Margaret thus occupied a devotional space that was available to both men and women. And yet, as Margaret's body is shown to vacillate between gendered roles, positions of power and categories of embodiment, she demonstrates the potential for both social disruption and transgressive forms of empowerment that may have been especially relevant to audiences of both religious and lay women. As I go on to demonstrate, analysis of these different groups is pertinent to a better understanding of these images and their possible impact on viewers.

5.1 *The Passion of St Margaret*, fol. 63v–64r Bayerische Staatsbibliothek
Clm. 1133, twelfth century. Photo credit: Bayerische Staatsbibliothek

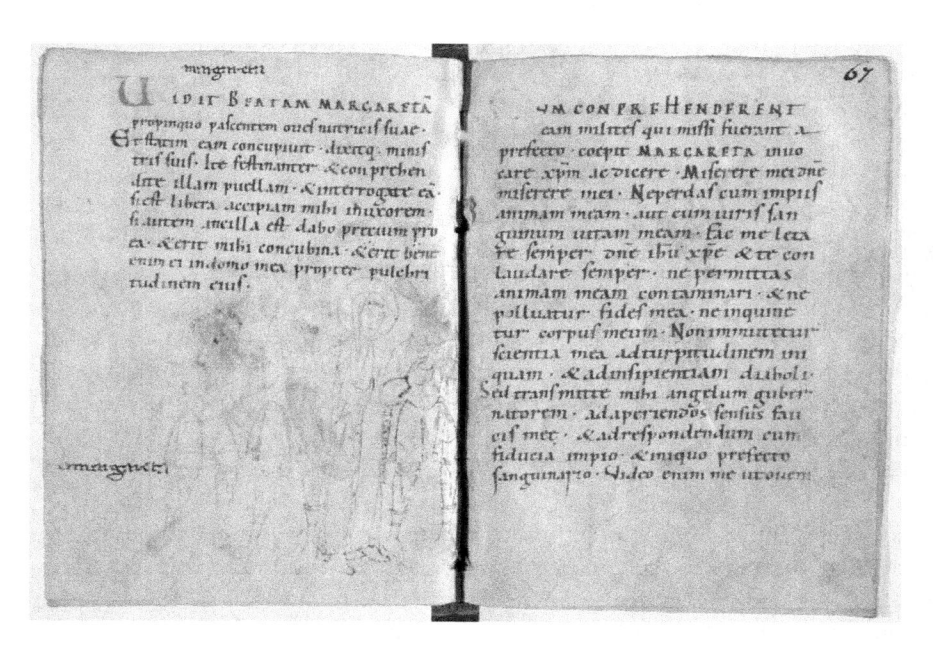

5.2 *The Passion of St Margaret*, fol. 66v–67r Bayerische Staatsbibliothek
Clm. 1133, twelfth century. Photo credit: Bayerische Staatsbibliothek

5.3 *The Passion of St Margaret*, fol. 67v–68r Bayerische Staatsbibliothek Clm. 1133, twelfth century. Photo credit: Bayerische Staatsbibliothek

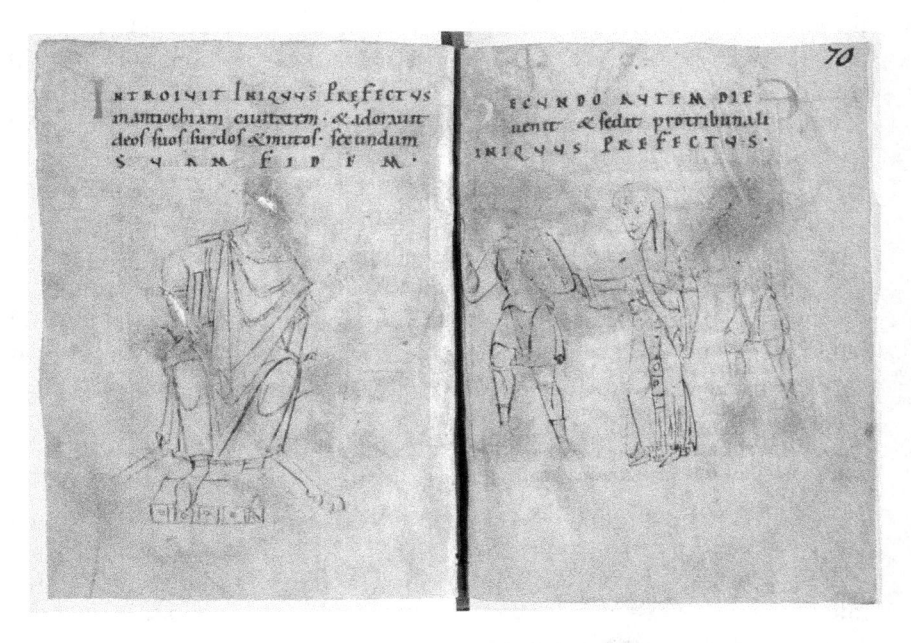

5.4 *The Passion of St Margaret*, fol. 69v–70r Bayerische Staatsbibliothek Clm. 1133, twelfth century. Photo credit: Bayerische Staatsbibliothek

The Manuscript and its Images

St Margaret's *Life* is one of twenty-seven texts included in this manuscript. Of these texts, sixteen deal with saints – their *Lives* and/or their martyrdoms. The items included in the book range from the twelfth through to the fourteenth centuries, but it appears that the majority of the book is from the twelfth century.[2] Margaret's *Life* is fourth in the book, and is one of the longer texts, extending over thirty-seven folios. *The Passion of St Margaret* tells the story of a virgin martyr who was tortured and killed because she would not submit to the advances of a Roman prefect, Olibrius, and renounce her Christianity. Although a familiar hagiographic narrative, the *Life of St Margaret of Antioch* and the details of this set of illustrations, draw attention to the unique aspects of this particular Passion. A small book, 11.4 cm tall and 7.9 cm wide, this manuscript would have been easily portable and shows evidence of frequent use. Among the twenty-seven texts included, Margaret's *Life* is the only one that is illustrated. This fact is significant because it suggests that for the patron and/or intended reader, Margaret's story warranted special attention.[3] The expense of generating pages dedicated to illustrations and the additional effort necessary to complete them was not negligible, even for a small and relatively modest volume. As an art historian, I am especially intrigued by the motives behind the inclusion of an extensive cycle of images for just one of the manuscript's *vitae,* as well as the effects for the reader(s) of such a decision. The effort and expense demonstrate that these images were not simply inconsequential illustrations of the text, but rather fundamental components involved in the manuscript's function and communication of specific ideas and messages.

The legend of St Margaret can be traced at least as far back as the eighth century, which is the date of the earliest extant Latin manuscript containing a version of Margaret's *passio.*[4] Unfortunately, no critical edition of the Latin *Passio S. Margaretae* has been produced to date. The most recent survey of the various Latin versions can be found in the work of Mary Clayton and Hugh Magennis. The text included in the Munich manuscript is very similar to the most widespread and influential version cited in the *Bibliotheca Hagiographica Latina, BHL* no. 5303, 'Version 1 (a)'.[5] Clayton and Magennis have printed the text of Paris BN lat. 5574, a manuscript of version *BHL* no. 5303, which is accompanied by an English translation and commentary.[6] The text of the Munich manuscript occasionally diverges from the version it otherwise copies rather closely.

It is clear that the creator(s) of the Munich version of Margaret's Passion intended it to be extensively, though simply, illustrated: in addition to the seven drawings currently found in the manuscript, twenty-seven more folios in the section dedicated to Margaret's *vita* have large areas left blank, presumably for further illustration that was never completed (four of the existing images are included here; see figs 5.1–5.4). Despite the limited number of images, the location of the blank pages provides a glimpse into the programme of illustration originally intended.[7] The illuminations that are included spread over several consecutive folios, beginning on the second page of the Margaret text. Integrated with the text, the images are primarily line drawings of the main characters of the narrative, and do not depict any external architectural or spatial details such as framing or lines indicating the ground.[8] The figures are drawn in light brown ink, and the manuscript is without other colour except for the occasional rubrication used for the initials. There is also overdrawing evident on several of the images, which seems to be of similar ink to the additional identifications that also appear on several of these folios.[9]

In the first scene, Margaret is shown as a model of virtue alongside two other saintly virgins, Thecla and Susanna (fols 63v–64r; fig. 5.1). These three are placed opposite a man, probably Margaret's father Theodosius, who is shown to be held in the grip of the devil, worshipping idols.[10] Located to the right and facing away from Margaret, this man looks at an idol, which is depicted as a beastly creature, standing upright and about half the height of the man. Margaret is shown with her foster mother in the *vita*'s second scene (fol. 64v), in which two female figures face one another. The text suggests that Margaret loved her foster mother, who was also Christian. In the third image (65v–66r), Margaret tends to her sheep as a man on horseback (Olibrius), followed by a group of soldiers, approaches her. As logically follows, the fourth scene shows Margaret surrounded by three soldiers, who follow Olibrius' command to seize her so that he might take her either as his wife or concubine (fol. 66v; fig. 5.2). On folio 67v, a winged creature and Margaret stand facing one another (fig. 5.3). Although we might be inclined to read this image as one of the beasts that visits Margaret while she is incarcerated, the figure is depicted sitting on a faldstool (folding chair), and is described in the text as the prefect Olibrius. In the sixth scene (fol. 69r), a small crowd of men, probably guards, stand in front of a tower, identified as the prison in which Margaret has been shut up. Finally, the remaining scene illustrated in this manuscript depicts the enthroned prefect opposite Margaret, who faces him as she is held by two guards, one on either side of her (fols 69v–70r; fig. 5.4).

Although the torture of Margaret's own body is not depicted in the existing images (the illustrations cease before her trials are underway), the bodies that are represented are fraught with complications. Margaret frequently encounters beings that represent the interplay between body and spirit, natural and supernatural, human and non-human. There is the monstrous idol represented in the first scene, and demonic or beastly bodies are depicted in at least three visualized scenes; they continue to appear to

5.5   Christ Trampling Beasts, Amiens Cathedral, thirteenth century. Photo credit: Foto Marburg/Art Resource, NY

Margaret throughout the narrative of her tortures and incarceration (figs 5.2–5.4). As will become apparent, these evil bodies play an important role in the way in which the audience reacts to both the manuscript and Margaret herself.

The devil's presence is uncommon in the *Lives* of early Christian female saints, but he makes repeated appearances in Margaret's story.[11] In fact, Margaret's primary ordeal as described by Theotimus, the author of the Latin *Passio S. Margaretae*, was how she 'fought the demon and overcame this world', rather than her perseverance and victory over her tortures.[12] In the two scenes in which Margaret stands in front of Olibrius, the prefect is represented as particularly monstrous: even his faldstool represents a monstrous hybrid of animal parts (two heads and two legs) sticking out from behind him (figs 5.3–5.4). Along with the threat, and eventual occurrence, of tortures and imprisonment, Margaret's ordeal, as laid out in the text but not illustrated in this manuscript, involves two encounters with particularly beastly entities: a dragon that appears to her in prison, and another devil, in the form of a black figure, who claims to be the brother of the dragon. In the first case, Margaret is swallowed whole by the dragon, but by making the sign of the cross, Margaret grows and splits the dragon 'into two parts', emerging from his body unscathed.[13] It is this successful emergence that caused Margaret eventually to become known as a patron saint of birth and motherhood, especially in France and England.[14]

When the second devil appears to her Margaret warns him to be gone: 'Let what you have done be sufficient to you. Depart from me now. You have performed many evils.' The holy maiden then 'seized the demon by the hair and smashed him to the ground. She placed her right foot on his neck and said to him, "Abandon now, evil one, your attempts against my chastity"'.[15] Although left undepicted in this manuscript, the gesture described in the text alludes to images of Christ trampling beasts or St Michael killing the dragon which is seen other medieval representations. Margaret's actions thus evoke both Christ and the behaviours of triumphal Roman warriors from which this motif was originally derived (fig. 5.5).[16] But Margaret's gesture as described in the text is unique – actively throwing down her enemy and pinning him to the ground. We might imagine, therefore, that the projected illustration would have shown Margaret in a pose that differed somewhat from the static, frontal depictions of the trampling Christ.

A closer iconographic connection might be made with the armoured female figures of Victory and Fortitude in Hildegard of Bingen's *Scivias* (*Scito vias Domini*).[17] Both figures appear in the *Scivias*, trampling stand-ins for the Devil: Victory destroying a lion, Fortitude crushing a dragon (figs 5.6–5.7).[18] Hildegard was a well-known figure in the twelfth century and her works provide an important context for other manuscripts from the

5.6   *Liber Scivias*, fol. 139r, Victory (detail), Vision III.3 Eibingen, c. 1160–75
(twentieth-century copy of lost original). Photo credit: Rheinisches Bildarchiv, Cologne

5.7   *Liber Scivias*, fol.192r, Fortitude (detail), Vision III.9 Eibingen, c. 1160–75
(twentieth-century copy of lost original). Photo credit: Rheinisches Bildarchiv, Cologne

period. In the *Scivias*, her first book of visions, feminine bodies often display transgression through corporeal fragmentation, although the problems of female authority play out differently here than in the Munich manuscript. Nevertheless, both cases demonstrate that such female heroics transgress norms. Just as Hildegard asserts the truly desperate nature of the Church because God blessed her, a lowly woman, with visions, so too is the power of the devil in Margaret's *Life* 'worth nothing', because, as the devil himself claims, 'we have been defeated by an insignificant girl'.[19] Both examples suggest that such behaviour was culturally categorized as problematic. Margaret's actions and the devil's response thus attest to the transformative nature of her unique position in this book.

The Presence of the Viewer

Margaret's prominent position in these images is further emphasized by the effects of the literal hand of the viewer(s). Numerous heads, faces and limbs have been rubbed out throughout this manuscript's pages, to the degree that several spots have become large holes in the vellum (figs 5.1–5.4). Although it is difficult to know when the damage was made, we can assume that it occurred before the book was acquired by the Bayerische Staatsbibliothek in 1803.[20] Furthermore, as a common phenomenon in medieval manuscripts, such defacement is often presumed to have been done in the later Middle Ages.[21] Josepha Weitzmann-Fiedler has pointed out the similarities between several roughly contemporaneous manuscripts of Margaret's cycle from this region, and in some cases (though not all of them), Olibrius is also the recipient of censorship. Such examples may indicate trends of defacement particular to this region or historical moment.[22] Contributing to the difficulty of reading these images, the vigorous defacing and dismemberment focuses specifically on those bodies that are evil or beastly: including every demon or monster figure, the soldiers or guards who arrest Margaret, and the prefect. Such active destruction of these bodies demonstrates the moral position of the characters, as well as the desire of the reader to be morally aligned with the saint – whose body remains untouched. In contrast to other twelfth-century manuscript images of female saints in which women's bodies are often tortured, physically assaulted and dismembered (fig. 5.8), Margaret's body remains *more* intact than the erased and fragmented bodies of the wicked.

In the first of the manuscript's images, the face of Margaret's father is virtually erased (fig. 5.1), but the vigour of the rubbing here is minimal compared to other places in the manuscript. Indeed, on the same page the idol's face has been worn completely through. The idol's hand and foot are also erased, gray smudges appearing where these extremities once were.

A gata dix. ǫa ancilla xpi ſū ideo me oſtendo ſeruilē pſonā. qn̄
cian⁹ dix̄. certe ingenua eraſ ⁊ nobiliſ. ǫmodo te ācilla cōme
moraſ.

Quintian⁹

Agata

Quintian⁹

agata

mamilla

T ūc irat⁹ ǫncian⁹ iuſſit ea in mamillā torqueri ⁊ tortā diu
iuſſit eā excidi. agata dix̄. impie crudeliſ ⁊ dire tirāne nō
eſ cōfuſuſ hoc amputare ī femina qð ipſe ī matre ſuxiſti.

5.8   Pamplona Bible martyrology, fol. 247v (Agatha cycle, detail) Augsburg
Cod. I.2.4°15, 1199–1212. Photo credit: Augsburg, University Library

On folio 67v, nearly the entire body of this figure has been smeared away, leaving only the faintest hint of its presence (fig. 5.3). The most prominent example of defacement appears in a later image in the manuscript, which depicts Olibrius on his throne on the verso folio, as two guards escort Margaret to him on the recto folio (fig. 5.4). The prefect's face, right hand and arm are rubbed completely through, as are parts of his throne including one of the bestial feet. In this case, even the markers of Olibrius's authority are removed by the diligent defacer(s). Across from this image, Margaret remains visible while the two guards appear as headless henchmen without hands, or even feet to stand on. The figure on the right is especially dissolved, with only a pelvis and stumps of his legs remaining.

The destruction of these figures' faces succeeds in removing their identity, but it also takes away the signifiers of their capabilities for both sight and communication. Defacement of figures occurs occasionally in medieval manuscripts, and often the eyes are rubbed out, suggesting an attempt to remove the 'evil eye' or powerful gaze of a malevolent figure. The erasure of the hands and feet are equally telling. By removing the hands, the reader took away another sense from these bodies, which remain unable to touch or feel.[23] Moreover, the figures that have had their feet erased have become unable to move. In other twelfth-century images of female saints, movement also seems directly linked to power – the power to move through spaces, to transcend earthliness, to transgress boundaries. The fact that these figures have been made immobile suggests they no longer have power to manoeuvre as Margaret is still able to do. But this diligent handler, who carefully rubbed away nearly every wicked face, hand and foot on these pages, succeeded in usurping from them the power that Margaret was denied by the prefect. The handler's activity also reveals the particular tactility and immediacy of medieval viewing practices, for the reciprocal understanding of sight as an exchange between viewer and viewed further implicates the audience in Margaret's transgressive status.[24]

Despite the repeated series of tortures ordered by Olibrius, including being suspended naked and lacerated by rods, burned with torches and tied up to be drowned in a great vessel, only a final beheading succeeded in killing Margaret. This death by the sword was itself almost avoided, as the soldier responsible for decapitating Margaret at first refuses to kill a holy virgin, and she eventually persuades him to participate in her martyrdom: 'If you do not do this you will not have your share with me in the paradise of God'.[25] Just as Margaret's perseverance is evident in the text, through the many tortures and demonic encounters she endures, her physical incorruptibility is further emphasized by her wholeness in the existing images. This treatment indicates that the readers were aware that corporeal integrity was seen as a virtue, intentionally leaving Margaret's parchment body unscathed.

This *Life* of St Margaret is filled with evidence of the physical interaction between its readers and the book itself. By rubbing and defacing the demons and evil figures on these pages, the reader in a sense re-enacted the heroic, saintly acts of Margaret.[26] The images seem to have evoked a physical response, one that was likely solicited repeatedly, each time a reader came to engage with the manuscript and its images. Similar responses have been described for other medieval objects such as ivories and statues that were repeatedly rubbed or kissed. For example, the wear displayed by Byzantine ivories indicates not only frequent handling, but also sometimes the caressing or kissing of specific elements within the image.[27] In her essay on the relationship between the flayed body in medieval narratives and the flayed animal skins on which those stories are written, Sarah Kay wonders if these 'inarticulate material witnesses' affected their readers as much as the texts.[28] Given the tangible immediacy of such objects and images, it seems likely that such representations had an impact on medieval audiences and involved them in the production of the images' meanings. The viewers of this manuscript expressed their presence directly onto the fabric of the book's pages and, in doing so, they facilitated the inviolate nature of Margaret's body and thus her transcendence above the restrictions of her imprisonment. The resulting depiction of Margaret demonstrates her transgression of earthly categories and constraints, oscillating between such divisions in the images as well as the text.

According to the catalogues of the collections of the Bayerische Staatsbibliothek, this humble manuscript was probably one of over 400 manuscripts that were accessioned into the state library in the early nineteenth century, when the Benedictine abbey in Benediktbeuern, in southern Bavaria, was secularized in 1803.[29] Therefore, the likely readers for centuries were probably monks and nuns, but of course we cannot rule out the possibility that other visitors may have had access to this manuscript as well.[30] Although we do not know for certain who made up the audience for this book, there can be little question that Margaret's *Life* was significant to the designer and/ or intended reader(s) of this manuscript.

Ambiguous Bodies

The accompanying text, nearly identical to the most popular version of Margaret's Passion (*BHL* no. 5303), nevertheless contains some departures from that version, and these changes may reflect the manuscript's original context or the audience for whom it was made.[31] Several of these instances foster specific questions about the manuscript's intended audience, and although details about these viewers remain unknown, the allusions made in the text corroborate the ambiguities and theme of transformation that we have already seen in the illuminations.

There are distinct facets of the text that speak to the possibility of a female lay audience. For example, Margaret's association with childbirth, which becomes more pronounced in later centuries, is nevertheless implied here. Just before she is beheaded, Margaret prays to God; in this section, the idea of a cult growing around her martyrdom and sainthood is clearly established:

[...] whoever comes with his light to the church where my relics are [...] may his sins be blotted out [...] whoever reads it [i.e. the Passion] or carries it in his hand or hears it read, from that hour may his sins be blotted out [...] whoever builds a basilica in my name or from his labour furnishes a manuscript of my passion, fill him with the Holy Spirit, the spirit of truth, *and in his home let there not be born an infant lame or blind or dumb*.[32]

Although the link between Margaret and childbirth has not yet become concrete, the text here does suggest that her relics and Passion books may be capable of producing birth-related, and thus female-oriented, miracles.[33]

A female audience is also implied earlier in the text, which reads, 'Omnes aure audite, corde intelligite, viri virgines pro bonitate vera velut puelle lectionem tenere legentes' ('Just as [young] girls softly reading [sacred] lections for true moral goodness, all [you] honourable men [and] virgins, listen with the ears, understand with the heart').[34] Although this may seem to suggest that the author speaks of male virgins, in the version on which it was based, the comment is similarly made to 'men, women and maidens' ('*vir, mulieres, virgines*').[35] As is explored in Cassandra Rhodes essay in this volume, the term 'virgin' was usually used to refer to a woman throughout the Middle Ages. The *Speculum virginum* was a widely read text written around 1140 specifically for nuns, and Alan of Lille's late twelfth-century *Summa on the Art of Preaching* includes sample sermons for specific audiences, addressed *ad claustrales* (to monks or canons) and *ad virgines* (to nuns).[36] As Maud Burnett McInerney has explained, certainly both men and women lived as virgins, but 'the various words used for virgin in learned and vernacular languages [...] all have as their primary meaning the sexually intact body of the female of the human species'.[37] Rhodes builds on this observation and answers McInerney's provocative question: 'What, after all, is a male virgin?' The second person address makes it clear that this text is speaking directly to the readers and audience for the images; at the same time, the excerpt above suggests these readers may have included both men and women. Margaret's movement between categories (such as gender) is thus reflected in this multifaceted audience.

A noteworthy alteration to the original Latin version has been made to the Munich version which also suggests the possibility that this manuscript could have been intended to include woman readers. The first image of Margaret's *Life* shows her standing with the saints Thecla and Susanna (fig. 5.1). This image accompanies the text which tells the reader to 'so strive that you may receive the salvation *and you may be deserving of entry to* eternal rest with *the Blessed Tecla and Saint Susanna*'.[38] In the Latin version of the text on which this is based, that phrase concludes 'receive the salvation *of your soul* and eternal rest with *the just who have been crowned by the Lord*'.[39] Entering an assembly of specific female saints, also associated with the early Church, in lieu of the general group of those 'crowned by God', suggests that a reader of this manuscript is invited to join a saintly assembly of her own gender in the eternal kingdom.[40]

The indications in the text of a mixed audience seem to echo the multiplicity inherent in Margaret's illustrated body. But the links between audience and saint do not end there. The handling of this manuscript, through which the viewer(s) actively participated in the facilitation of the saint's oscillating position, demonstrates the important connection between this book's multifaceted audience and its transgressive and even contradictory saint.

Trangression and Transformation

The conflations and ambiguities of gender evident in this manuscript's images of Margaret as well as in the potential audience for the book indicate that its complex set of messages and associations probably varied for different audiences. In addition to the torments of martyrs, gendered readings of other dimensions of traditional tropes of violence may have also reinforced social difference. Such literary tropes include blood, a corporeal substance that Peggy McCracken has investigated in the context of romance literature.[41] McCracken's analysis focuses on the complications of the opposition between public masculine bloodshed (seen as heroic) and the hidden blood of women (i.e. menstruation, understood as shameful and polluting). A natural sub-theme for such an argument demonstrates the contradictions of this dichotomy. For instance, women warriors present a curious conflation of these two forms of bloodshed; narratives about such women involve sacrifice and public, heroic bloodshed while nevertheless categorizing them as unnatural and problematic. Stories of martyrs are often stories of bloodshed as well. Although the blood spilt by Margaret's body in the various tortures ordered by Olibrius is never portrayed in the Munich manuscript, the potential connection between women's blood and heroism is a fruitful one.

Margaret's aggressive handling of the demons who torment her in prison, including her obliteration of the dragon as well as the victorious gesture of dominance over the man-like devil, presented her as more complex than simply the virginal victim of a godless tyrant. Margaret was portrayed as someone who achieves surprising physical, as well as emotional, strength in the face of oppression and eventual martyrdom. The images facilitate this unrestrained corporeality, showing Margaret as free from the visual frames of traditional manuscript composition – such as the rectangular frames delineating each scene, or forms of framing created by trees, buildings and other environmental elements. Margaret is spatially uncontained, and her formal lack of enclosure in the images' composition signals both her narrative independence and an embodied motility, which was denied her enemies through their amputated limbs.

Related to this, some medieval scholars have pointed out the masculinization invoked through the virtue achieved by virgin saints and other martyrs, suggesting that such women were often portrayed as becoming male in order to transcend their inherently faulty womanhood.[42] However, what Margaret represents is more complex than simple masculinization. The threat indicated by Margaret's physical power is not that of a straightforward transformation from female to male; on the contrary, her threatening power is in her straddling of the categories of victim and hero and refusing to stay in a position that is identifiable in terms of gendered norms. The curious textual contiguity of '*viri virgines*', meaning literally 'men [and] virgins', also evokes Margaret's oscillation or morphing between gendered realms.[43] Such categorical slippage transgresses both gender stereotypes and narrative functions, potentially upsetting the roles with which specific audiences may have identified, and as Alison More's essay in this volume illustrates, sets the saint apart as having moved towards holiness.

Undermining the definitive roles of victim and hero, Margaret's *Life* confuses the clear boundaries between violation and transcendence. There might seem to be a contradiction between Margaret's resilience throughout her various ordeals, or her material wholeness in the manuscript itself, and the uncontained aspects of her narrative position, which is further supported by the loose ephemerality of the drawing. Rather than a simple 'gender-bending' for the purpose of appearing more masculine, Margaret is presented as difficult to pin down, oscillating between (gendered) roles, positions of power, and categories of embodiment. In fact, Margaret's victim status is what provides her power. As she is tortured, she succeeds in both thwarting Olibrius' numerous attempts on her life and defeating the devils. In a way, all martyrs are by nature both victim and hero, for their power, evident at death, is inherently dependent upon their victimization. Beyond her holy death, moreover, Margaret uses her victimization to gain more power throughout the story, performing more than one role at a time. Vacillation itself is not wholly unique to this manuscript, and in fact appears repeatedly in twelfth-century manuscripts of female saints' *Lives*.[44] The images in such manuscripts reinforce the difficulties of reconciling the contradictions of the female saint's embodiment by presenting figures that both transcend and transgress. The visualized body of the female saint was problematic precisely because it vacillates between being inviolate and being penetrated, between solidity and ephemerality, between wholeness and fragmentation.

The unpredictability of Margaret's oscillating position might have been potentially disruptive to an audience of monks or ecclesiastical readers. We might theorize that religious women would have been more responsive to both the somatic and spiritual power of Margaret's story. But male or female, the religious members of the monastery were probably not the only the recipients of the devotional benefits facilitated by the defacement. Thus another group comes into play: the biological beneficiaries of Margaret's association with healthy birth. While it seems unlikely that many lay women would have been readers of the Latin text in this manuscript, a number of other scenarios are possible in which such individuals might have had a connection to the book. The prayers of a nun or monk could focus on the well-being of those outside the monastery. Female religious communities often maintained close ties with the noble families who supported these institutions in part to provide appropriate places for daughters, often as lay sisters.[45] Access to such manuscripts, especially those that were illustrated or that contained familiar material such as prayers or saints' *Lives*, may have been one of the benefits of such patronage. In addition to such forms of 'reading', users may have considered simple physical proximity to books to be desirable. As Jocelyn Wogan-Browne has argued, the transmission of the *Lives* of saints such as Margaret should be seen to extend beyond textual transmission to include 'perishable' modes such as touching, seeing or wearing.[46] While the decisions behind the defacement of the images seems to reflect a knowledge of the Latin text, these actions may have been tied to alternative forms of reading as well as a wider range of audiences, possibly used together by audiences both literate and non-literate, religious and secular.

In the Munich manuscript of Margaret's *Life*, the physical destruction of evildoers was literally enacted by the reader-viewer, the figures being present to the reader and thus vulnerable to attack. Indeed, the audience is encouraged to experience the reading of the book as an activity that encompassed body, mind and soul while engaging multiple senses. The 'tangible materiality'[47] of a manuscript like this one is even referenced directly by the text of Margaret's *Life*, in that healing properties of both Margaret's Passion (when read aloud) and her relics are espoused, claiming that 'no infant will be born lame, blind or dumb', and anyone responsible for penning her story would also benefit as if they had visited her relics themselves.[48] Finally, the voice of God, in the form of a dove, informs her just before her death that 'where your relics are, or a book of your Passion, a sinner [...] will find remission of his sins'.[49] The text presents the manuscript as equivalent to her relics, physical objects that are trappings of the earthly realm, but which nevertheless hold transformative capacities.[50]

A reminder of Margaret's associations with successful childbirth and other healing, the miraculous quality attributed to her story demonstrates that books precisely like the one considered here may have been conceptualized as relics in and of themselves. If this book was used as a kind of talisman or relic, held and rubbed to conjure the blessings or healing powers of Margaret, a viewer is envisioned who facilitated Margaret's aid by helping her fight the evil entities depicted. Any number of possible members of the audience could have been enlisted to embark upon such actions, either for their own health or on behalf of another member of society. In contrast, however, to the logical scenario of venerating Margaret with kissing and touching, in the Munich manuscript the touching is used for the bad characters. Perhaps this can be interpreted as a concern that if left intact, the evil figures would in some sense cancel out Margaret's power with their physical presence.

Both Margaret and the dove, in the phrases quoted above, associated a book of her Passion with her relics and the location of her shrine, asserting the apoptropaic power embedded in the physical manifestation of such manuscripts. This book seems to have served a similar function – that of bringing the viewer together with the saint through the physical or spatial proximity to a sacred object – to the role of relics in the cults of saints. This not only verifies the physical importance of such manuscripts and how they were handled and experienced, but also suggests they were instrumental for one of the physical manifestations of the saint on this earth: healing people's bodies. Especially as Margaret's legend evolved into one that highlighted her healing power for the physical bodies of women and their babies, the physicality of her relics and Passion book commingled with the transgressive nature of her otherworldliness, unrestrained motion and miracles to reinforce the volatility of her existence in numerous spheres and categories at the same time.

Conclusion

Margaret's particular transformative capacities, as expressed through the uncontained and transgressive nature of her portrayal, can also be linked to the similar propensities observed more generally in saints' cults. For example, Barbara Abou-El-Haj has described what she sees as a scholarly 'underestimation' of the 'volatility and instability' of saints' cults.[51] Involving ritual and spectacle, and competition between monastic and ecclesiastical clergy, between clerical and lay audiences, and even between the saints themselves, these cults were inevitably vulnerable to the chaos and spontaneity of the public sphere in which they thrived. Speaking more directly to female saints' *Lives*, the narratives that spawned or were spawned by the cults, Jane Tibbetts Schulenburg mentions the transgressive nature of women saints. Although held up as the epitome of holiness, these saints were nevertheless problematic as both women and extremists, hovering around a finely drawn line between characteristics that were either celebrated or deemed highly dangerous.[52] The ambiguities expressed in Margaret's portrayal demonstrate precisely such straddling of saintly roles.

I have suggested that the audience for this illustrated version of Margaret's *Life* was probably mixed. At the same time, much medieval evidence suggests that 'female saints tend to be perceived as particularly relevant models for female audiences'.[53] This becomes keenly evident in some manuscripts more than others, but is demonstrated clearly by a pair of twelfth-century manuscripts depicting female saints' *Lives* called the Pamplona Picture Bibles. The Pamplona Picture Bibles were commissioned by King Sancho VIII el Fuerte of Navarre (1153–1234), which are nearly identical and both include a similar version of the Bible followed by a martyrology.[54] The second manuscript, however, which is believed to have been made for a female member of Sancho's court, contains a significantly expanded section on female saints.[55] Thus it provides a more nuanced and complete portrayal of the saints' Passions, and is collectively less gratuitous than the unrelieved sequence of tortures depicted in the first manuscript's martyrology of female saints. At the same time, however, the second book also articulates a powerful message about the physical dangers of the real world, largely at the hands of men, in contrast to the sanctuary attained upon 'giving up one's ghost'. As the Munich manuscript likewise demonstrates, pictured bodies of female saints seem to appeal to the specific experiences of women in their paradoxical negotiation of corporeality and transcendence.

Notes

1. This has been explored in a number of works, such as Barbara Fay Abou-El-Haj, *The Medieval Cult of Saints: Formations and Transformations* (Cambridge: Cambridge University Press, 1994); Barbara Newman, *From Virile Woman to WomanChrist: Studies in Medieval Religion and Literature* (Philadelphia: University of Pennsylvania Press, 1995); Jane Tibbetts Schulenburg, *Forgetful of Their Sex: Female Sanctity and Society, ca. 500–1100* (Chicago: University of Chicago Press, 1998); *Gender and Difference in the Middle Ages*, ed. Sharon Farmer and Carol Braun Pasternack (Minneapolis and London: University of Minnesota Press, 2003).

2. It is unclear if the order is original, although it seems that the later texts are towards the end.

3. The focus on Margaret's story itself is not terribly helpful in determining audience or possible users of this manuscript. Margaret was a popular saint in this period, as indicated by other manuscripts devoted to her as well as the frequency with which her relics were venerated. The Latin *Life* of St Margaret dates from late eighth century, and there are some illuminated manuscripts from as early as the ninth and tenth centuries. She was especially popular from the twelfth century on. See Brigitte Cazelles, *The Lady as Saint: A Collection of French Hagiographic Romances of the Thirteenth Century* (Philadelphia: University of Pennsylvania Press, 1991); Mary Clayton and Hugh Magennis, *The Old English Lives of St Margaret* (Cambridge: Cambridge University Press, 1994); Elizabeth Robertson, 'The Corporeality of Female Sanctity in the *Life of Saint Margaret*', in *Images of Sainthood in Medieval Europe*, ed. Renate Blumenfeld-Kosinski and Timea Klara Szell (Ithaca: Cornell University Press, 1991), 268–87; Elaine Treharne, '"They Should Not Worship Devils…Which Neither Can See, nor Hear, nor Walk": The Sensibility of the Virtuous and the *Life of St Margaret*', *Proceedings of the PMR Conference*, 15 (1990), 221–36.

4. Clayton and Magennis, *Old English Lives*, p. 195.

5. *Bibliotheca Hagiographica Latina*, v. 2, pp. 787–88; Clayton and Magennis, *Old English Lives*, p. 7. This Latin version can also be found in *Sanctuarium seu Vitae Sanctorum*, ed. Boninus Mombritius, 2 vols (Paris: Fontemoing et Socios, 1910), II, pp. 190–96.

6. An English translation of the Latin 'Passio S. Margaretae' can be found in Clayton and Magennis, *Old English Lives*, Appendix 2; my translation of the manuscript's text is read against this translation. Their translation is based on a tenth-century Latin text, a text quite similar to that in Clm. 1133. Notable exceptions include my own translations, when the Latin text of Bayerische Staatsbibliothek Clm. 1133 differs significantly from *BHL* no. 5303; see Clayton and Magennis, *Old English Lives*, pp. 7–23, and Appendix 2, pp. 191–223. Another strand of Version 1 in Latin is classified as *BHL* no. 5304, 'Version 1(b),' also referred to as the Casinensis version, and departs in some ways from the *BHL* no. 5303 (or the Mombritius version); see Clayton and Magennis, *Old English Lives*, pp. 13–16, and Appendix 3, pp. 224–34. In the Munich manuscript, some of the departures from *BHL* no. 5303 seem to evoke unique aspects of *BHL* no. 5304 instead, although such inferences are not identical to this alternative Latin version either.

7. Josepha Weitzmann-Fiedler, 'Zur Illustration Der Margaretenlegende', *Münchner Jahrbuch der Bildenden Kunst*, 17 (1966), 17–48. Weitzmann-Fiedler does an extensive analysis of the probable scenes each blank space would have contained. There may have been a number of reasons why these images were left incomplete (we can only hypothesize what they might have been). At the same time, it is not uncommon for illuminated manuscripts to have been left incomplete, since this was one of the last stages of the production of the book.

8. The one exception is the prison tower depicted on fol. 69r.

9. These 'captions' or identifications include: *S. Margareta* on fol. 64r, *S. Margareta* and *Oues* on 66r, *S. Margareta* on 66v, *Carcus* on 69r.

10. On the next page, 64v, the text states 'Beatissima enim Margareta erat Theodosii filia qui erat patriarcha gentilium et idola ad orabat' (The most blessed Margaret, then, was the daughter of Theodosius, who was chief priest of the pagans and worshipped idols); Clayton and Magennis, *Old English Lives*, p. 195.

11. Clayton and Magennis (*Old English Lives*, p. 6) suggest that this facet of Margaret's story resembles the Passion of St Juliana, who also had verbal contests with the devil.

12. Clayton and Magennis, *Old English Lives*, p. 195.

13. Clayton and Magennis, *Old English Lives*, p. 207.

14. See, for instance, Robertson, 'The Corporeality of Female Sanctity', p. 285. Also see Cazelles, *The Lady as Saint*, p. 218. With regard to the apparent contradiction in Margaret's emergence, in which she seems to evoke infant rather than mother, Wendy Larson explains that 'as the legend was modified and the connection to childbirth made more explicit, the image of the saint being delivered whole from the belly of the beast came to represent a mother's similar fate for her child'; see Wendy Larson, 'Who is the Master of This Narrative? Maternal Patronage and the Cult of St Margaret', in *Gendering the Master Narrative: Women and Power in the Middle Ages*, ed. Mary C. Erler and Maryanne Kowaleski (Ithaca: Cornell University Press, 2003), pp. 94–104.

15. Clayton and Magennis, *Old English Lives*, p. 207.

16. See André Grabar, *Christian Iconography: A Study of Its Origins* (Princeton: Princeton University Press, 1968) and Gertrud Schiller, *Iconography of Christian Art*, trans. Janet Seligman (Greenwich, CT: New York Graphic Society, 1971).

17. Hildegard finished the text of the *Scivias* in 1151; the illustrated manuscript of the *Scivias* (Eibingen, Abtei St. Hildegard, Cod. 1) is dated to between 1160 and 1175.

18. *Scivias*, III.3 and III.9.

19. Clayton and Magennis, *Old English Lives*, p. 209.

20. See note 28 below.

21. For more on medieval censorship, see Michael Camille, 'Obscenity under Erasure: Censorship in Medieval Illuminated Manuscripts', in *Obscenity: Social Control and Artistic Creation in the European Middle Ages*, ed. Jan M. Ziolkowski (Leiden: Brill, 1998), 139–54, and figs 1–13.

22. Just prior to publication, a source was brought to my attention suggesting an earlier dating for the manuscript (eleventh–thirteenth centuries): Elisabeth Klemm, *Die Illuminierten Handschriften des 13. Jahrhunderts Deutscher Herkunft in der Bayerischen Staatsbibliothek*, 2 vols (Wiesbaden: L. Reichert,

1998), p. 290. Time and space mean that it has not been possible to explore these suggestions further here.

23.   Elaine Treharne has discussed the connection between evil and the lack of senses in an Old English version of Margaret's *Life* in Corpus Christi College, Cambridge MS 303; see Treharne, '"They Should Not Worship Devils"'.

24.   Medieval understandings of vision and perception were conceptualized as active exchange between seer and seen, as is articulated by two theories regarding how sight worked: extramission and intromission. Extramission involved 'the idea that a beam of light radiates outward from the eye illuminating what it falls on', while intromission was the notion 'that all matter replicates its own image through intervening media until the image strikes the human eye'; Carolyn P. Collette, *Species, Phantasms, and Images: Vision and Medieval Psychology in the Canterbury Tales* (Ann Arbor: University of Michigan Press, 2001), p. 15. See also Suzannah Biernoff, *Sight and Embodiment in the Middle Ages* (New York: Palgrave Macmillan, 2002).

25.   Clayton and Magennis, *Old English Lives*, p. 217.

26.   Although the rubbing was probably done initially by one person, each reader was nevertheless reminded of this somewhat iconoclastic behaviour, and may have been inclined to repeat it.

27.   Anthony Cutler, *The Hand of the Master: Craftsmanship, Ivory, and Society in Byzantium (9th–11th Centuries)* (Princeton: Princeton University Press, 1994), pp. 23–29, 39.

28.   Sarah Kay, 'Original Skin: Flaying, Reading, and Thinking in the Legend of Saint Bartholomew and Other Works', *Journal of Medieval and Early Modern Studies*, 36 (2006), 35–73 (p. 38).

29.   *Das Bistum Augsburg I: Die Benediktinerabtei Benediktbeuern, Germania Sacra*, ed. Josef Hemmerle (Berlin and New York: Walter de Gruyter, 1991), p. 118. See also the electronic catalogue Halmii Codices Latini Monacenses: <http://webserver.erwin-rauner.de/halm/vsign_saec. asp?provenienz=Bened> [accessed 8 November 2008].

30.   There is documentation dated to 1116 of a double monastery at Benediktbeuern, presumably related to reforms enacted by Abbot Konrad (c. 1100–1122), while nearby Kochel was apparently the site of a twelfth-century church, nuns' cloister (both destroyed in a 1248 fire) as well as a scriptorium; see Hemmerle, *Die Benediktinerabtei* pp. 42, 80, 95, 270. Bavaria was a notable centre of Latinate book production by and for religious women by the twelfth century, with a longer history of educating women; see Alison I. Beach, *Women as Scribes: Book Production and Monastic Reform in Twelfth-Century Bavaria* (Cambridge: Cambridge University Press, 2004). Beach explores manuscripts from several communities that would have been in close proximity to Benediktbeuern, including Schäftlarn and Wessobrunn, and cites examples of exchanges between many Bavarian institutions for the purposes of copying texts (p. 22).

31.   As mentioned above, the Munich manuscript occasionally demonstrates similarities to *BHL* no. 5304 in some of these diversions as well.

32.   Clayton and Magennis, *Old English Lives*, p. 215 (emphasis mine).

33.   Both Larson and Don C. Skemer speak to the prevalence of such texts on various objects including amulets, amulet rolls, and Books of Hours – objects that are frequently associated with female patrons and especially prominent in the later Middle Ages; many of these objects also include dedications to St Margaret. See Don C. Skemer, 'Amulet Rolls and Female Devotion in the Late Middle Ages', *Scriptorium*, 55 (2001), 197–227, and Larson, 'Who is the Master of This Narrative?', pp. 94–104.

34.   'Omnes aure audite, corde intelligite, viri virgines pro bonitate vera velut puelle lectionem tenere legentes' (Clm. 1133, f. 63).

35.   Clayton and Magennis, *Old English Lives*, p. 194. It is worth noting that in the *BHL* no. 5304 Latin version, 'viri et virgines' appears in this line (p. 225). The grammatically feminine word *virgines* almost invariably refers to female virgins. The positioning of *viri* here is misleading, but does not indicate that these virgins are male. The Latin *vir* refers to 'a male person, a man', rather than to the adjective 'masculine' or 'male' (*Lewis and Short* s. v. *vir, viri*). The adjectival form is either *masculus, a, um*, or *mas, maris* (*Lewis and Short* s. v. *masculus*; ibid., s.v. *mas maris*). In order for the text to be referring to 'male virgins' it would be necessary to read *Masculas virgines* or *mares virgines*.

36.   *Speculum Virginum, Corpus Christianorum Continuatio Mediaevalis 5*, ed. Jutta Seyfarth (Turnhout: Brepols, 1990); Newman, *From Virile Woman to WomanChrist*, p. 35. See Alan of Lille, *Summa de arte praedicatoria* 43, 47, *PL*, p. 210.

37.   Maud Burnett McInerney, *Eloquent Virgins from Thecla to Joan of Arc* (New York: Palgrave Macmillan, 2003), p. 7.

38. Ita laborate ut accipiatis salutem et *ut mereamini* requiem sempiternam *cum beata Tecla et sancta Susanna*. (Clayton and Magennis, *Old English Lives*, pp. 194–95, emphasis mine).

39. '[...] accipiatis salutem *anime uestrae* et requiem sempiternam *cum iustis a Domino coronatis*' (Clayton and Magennis, *Old English Lives*, pp. 194–95).

40. Again, this reference seems to suggest a connection to the *BHL* no. 5304 version, which also mentions Tecla and Susanna; however, the Munich manuscript does not quote verbatim from that version. See Clayton and Magennis, *Old English Lives*, p. 225.

41. Peggy McCracken, *The Curse of Eve, the Wound of the Hero: Blood, Gender, and Medieval Literature* (Philadelphia: University of Pennsylvania Press, 2003).

42. A frequently cited and impressive example is Newman, *From Virile Woman to WomanChrist*.

43. Although not saints or martyrs, Hildegard's visualization of the virtues Victory and Fortitude also plays with the ambiguity surrounding female warriors – these two virtues appear as male knights in full armour and with weapons, although the text confirms she understood these figures as female.

44. For example, in a particular manuscript of the *Passion of Lucy* (Berlin, Staatliche Museen, Kupferstichkabinett 78 A 4), Lucy is depicted as moving between the earthy and heavenly realms in a variety of ways.

45. Beach, *Women as Scribes*, p. 114.

46. Jocelyn Wogan-Browne, 'The Apple's Message: Some Post-Conquest Accounts of Hagiographic Transmission', in *Late Medieval Religious Texts and Their Transmissions*, ed. Alistair Minnis (Cambridge: D.S. Brewer, 1993), pp. 39–53 (pp. 40, 53).

47. Magdalena Elizabeth Carrasco, 'Spirituality in Context: The Romanesque Illustrated Life of St. Radegund of Poitiers (Poitiers, Bibl. Mun., Ms 250)', *Art Bulletin*, 72 (1990), 414–35 (p. 430). Carrasco is speaking specifically to the accessibility of saints through shrines, relics, and other trappings associated with their cults, but the term seems equally relevant to the manuscripts which relayed the stories upon which these cults were based.

48. The links between the rubbing and the text's characterizations of the evil entities is explored more fully in my forthcoming essay 'Unruly Reading' (see note 22 above). Cf. Clayton and Magennis, *Old English Lives*, p. 213.

49. Clayton and Magennis, *Old English Lives*, p. 215.

50. Indeed, manuscripts were often worn or placed on the body in much the same manner as other kinds of talismans, amulet rolls, etc.; often these were small books of hours of a scale similar to the Munich codex; Skemer, pp. 201, 209–10, 213, 215–16, and Wogan-Browne, 'The Apple's Message'.

51. Abou-El-Haj, *The Medieval Cult of Saints*, p. 3.

52. Schulenburg, *Forgetful of Their Sex*, p. 2.

53. Jocelyn Wogan-Browne, 'Saints' *Lives* and the Female Reader', *Forum for Modern Language Studies*, 27 (1991), 314–332 (p. 314).

54. Amiens, Bibliothèque communale, Manuscript Latin 108 (1197–98), and Augsburg Cod. I.2.4°15 (1199–1212).

55. In comparison to the first manuscript, which contains thirty-five female saints depicted in thirty-eight images, the second book depicts thirty-nine female saints in eighty-three illustrations. Agatha, Agnes, Cecilia, Eulalia, Leocadia, Christina and Lucy are all given extended treatment; Lucy's is the longest with twelve scenes; François Bucher, *The Pamplona Bibles; a Facsimile Compiled from Two Picture Bibles with Martyrologies Commissioned by King Sancho El Fuerte of Navarra (1194–1234): Amiens Manuscript Latin 108 and Harburg Ms. 1, 2, Lat. 4° 15* (New Haven: Yale University Press, 1971), p. 37.

6

'Pourquoy appellerions nous ces choses differentes, qu'une heure, un moment, un mouvement peuvent rendre du tout semblables?': Representing Gender Identity in the Late Medieval French *Querelle des femmes*

Helen Swift

A late sixteenth-century treatise entitled *Le Triomphe des dames* (1599), ostensibly written by a woman in defence of women, poses at one point a somewhat radical question:

Why should we call these things by different names that an hour, a moment, a single movement can make absolutely the same?[1]

She appears to be calling here for the abolition of different signifiers to designate 'man' and 'woman'. Indeed, it is not just the cultural distinction between 'masculine' and 'feminine' gender identities, imposed by a masculine hegemony, with which she takes issue here, but the basic concept of biologically determined sexual difference, dividing human identity between 'male' and 'female'. She supports her point by citing several exemplary tales of hermaphrodism, sexual transformation and mistaken sexual identity. These examples fuel her argument for the contingent, accidental and fundamentally unstable nature of sex, for instance in the case of Iphis, daughter of Telethusa, an example drawn from Ovid's *Metamorphoses*.[2] Iphis happened to change from a woman into a man: 'en lieu d'une pucelle elle devint homme'.[3] Neither identity is represented as Iphis's proper sexual being; each is a position she holds or performs.

The *Triomphe* narrator's perspective on gender and sexual identities, which might seem, to use Judith Butler's phrase, to be 'undoing gender' in some measure, is not an isolated occurrence amongst the corpus of late medieval writings in support of the case for women, the body of works now referred to under the umbrella term *la querelle des femmes*.[4] Understanding how sex and gender were viewed scientifically, construed culturally and represented in literary contexts at any point in the Middle Ages is a complex matter. Scholars of various disciplines, in approaching the subject, have acknowledged that there is no consistent, unitary source and no single model that accounts for the range of evidence available.[5] Thomas Laqueur contended that a one-sex model dominated in the pre-modern era, positing identity in kind but difference in degree between male and female. An alternative, described by Cadden, would be to apply a two-sex paradigm, maintaining the incommensurability and opposing natures of man and woman. A further possibility would be to recognize that neither model suffices, though both have problems and possibilities: both can give rise to a gender hierarchy in binary terms that privileges the masculine part in pairs of ordered contrarieties such as honourable/dishonourable, active/passive, legitimate/illegitimate; equally, though, both models offer possibilities for the disruption of established categories, through hermaphrodism or transvestism. Neither structure is inherently misogynistic.

We shall see in this essay how the representation of woman's identity became a principal site of hermeneutic interest for certain writers in the late medieval *querelle des femmes*, the trend for literary defences of women which began, in large part, with the writings of Christine de Pizan and continued into the sixteenth century.[6] These writers – who were, with the exception of Christine and, later, Anne de France, all men – composed catalogues of virtuous women.[7] In most prose works their *exempla* featured as sequences of discrete biographies; in verse they were often embedded in a narrative fiction. Christine de Pizan's *Livre de la cité des dames* (1405) is the most celebrated catalogue, but Martin Le Franc's *Le Champion des dames* (c. 1442) and Antoine Dufour's *Les Vies des femmes célèbres* (1504), the two *querelle* works considered here, deserve to be equally well known for the sophisticated ways they present positive portraits of women drawn from scripture, classical legend, contemporary literature and French history. All three authors were writing against the tradition of Boccaccio's *De mulieribus claris*, the fourteenth-century catalogue of women which was widely transmitted in both the original Latin and in French translation throughout the fifteenth century.[8] This tradition valued women in as much as they were able to emulate the behaviour of men; in Boccaccio, as Liliane Dulac has noted, 'le modèle héroïque masculin est indispensable à l'éloge superlatif'.[9] Boccaccio's lexeme of choice for praising woman's accomplishments is *virilis*, a term implying that her supreme achievement as a woman lies in overcoming the expectations of her sex.[10] By contrast, the later, *querelle* writers seem dissatisfied with this 'immasculating' viewpoint, which, by praising the man in woman, correspondingly denigrated the woman, the femininity, in her.[11] *Femina* and its cognates connoted for Boccaccio effeminacy and weakness, aspects of character that were undesirable and must be suppressed if a woman wished to earn praise. The *querelle* bears witness to a concerted *mise en question* of the value-laden nature of vocabulary used to define woman's achievements. It has been observed, for example, that Christine de Pizan eschews entirely the lexeme *viril*, except when quoting Boccaccio directly.[12] Rosalind Brown-Grant and Thelma Fenster have made convincing cases for examining in detail Christine's use of the vocabulary of gender.[13] Fenster in particular has shown how Christine seems to revalorize *femina*, that is, woman's body, to re-model it as a positive term because, not in spite of its assigned connotations of weakness.

Building on such studies as Brown-Grant's and Fenster's, this essay analyzes the vocabulary of gender behaviour and sexual identity employed by two later, male writers, Martin Le Franc and Antoine Dufour. Le Franc and Dufour appear, consciously or otherwise, to be tapping into the same literary and linguistic strategies that Christine instigates as ways to praise women's greatness *qua women*, not as aspirant men. The result is to open up femininity to new symbolic possibilities. This essay falls into two sections. The first part considers how the masculine gold standard of gender behaviour is challenged by Dufour. It focuses specifically on the problematic case of praising women whose virtue derives from their fulfilment of an active, often military, office that is culturally defined as masculine. The examples of Hypsicratea and Artemis have been selected for study.[14] In these biographies, Dufour's use of gender vocabulary displays a flexibility that can be approached in terms of gender performance, involving various types of transvestism: the expedient wearing and taking off of masculine and feminine characteristics, from cross-dressing clothes to putting on a man's or woman's heart. In modern theorization of gender identity, Butler's writing on drag has been especially influential in shaping understanding of the implications of transvestism.[15] Butler herself highlights how the possibilities for flexibility opened up by practices of gender re-signification such as drag can work subversively or, alternatively, can function merely to reinforce existing hierarchies in a masculine hegemony.[16] It will be important to consider carefully the degree of disruption implied by Dufour's deployment of literal and figurative cross-dressing, not least, again as Butler emphasizes, in the light of the distinction between 'performance' and 'performativity', the former presuming the existence of a subject whilst the latter contests the very idea of a subject.[17]

The second section of this essay takes up the title quotation to examine the representation of sexual identity: the biological, embodied status of man or woman. The male–female binary is imaginatively disrupted by the way Martin Le Franc enlists the discourse of hermaphrodism in an unconventional way, to promote female above male, conventionally her sexual superior in either one-sex or two-sex models. A passage in Le Franc's *Le Champion des dames* in which he rewrites Ovid's myth of Hermaphroditus and Salmacis, seems to advance a radically new 'modèle héroïque *féminin*', a new cultural framing of the female body.

To introduce Dufour's active women, it is helpful to begin with a moment from Christine's *Cité* which encapsulates the sort of disruption of normative 'intelligible gender', to use Butler's phrase, at which *querelle* writers seem to have been aiming.[18] Christine imagines how the besieged French queen Fredegonde might have addressed her troops on the eve of battle:

I've worked out a strategy that will enable us to win [...] I shall leave behind all feminine fear and arm my heart with manly courage in order to raise your spirits and those of our troops out of pity for your young prince[19]

This quotation is usually cited by critics as evidence that Christine, like Boccaccio, adhered to the principle that to receive praise a woman must be described as aspiring towards 'le modèle héroïque masculin'. But we should consider the particular context of Fredegonde's figurative transvestism, whether we should in fact see her taking on 'hardiece d'omme' merely as an expedient identity, a means to an end and not an end in itself, a route towards realizing an identity and not the identity itself. Fredegonde plans to perform masculinity in order to achieve a particular goal, what she herself refers to as 'celle fin'. She seeks to communicate more effectively with her (male) barons and thence proceed to military victory. In doing so, though, she acts out of one of the most essentially feminine motives, namely maternal 'pitié' for the prince, her son.[20] She thus advances into battle as both warrior and mother, a duality Christine expresses through the iconic image of Fredegonde riding forth as commander of her troops whilst carrying her son in her arms: 'She set all the troops in good and fine order, then positioned herself in front, securely mounted, her son in her arms, the barons following after'.[21] Here we can see that the 'maleness' she puts on is no more than a contingently useful metaphor or expedient masquerade. Similarly, in her *Livre des trois vertus* (1405), Christine describes how a widowed chatelaine 'doit avoir cuer d'omme, c'est qu'elle doit savoir les drois d'armes'.[22] Here, the appended explanation ('c'est que...') makes explicit how 'cuer d'omme' is simply a convenient shorthand notation, for want of anything better, for the taking up of a military role with a specific objective in sight. It is perhaps illuminating to see in Christine's rhetorical manoeuvres with expressions like 'cuer d'omme' an adumbration of the sort of 'gender trouble' theorized by Butler. In this light, we can see Christine's perspective on gender identity to have been constrained by what Butler calls a male-normative 'cultural matrix' through which gender identity becomes 'intelligible'; Butler comments how

Regulatory practices [...] generate coherent identities through the matrix of coherent gender norms [...], the production of discrete and asymmetrical oppositions between 'feminine' and 'masculine', where they are understood as expressive attributes of 'male' and 'female'.[23]

Christine appears to be trying to disrupt this matrix of coherent binaries, engaging with its terminology in order to effect from within a critique of this culturally pre-determined binary thinking and its manifestation in language. Her stumbling block is a lack of alternative gender vocabulary outside the masculine–feminine opposition that would break down this dichotomous matrix. Though wanting to oppose the Boccaccian normative system, Christine is still obliged to define her women's positions in relation to it. She seems to have very little room for rhetorical manoeuvre, to be caught in what Butler calls 'a restrictive discourse on gender that […] forecloses the thinkability of its disruption'.[24] However, such 'thinkability' is not entirely foreclosed for Christine. In her *Cité*, her spokeswoman Dame Raison, reflecting on the relationship between gender and physical bravery, gestures towards a fracturing of the binary structure:

Even if women don't at all possess the same strength and physical boldness that men generally have, they absolutely must not say or think that this is because all strength and bodily courage are excluded from the feminine sex.[25]

Raison's argument is thus: physical bravery does not necessarily correspond to intelligible gender identity; there is space within the concept of 'sexe femenin' to accommodate, re-make, even appropriate, a virtue that is culturally mapped 'masculine'. Whilst this sharing of virtues can be maintained conceptually, its representation in language is hampered by the oppositional terms of discourse the writer is obliged to employ, as well as by the slippage that occurs between the neutrally 'denotative' and positively or negatively 'connotative' adjectives *masculin* and *féminin*. It is in this light that we may understand Christine's preference for descriptive phrases involving noun collocation, like 'cuer d'omme', rather than the adjectives *masculin* and *féminin*. As well as designating a quality intrinsic to men, the noun collocations denote a masculine gender role that women can adopt in order to achieve their own, feminine ends.[26] Such formulations have the benefit of avoiding already value-laden terms; Christine wants to shake off the Boccaccian semantic baggage of *masculin* and *féminin* which would hinder her literary project: her desire to tear down existing rhetoric for representing women's achievements in order to lay new foundations for defending her sex, to use the architectural metaphor that governs the *Cité*.

Christine represents the taking on of 'cuer d'omme' as an expedient implemented by a woman, who remains very much female, and positively so, in her achievement of honour.[27] We thus come to see the verbal construction of gender identity as a carefully thought out negotiation within a limited vocabulary of gender-signifying terms.[28] In the *Cité* this negotiation is complicated by the fact that Christine's choice of vocabulary is not simply a linguistic selection of free-floating signifiers, but is necessarily an engagement with the literary context in which these terms have already been deployed, notably the principal source of her *Cité*, Boccaccio's *De mulieribus*. Such negotiation becomes even more complex at the turn of the sixteenth century when Antoine Dufour undertakes his *Vies des femmes célèbres*. The sources he is writing against include not only Boccaccio but also a late fifteenth-century reworking of *De mulieribus* by Jacopo Filippo Foresti, *De plurimis claris selectibus mulieribus* (1497).[29] This essential intertextual dimension to the representation of women can perhaps be seen as a specifically literary manifestation of the notion of gender performativity as a citational practice: the exemplary woman in question is both reiterated and called into question in the same moment that she is re-presented in the new *querelle* text. Dufour's representations of two active women, Hypsicratea and Artemis, will be my focus here. They constitute an apt pair of examples since Hypsicratea illustrates Dufour's use of literal, vestimentary transvestism as a discourse of gender definition, while his Artemis involves a more figurative transvestism as she is represented taking on 'cuer d'omme', to use Christine's term, when she fights in battle alongside Xerxes.

Hypsicratea is a devoted wife who follows her husband into war by disguising herself as a soldier:

Hypsicratea was the wife of Mithridates the Great, who filled with a mighty heart, upon seeing her husband subjugated and banished by Pompey in this fashion, went off [...] to look for her beloved husband. And because her beauty provoked desire in every man, and because, two or three times, passing through the kingdom, she thought she was going to be raped, in order to deal with this threat and to remain faithful to her husband, she changed her clothes and cut her hair [...], putting on full body armour so that she would no longer be importuned or solicited. Moreover, the better to find him whilst passing through Roman lands, she pretended to be one of Pompey's soldiers who was pursuing Mithridates [...] Eventually she found him [...] she declared herself to be his wife, and thus divested herself in order to put on her feminine attire, which was such a great joy to Mithridates [...][30]

Dufour's innovation to her representation is to inscribe a symmetry of transvestite acts in the narrative recounting her pursuit of Mithridates on the battlefield. When she sets out, she changes her clothes and cuts her hair for the respectable reason that she fears for her chastity; her transvestism is approved as the act of a loyal spouse. Once reunited with her husband, she can therefore divest herself freely and resume feminine attire. Hypsicratea's doffing and donning of garments highlights her external transvestism, not only as acts motivated by prudence and propriety, but also as an art of role-playing: she temporarily performs a male identity in order to get what she wants. This idea of performance is all the more significant as Dufour stresses the superficiality of her transvestism. Unlike his sources, he does not characterize the courtly wife's transformation into a warrior as an acquisition of the internal qualities of a 'manly spirit', *animus virili*.[31] Similarly, he changes her motives for wanting to disguise herself. Dufour's sources held that it was a question of decorum; to appear as a woman on the battlefield would have been indecent.[32] In the *Vies*, however, Hypsicratea is motivated, not by regulatory social norms, but by what we might see as the more active, practical and immediate reason of wanting to protect herself from sexual attack in order to remain a loyal wife. Dufour's alteration here could, of course, be seen as a retrograde step, a way of circumscribing Hypsicratea's activity to her accepted social role as faithful spouse.[33] However, in the same way that Dufour's selection of vocabulary must be considered within his work's intertextual context, it is also necessary to consider any extratextual influence operating upon his choices, specifically as regards his patronage. Dufour was writing his *Vies* as a commission from Anne of Brittany (d. 1514), wife of King Louis XII (d. 1515) and, formerly, of Louis's predecessor, Charles VIII (d. 1498). Thus his alteration of the motive of decorum could be seen as a strategic deletion of any acknowledgement of female inferiority since such an acknowledgement would hardly be appropriate for a patron who herself twice held the role of queen of France. The nature of the alteration, changing it to praise of wifely devotion, may thus have been intended to flatter Anne's commitment both to Louis and to France itself via this marriage to her late husband's successor.[34]

The second example of Dufour's active women is Artemis. It is notable that Christine, Dufour and most other *querelle* contributors address Artemis as a hybrid example of virtue, both feminine and chivalric. This hybridity results from their conflation of two distinct figures: Artemis devoted widow of Mauseolus, and Artemis (or Artemidora) who fought in battle on behalf of Xerxes.[35] Her character thus lends itself to definition in gendered terms: her immasculated role as a virtuous widow taking up arms, like Christine's chatelaine, succeeds her role as loyal wife. Boccaccio forges Artemis's hybridity by acknowledging that 'each undertaking was still that of a woman' ('opus quippe fuit femineum unumquodque'), but he uses this duality to point up a contradiction:

As we admire the deeds of Artemisia, what can we think except that the workings of nature erred in bestowing female sex on a body which God had endowed with a virile and lofty spirit?[36]

He portrays her virile spirit encased in woman's flesh as a freakish anomaly; her femininity is utterly at odds with her military accomplishment. The contradiction he perceives in her gender identity works to the detriment of her femininity. Later French *querelle* writers use Artemis's hybrid identity for the same purpose as Boccaccio, to open up the question of gendered conduct, but diverge from him in that they do not perceive Artemis's femininity to be at odds with her achievement. An even more complex perspective emerges in the *Vies*. Dufour concludes his *vita* with a curious homage:

…she performed in so virile a manner that she put to flight Xerxes and his great army, who cried out whilst fleeing: 'I do not believe that Artemis is [not] an angel or a devil!' Having ruled her kingdom in peace, she died a well esteemed and renowned woman.[37]

Apparently unique amongst *querelle* biographies of Artemis, this concluding anecdote seems almost calculated to focus attention on the question, not just of her gender, but of her very being. She fights as a man, dies as a woman and, just to complicate further her ontological status, seems to exceed both male and female natures. Her accomplishments make her *super*natural. Although Dufour uses here the heavily loaded Latinate term 'viril', translating Boccaccio's lexeme of choice, he uses it somewhat oddly: it appears in a context which suggests the transitory nature of Artemis's virility, as an expedient performance rather than a permanent feature of her spirit that is at odds with her female nature. Moreover, Dufour omits the transsexualizing comment made in praise of Artemis which is present in all his sources, that she fought 'quasi cum Xerxe sexum mutasset'.[38] He seems deliberately not to impose this ultimate virility on Artemis.

Dufour's representation of Artemis seems to endow her with a malleability of gender identity redolent of Christine's Fredegonde, proposing a configuration of masculinity-and-femininity which, whilst in no way collapsing the terms of a gender binary, does play with them. In Dufour's account, not only Artemis's gender, but also her human status is illegible; she cannot be recognized, and Dufour resists the logic that assimilates her conduct to a masculine ideal, thereby resisting the imposition of such a normative view of gender behaviour. Artemis is endowed with a measure of uncertainty in her gender identity; her 'doings' do not add up to a unitary being, but she is still designated *elle*, a feminine she, indicating at base an unshaken confidence in essential femininity.

The above examples show how *querelle* writers concerned with lauding the endeavours of active women engaged with the limited, dichotomous vocabulary of gender identity to negotiate what we might call a recognizable discursive position for these women to occupy. This position allows conventionally masculine virtues to be incorporated into a configuration of femininity so a woman can be praised *qua woman* for her heroic deeds. Admittedly this new position is being defined in relation to the established binary norm and is thus still being regulated by it, though not straightforwardly or without experiment. The linguistic activity performed by Dufour in his portraits of Hypsicratea and Artemis manipulates the terms by which gender representation is constrained in order to open up, albeit to varying degrees, different discursive possibilities. There is, as we saw briefly with regard to Hypsicratea, a political edge to Dufour's literary project, in the way his biographies were calibrated according to his target audience, his patron, Queen Anne. In this sense, *she* is the dominant norm against which his exemplary tales are modelled. They, in turn, stand as performances of aspects of her identity, intended to produce a personhood that the queen recognizes as her own performances. They are designed to project her own desired public image as an authoritative, strictly principled manager of court life, a devoted wife, a caring and educative mother.[39] Dufour imagines possibilities of woman's accomplishments which represent, in fact, the possibilities lived out, or imagined to be liveable out, by Anne, on her terms as his patron and his queen. It is interesting to speculate whether Dufour's projected image would have corresponded to Anne's own image of herself, whether she saw herself in exactly the same terms as he wanted to present her.[40]

The *querelle des femmes* instigated an interrogation not only of gendered behaviour but also of sexual identity, biological male- or femaleness. The present essay's title quotation from the *Triomphe des dames* challenges the presumed usefulness of separate signifiers for denoting 'male' and 'female':

Pourquoy appellerions nous ces choses differentes, qu'une heure, un moment, un mouvement peuvent rendre du tout semblables?[41]

The context of this question, extracted from a defence of women, indicates how the discourse of sexual instability was being mobilized by woman's champions in their efforts to portray *femina* – woman's body and sexuality – in a positive light. One striking example of this mobilization occurs in Martin Le Franc's *Le Champion des dames*. Le Franc, provost of Lausanne, dedicated his narrative verse fiction to Philip the Good, duke of Burgundy. The poem develops around a lengthy debate between the eponymous Champion of Ladies, Franc Vouloir ('Free Will'), and a series of misogynist opponents whom the Champion ultimately defeats. At one point, Franc Vouloir enlists the Ovidian tale of Hermaphroditus and Salmacis in support both of women and of marriage as virtuous and desirable entities; thus he kills with one rhetorical stone, so to speak, the two literary birds of misogyny and misogamy.

In the history of ideas, hermaphrodism and androgyny are distinct concepts: Plato's androgyne is an ideal, third kind of human being, not male or female, but a harmonious combination of the two as halves reunited in the perfection of a circular whole; they are conjoint in body but separate in sex.[42] By contrast, the Ovidian hermaphrodite is neither fully male nor fully female and results from a violent merging of the two sexes into a new body.[43] The following section demonstrates how Le Franc's representation of sexual fusion seems, at least to modern eyes, to appropriate both Platonic and Ovidian mythographies as part of a discourse of praising women.[44] He weaves together a number of different mythographies of sexual fusion, much like Dufour dexterously handled the various sources for his *vitae*. Le Franc contrives thereby to rehabilitate the Ovidian myth of monstrous transformation in woman's favour.

Franc Vouloir prefaces his account of the youth Hermaphroditus's fusion with the nymph Salmacis by discussing St Augustine's commentary on the creation of woman, using this as a springboard to introduce his own idea of marriage as a rightful communion of body and soul. He depicts the 'conjunction' of man and woman as husband and wife: formed from the common flesh of Adam, they are joined in an 'alliance' that entails the mystic union of soul and body into one being: 'qu'ilz facent ung et ens et hors'.[45] Platonic resonances of harmonious fusion are discernible in the sort of androgynous unity Franc Vouloir sees marriage to represent. The story of Hermaphroditus and Salmacis is thus set up to illustrate this felicitous reading of male–female communion. The Champion recounts how the nymph fused into Hermaphroditus to create another sexual identity:

> She was merged into him and became a new man/person, male and female. Thus he/it was both a beautiful woman and a handsome man, being made up of both all jumbled together.[46]

The pattern of alternating masculine and feminine rhymes in the original French supports prosodically the stanza's thematic depiction of sexual fusion.[47] A little later, he explicitly equates the fountain of Salmacis with the estate of marriage: 'Marriage is a fountain/spring in which one body merges with/moves into another'.[48] The language of physical movement demonstrates that the marital ideal promoted by Franc Vouloir is not chaste chivalric love, the supposed clerical ideal, but consummated conjugal desire.

It is already clear that the Champion is not following Ovid's tale, either the Latin original or the fourteenth-century vernacular *Ovide moralisé*, to the letter. The latter was an especially popular mythographical source for late medieval writers like Guillaume de Machaut, so may well have been Le Franc's principal reference for his version of the tale. The first deviation from Ovid concerns the character of the nymph Salmacis. She is severely reproved by Ovid for her rapacious desire, and is similarly glossed in the *Ovide moralisé*.[49] By contrast, she represents in the *Champion* a legitimate amorous joy ('amoureuse liesse') that befits one half of the conjugal couple.[50] The second difference concerns the figure produced by the fusion of man and woman. Ovid presents a negative, monstrous image of the conjoining of male and female sexual organs in a sort of asexuality: they were not two, but they had a dual form that could be said to be neither woman nor boy, they seemed to be neither and both.[51]

The *Ovide moralisé* follows suit:

> They are both male and female:
> they are both one and the other together;
> they are neither one nor the other completely.[52]

The *Champion*'s hermaphrodite, on the other hand, is both one and the other as a positive, fertile state, and a complete, perfected whole. Where the *Ovide moralisé* has Hermaphroditus seeing himself as a 'demi malle', Le Franc visualizes a 'nouvel homme' who is not a compromised version of both sexes, but a celebration of each in their fullness.[53]

This re-working of Ovid's negative image continues as the Champion characterizes positively the femininizing power of the Salmacis fountain. In doing so, he enlists a further source relating to the Hermaphrodite myth, John of Salisbury's *Policraticus*:

> Furthermore, says the *Policraticus*,
> the Salmacis fountain is found in Greece,
> where, without any know-how,
> one is transformed into a woman
> and gains a fine and elegant body
> by bathing in it. I wish to God
> that I were in that fountain right now,
> fully clothed, or that such water should fall on me![54]

Quoting this stanza in full draws attention to the audacious, radical manner in which Franc Vouloir here subverts both his explicit and implicit sources – that is, the *Policraticus* and the *Metamorphoses* – in order to advance a pro-feminine argument grounded in the hermaphrodite myth. The Champion's quotation of John of Salisbury is accurate, as far as it goes: the feminizing effect of the fountain's waters is indeed described in the *Policraticus*, but what the Champion deliberately overlooks is the negative tenor of its transformative power:

> [...] the fountain of Salmacis [...] is notorious for weakening virility [...] those who enter it are enervated to such a degree of weakness that like effeminate men they are deprived of the nobler sex.[55]

For John of Salisbury, the feminizing effect of the fountain is a perfect analogy for denouncing the decadent influence of the degenerate courtier who 'pollutes and dishonours virility with effeminacy' in a moral, rather than a sexual, sense.[56] The specific sphere of reference of the medieval court is simply Salisbury's application to a particular, moral context of the literal, physical effeminacy present in Ovid's tale, where the fountain acquired an 'evil name' for causing the men who take its waters to diminish their sexuality to that of a 'semiuir': 'Why Salmacis is thought ill of, how the evil strength of its waters enfeebles and softens the limbs they touch you must learn.'[57] The radical, revisionist nature of the position taken in the *Champion* now becomes clear: far from shunning the fountain's waters as a vitiating force, Franc Vouloir embraces their transformative power as a virtue, going so far as to exclaim that he himself wishes to partake of them and become, thereby, a woman. In this, he radically overturns the conventional sexual hierarchy that places man qualitatively above woman, by valorizing his inferior on Creation's ladder: Dulac's 'idéal héroïque' here becomes emphatically 'féminin'.

The question arises as to why Le Franc should devote such attention to this mythographic moment, and how this may relate to his aims in targeting Philip the Good with his pro-feminine text. The Salmacis episode is but a brief instant in the 24,000-line *Champion*, a work whose status as a defence of women per se is admittedly ambiguous. The poem, divided into five books, certainly pays tribute to a host of valiant, learned and artistic women, foregrounding those from contemporary culture in the catalogue style of Book IV; Book V is given over to a detailed theological defence of the doctrine of Immaculate Conception, and Books I–III address women in the context of love relationships, promoting the institution of marriage as the spiritual union of equals. There are also, however, certain political threads which suggest that pro-feminine argument is being deployed in the service of an agenda other than the defence of women in its own right: Le Franc's staunch support of papal reform and hence vehement opposition to Philip's withdrawal of his prelates from the Council of Basel is most evident in Book V; an ironizing portrait of the Treaty of Troyes is discernible in Book I and a vein of anti-curial criticism simmers throughout. It is therefore possible that the intended focus of the Salmacis episode is not the re-working of gender, but the manipulation of intertextual material that is foregrounded by this striking treatment of the myth. If our attention is, in fact, supposed to be drawn to the *Policraticus* at this point, an entirely different reading of Le Franc's apparent valorization of women emerges: his character's desire for femininity may be construed as a satirical expression of the moral turpitude of the Burgundian court and of the author's wish to be patronized by it, to have its water fall on him. Such a reading requires us to see Le Franc endorsing rather than reversing the misogynist thrust of the tale and John of Salisbury's enlistment of it; it is an intriguing possibility, but somewhat incongruent with the careful re-writing of woman's status in marriage, both here and elsewhere.

Much about the *Champion* remains intriguing, not least the reasons for its apparently chilly reception by its dedicatee. At least according to the evidence of a short sequel, *La Complainte du livre du Champion des dames à maistre Martin Le Franc son acteur*, the *Champion* was spurned by the court on account of its position on matters of 'Holy Church'; but we should be wary of taking at its word this later dream-vision poem, given that nine, often copiously illustrated, manuscript copies of the *Champion* survive, of which a significant number are believed to have been produced in contemporary Burgundian circles.[58] It is clear that, as with Dufour's *Vies*, extratextual factors and issues of ideological context must be borne in mind when interpreting late medieval texts advancing pro-feminine arguments, albeit that speculation and ambiguity may be the only sure fruits of such reflection.

Whatever agenda the Salmacis episode may be serving in the *Champion*, Le Franc's treatment of hermaphrodite mythography proposes both an ideal of equality and harmonious sexual fusion, and, through the Champion's wish to become a woman, an inversion of established sexual relations that revalorizes effeminacy as positive *femina*. We might reflect on this coalescence of the sexes in the context of the *querelle*'s negotiation of discursive spaces that a positive identity for woman may occupy. Le Franc's 'nouvel homme', if we understand 'homme' in a gender universal sense, can be seen on a linguistic level to offer a solution to the problem of defining woman's excellence within restricted discursive boundaries. We should not call this collocation a 'third term' since it does not after all designate a 'third sex', more an integration of two sexes which prevents the normative insistence on one or two.[59] It is a solution in the same vein as Christine de Pizan's attempts to integrate 'hardiesce' into the definition of 'sexe femenin', or Dufour's rhetorical gymnastics when he defines Artemis's identity as a supernatural being. There is a disruption and a re-making that is neither an appropriation nor a transformation. This disruption resists definition according to binary terms of logic, but is nevertheless legible and capable of linguistic expression.

Le Franc's use of the discourse of hermaphrodism to promote the case for women can be seen to anticipate the argument advanced by the female speaker of the *Triomphe des dames*. She develops her point about sexual instability, with which this paper opened, to make a case for woman's superiority. Having posited a non-hierarchical, dialogic relationship between the sexes, her polemic changes tack. She shifts from advocating a sort of egalitarian identity, 'la ressemblance de l'homme et de la femme',[60] to a line of reasoning which reinstates a hierarchy, but now in woman's favour:

I don't want to spend any more time demonstrating that we can be men – that adds nothing to our honour, and so I don't intend to boast about it, except to say that we can be what they are, and they cannot be what we are.[61]

It is clear that, in this speaker's eyes, women have the upper hand in the negotiation of gender identity, and I think we must understand the narrator to have switched here from talking about biologically determined sexuality to discussing socially constructed gender identity. She seems to propose the flexibility of gender, the possibility to perform as a man or as a woman, as an enabling condition that is the prerogative of the female sex. There are several possible interpretations of this proclaimed prerogative, including a possible allusion to Herodotus' account of interactions between Scythian men and Amazon women: the men could not learn the women's language, but the women mastered the speech of the men.[62] Is she perhaps alluding ironically to the hierarchy of Creation, exploiting the perception that man cannot 'become woman' by wearing feminine attire as that would constitute lowering himself on the ladder? In any case, she draws a further conclusion here which bears most pertinently on the debate launched by Dulac regarding 'le modèle héroïque'. According to the *Triomphe*, far from being 'indispensable à l'éloge superlatif', a masculine ideal is presented as being utterly dispensable; acquiring masculine qualities by 'being man' adds nothing to woman's honour. 'Cela n'adjouste rien à nostre honneur', she proudly declares, and thereby evokes an independent, uniquely and wholly feminine route to virtue and renown. Her closing words 'sinon entant…' qualify the ability to become man as a question of latent potential rather than its realization; the speaker does not promote the act of crossing gender, but only the power to act, and the fact that a reciprocal power is denied men. Such power implicitly accords woman the authority to regulate her own gender identity defined on her own terms.[63]

The *Triomphe* speaker's bold assertion of woman's superior gender flexibility can be seen to respond to Christine de Pizan's and Dufour's calls for the scope of 'sexe femenin' to be permitted to incorporate qualities of physical courage and strength that are culturally gendered masculine. The *Triomphe* takes up the two writers' desire in the same line of imaginative development as Le Franc's deployment of the hermaphrodite figure. Both the *Triomphe* and the *Champion* aim to valorize *femina* and essentially feminine qualities that might otherwise feature in an argument against woman's ability to access the highest virtue. They reinstate these attributes as the most noble and desirable route to attaining 'l'éloge superlatif'.

One further reflection on the *Triomphe* furnishes a fruitful conclusion to this exploration of how woman's identity is represented in the late medieval *querelle*. There is potentially a literary reflexive dimension to the speaker's rhetorical question 'pourquoy appellerions…?'. As mentioned above, the *Triomphe* is an anonymous work which purports to be voiced by a woman, who, identifying herself enigmatically as 'une Pucelle sans nom',[64] addresses a female audience: 'What I write has no other aim than to defend the justice of your cause that sex has made mine'.[65] The only indication of authorial identity we possess is the manner in which the work is signed at the end by the initials 'P.D.B', which have generally led authorship to be attributed to a man, Pierre de Brinon. If Brinon, or any other man, was the author, might we see him, through his female narrator's rhetorical question, to be proposing a sophisticated reflection on the gendering of authorial voice, on readerly preconceptions regarding authorship by different sexes and on the relationship between authorial and narrative voices when a shift in gender comes into play?

The *Triomphe*'s speaker seems to imply a series of questions that are germane to our reflections as modern critics of the late medieval *querelle des femmes*. Does the sex of an author matter when he or she is writing in defence of women? Does it matter whether the 'querelle' is really the 'mienne' of the first-person speaker? Having explored interrogations of gender behaviour and sexuality by both male and female contributors to the *querelle*, we might consider to what extent the two 'choses', man and woman, such as

Christine and Dufour, are 'du tout semblables' as writers, and for whom their identity or difference as such might matter: the author him/herself, a patron or contemporary audience or a modern readership. The narrative voice that speaks in the *Triomphe* may be that of a man who is putting into practice his ability to become a woman through the artifice of imaginative fiction. This may be seen as a treacherous act, an undermining of the authority the *Triomphe* apparently wishes to accord women. Alternatively, it may be understood less as an ethical problem than a linguistic and political act – a reflection on the positionality of gender as a narrative construct. Brinon may be seen to be performing in his literary work as both a man and a woman, with neither identity being more 'real', since both are equally performatively constituted, albeit within a framework of reference to existing gender subjects. Late medieval defences of women remain invested in an essentialism that renders inappropriate any attempt to assimilate these texts to Butler's gender performativity, a theory which challenges the notion of the subject and does not recognize a distinction between biological sex and cultural gender. However, facets of her 'undoing' of gender may nonetheless fruitfully be applied in order to provide a more nuanced appreciation of certain writers' linguistic manoeuvrings in their representations of women. These are issues to which future studies of the *querelle* corpus may wish to pay attention, bearing in mind that, as the present article has shown, any answers will involve a flexible and sophisticated understanding of gender, writing and performance in the *querelle des femmes*.[66]

Notes

1. 'Pourquoy appellerions nous ces choses differentes, qu'une heure, un moment, un mouvement peuvent rendre du tout semblables?', [Pierre de Brinon], *Le Triomphe des dames* (Rouen: Jean Osmont, 1599), p. 7. The ambiguity created by an authorial voice that is at once anonymous and purportedly female raises important questions of gender and authorship which are not the focus of this essay, but to which I shall return in conclusion. English translations of all foreign language quotations are my own, unless otherwise stated.

2. Ovid, *Metamorphoses*, ed. Richard J. Tarrant (Oxford: Oxford University Press, 2004), x, ll. 666–797.

3. *Triomphe*, p. 10.

4. Judith Butler, *Undoing Gender* (New York and London: Routledge, 2004). However, it is important to note that a distinction between biological sex and cultural gender does not apply in Butler's theories of gender performativity. Cf. p. 103.

5. See, for instance, Joan Cadden, *Meanings of Sex Difference in the Middle Ages: Medicine, Science and Culture* (Cambridge: Cambridge University Press, 1993), p. 3; Thomas Laqueur, *Making Sex: Body and Gender from the Greeks to Freud* (Cambridge, MA and London: Harvard University Press, 1990), p. 61.

6. The precise parameters of the *querelle* are open to debate; see Helen J. Swift, *Gender, Writing, and Performance: Men Defending Women in Late Medieval France (1440–1538)* (Oxford: Oxford University Press, 2008), pp. 227–48.

7. Anne de France, *Les Enseignements d'Anne de France, suivis de l'Histoire du siège de Brest*, ed. Tatiana Clavier and Éliane Viennot (Saint-Étienne: Publications de l'Université de Saint-Étienne, 2006). For discussion of the pro-feminine catalogue in the context of early modern encomiastic rhetoric,

see Renée-Claude Breitenstein, 'La rhétorique encomiastique dans les éloges collectifs de femmes imprimés de la première Renaissance française (1495–1555)' (unpublished doctoral thesis, McGill University, 2008).

8. Christine's expression of opposition towards Boccaccio through her re-writing of *exempla* has been well documented; see especially Patricia A. Phillippy, 'Establishing Authority: Boccaccio's *De claris mulieribus* and Christine de Pizan's *Le Livre de la cité des dames*', *Romanic Review*, 77 (1986), 167–94. Le Franc and Dufour evoke somewhat ambiguous relationships with their Italian predecessor: Le Franc's protagonist, the Champion, states how he compiles his arguments in favour of women 'with the help of (*a l'ayde de*) Jehan Bocasse' (*Le Champion des dames*, ed. Robert Deschaux (Paris: Champion, 1999), l. 10864); Dufour opens his prologue to the *Vies* by condemning Boccaccio as a detractor of women, but then states how he wishes to present to his patron a translation of Boccaccio's work into French (Dufour, *Les Vies des femmes célèbres*, ed. G. Jeanneau (Geneva: Droz, 1970), p. 1).

9. 'The masculine model of heroism is essential to superlative praise': 'Un mythe didactique chez Christine de Pizan: Sémiramis ou la veuve héroïque (du *De mulieribus claris* de Boccace à la *Cité des Dames*)', in *Mélanges de philologie romane offerts à Charles Camproux*, 2 vols (Montpellier: Centre d'Estudis Occitans, 1978), I, pp. 315–43 (p. 323). See also Jennifer Cavalli's contribution to this volume.

10. See *Famous Women*, ed. Virginia Brown (Cambridge, MA and London: Harvard University Press, 2001), pp. xviii–xix.

11. Judith Fetterley coins this term to describe how women must 'accept as normal and legitimate a male system of values' (*The Resisting Reader: A Feminist Approach to American Fiction* (Bloomington: Indiana University Press, 1978), p. xx). In the present context, immasculation signifies woman's assimilation to a masculine ideal of virile behaviour.

12. Rosalind Brown-Grant, 'Writing Beyond Gender: Christine de Pizan's Linguistic Strategies in the Defence of Women', in *Contexts and Continuities: Proceedings of the IVth International Colloquium on Christine de Pizan (Glasgow 21–27 July 2000), Published in Honour of Liliane Dulac*, ed. Angus J. Kennedy et al., 3 vols (Glasgow: University of Glasgow Press, 2002), I, pp. 155–69 (p. 167).

13. Brown-Grant, 'Writing Beyond Gender'; Thelma Fenster, 'Possible Odds: Christine de Pizan and the Paradoxes of Woman', in *Contexts and Continuities*, II, pp. 355–66.

14. This first section draws on materials included in Chapter 3 of my book: Swift, *Gender*.

15. Although Butler herself has been at pains to clarify that her original use of the figure was as an *example* of gender performativity, not as its paradigm: Peter Osborne and Lynne Segal, 'Gender as Performance: An Interview with Judith Butler', *Radical Philosophy*, 67 (1994), 32–39 (p. 33).

16. See Judith Butler, *Gender Trouble: Feminism and the Subversion of Identity* (London and New York: Routledge, 1990), pp. 174–75, and *Undoing Gender*, pp. 213–19.

17. Osborne and Segal, 'Gender as Performance', p. 33.

18. Judith Butler, *Gender Trouble*, p. 23.

19. 'J'ay pourpensé un barat par quoy nous vaincrons [...] Je lairay ester toute paour femenine et armeray mon cuer de hardiece d'omme a celle fin de croistre le courage de vous et de ceulx de nostre ost par pitié de vostre jeune prince' (*La Città delle dame*, ed. Patrizia Caraffi (Milan: Luni, 1997), p. 144).

20. For a discussion of Fredegonde's action that draws different conclusions, but from a linguistic line of argument similar to my own, see Brown-Grant, 'Writing Beyond Gender', p. 163.

21. 'Elle fist bien et bel ordener tout l'ost, puis se mist devant, bien montee, son filz entre ses bras, les barons après' (*Città*, p. 144).

22. Dulac cites Paris, Bibliothèque nationale, fonds français, 452, fol. 61v. '[She] must have a manly heart, that's to say, she must know how to use arms.'

23. Butler, *Gender Trouble*, p. 23.

24. Butler, *Undoing Gender*, p. 43; see also pp. 42, 197.

25. 'Pourtant se femmes n'ont mie toutes si grant force et hardiece corporelle que ont hommes communement, que ilz ne doivent mie dire ne croire que ce soit pour ce que du sexe femenin soit forclose toute force a hardiece corporelle' (*Città*, p. 104).

26. See Brown-Grant, 'Writing Beyond Gender', p. 163.

27. Brown-Grant and Fenster have shown how Christine resists the immasculation of women by men. Brown-Grant comments on Christine's semantic neutralization of adjectives such as *femenin* such that they 'carry no hint of value-judgment', whether positive *or* negative (p. 163), whilst Fenster reinstates certain connotations of *femina* to demonstrate that Christine valorizes the feebleness of woman's body as 'a model of human virtue-in-vulnerability'. Fenster, 'Possible Odds' (p. 366).

28. Cf. Valerie Hotchkiss, *Clothes Make the Man: Female Cross Dressing in Medieval Europe* (New York/London: Garland Publishing, 1996), pp. 125–27.

29. For the nature of this re-working, and the context in which it was produced, see Stephen Kolsky, *The Ghost of Boccaccio* (Turnhout: Brepols, 2005), pp. 117–47.

30. 'Ipsicrethea fut femme du grant roy Mithridates, laquelle, comme plaine de grant cueur, voyant son mary ainsi subjugué et banny par Pompée, s'en vint [...] cercher son bienaymé mary. Et pour ce que sa beaulté donnoit à ung chascun envie et que deux ou troys foys, en allant par le pays, cuyda estre viollée, pour y remédier et garder la loyaulté à son mary, mua ses habillemens et coupa ses cheveulx [...], se armant de toutes pièces, affin de n'estre plus priée ne solicitée. Et, pour mieulx le trouver, en passant par les terres des Rommains, faignoit estre chevalier de Pompée, qui suivoit Mithridates [...]. Tant fist qu'elle le trouva [...]. Après plusieurs parolles des Rommains, elle se déclaire estre sa femme et par ainsi se despoille pour prendre ses habitz fémenins, qui fut une si grande joye à Mythridates' (*Vies*, pp. 84–85).

31. *Famous Women*, p. 324; *De plurimis*, in Ravisius Textor, *De memorabilibus et claris mulieribus aliquot diversorum scriptorum opera* (Paris: Simon de Colines, 1521), fols 14v–160r (fol. 49r).

32. *Famous Women*, p. 322; *De plurimis*, fol. 49r.

33. Cf. Hotchkiss, *Clothes Make the Man*, Chapter 6, esp. p. 83.

34. For more detailed study of Anne's patronage in the context of other pro-feminine literature produced for her (notably Antoine Vérard's publication of a French translation of *De mulieribus*), see Cynthia J. Brown, 'Le mécénat d'Anne de Bretagne et la politique du livre', in *Patronnes et mécènes en France à la Renaissance*, ed. Kathleen Wilson-Chevalier (St Etienne: University of St Etienne Press, 2007), pp. 169–94.

35. *Città*, pp. 137–40, 263; *Vies*, pp. 73–75.

36. 'Sed quid [...] arbitrari possumus, nise nature laborantis errore factum ut corpori, cui Deus virilem et magnificam infuderat animam, sexus femineus datus sit?' (*Famous Women*, pp. 240–42). Translations of Boccaccio are Brown's: *Famous Women*, pp. 240–42.

37. '[...] tant virillement se monstra qu'elle chassa Xercès et sa grosse compaignie, qui en fuyant disoit: 'Je ne croy point que Arthémisie ne soit ung ange ou ung deable!' Après avoir pacifiquement son pays gouverné, mourut femme bien estimée et renommée' (*Vies*, p. 75). Dufour, like Christine, errs in having Artemis fighting *against* Xerxes, perhaps on account of ambiguity present in *De mulieribus* and *De plurimis*.

38. *Famous Women*, p. 240; *De plurimis*, fol. 46r. 'Almost as if she had changed sex with Xerxes.'

39. Anne lost all her children by Charles VIII and by the time of Dufour's commission she had only Claude (b. 1499). On the image of Anne's queenship constructed through book production at her court, see Cynthia J. Brown, *The Queen's Library: Image-Making at the Court of Anne of Brittany, 1477–1514* (Philadelphia and Oxford: University of Pennsylvania Press, 2011).

40. For a contemporary example of a failed correspondence, concerning Symphorien Champier's dedication of his *Nef des dames vertueuses* (1503) to Anne de France, Anne de Brittany's sister-in-law, see Swift, *Gender*, pp. 176–81.

41. *Triomphe*, p. 7.

42. Plato, *Symposium*, ed. Kenneth Dover (Cambridge: Cambridge University Press, 1980), 189c2–d6.

43. *Metamorphoses*, IV, ll. 285–388. Plato's image has traditionally been regarded as the emblem of a transcendent and harmonious union of opposites, whereas the figure of the hermaphrodite is typically regarded as a monstrous creation: see Marjorie Garber, *Vice Versa: Bisexuality and the Eroticism of Everyday Life* (London: Penguin, 1995), pp. 207–208.

44. It should be noted that hermaphrodism and androgyny are not always easy to distinguish in medieval writings engaging with the topic of sexual fusion. Cf. Floyd Gray, *Gender, Rhetoric and Print Culture in French Renaissance Writing* (Cambridge: Cambridge University Press, 2000), p. 151.

45. *Champion*, ll. 6961, 6957, 6976.

46.   'Fut muee en lui et nouvel / Homme devint masle et femelle. / Ainsi fut il et belle et bel, / L'ung et l'aultre ayant pellemelle' (*Champion*, ll. 6981–84).

47.   I am grateful to Miranda Griffin for pointing out this pattern.

48.   'Mariage est une fontaine / Ou ung corps en aultre se mue' (*Champion*, ll. 6993–94).

49.   *Ovide moralisé: poème du commencement du quatorzième siècle*, ed. Cornelius de Boer, 5 vols (Amsterdam: Müller, 1920), ii, ll. 2250–325.

50.   *Champion*, l. 6979. Cf. Christine de Pizan's use of Ovid's myth in her *Epistre Othea* (c. 1400), which, whilst not being pro-feminine in the same way as Le Franc's version, also comes down on the side of the nymph: ed. Gabriella Parussa (Geneva: Droz, 1999), p. 316.

51.   'nec duo sunt sed forma duplex, nec femina dici / nec puer ut posit, neutrumque et utrumque uidentur' (*Metamorphoses*, iv, ll. 378–79). Translations of Ovid's Latin text are taken from Tarrant.

52.   'Ambedui sont malle et femelle / Si sont ensamble l'un et l'autre, / Si ne sont parfet l'un ne l'autre' (*Ovide*, ii, ll. 2199–201).

53.   *Ovide*, ii, l. 2203. 'Half man.'

54.   'Encores, dist Policratique, / Est la fontaine Salmatis / En Grece ou sans quelque pratique / L'en est en femme convertis / Et a on corps beaulx et traictis / Par s'i baigner. Or a Dieu pleut / Que dedens fusse tout vestis / Ou que telle yaue sur moy pleut!' (*Champion*, ll. 6985–92).

55.   *Policraticus: Of the Frivolities of Courtiers and the Footprints of Philosophers* ed. Cary J. Nederman (Cambridge: Cambridge University Press, 1990), p. 90.

56.   *Policraticus*, p. 91.

57.   '[…] unde sit infamis, quare male fortibus undis / Salmacis eneruet tactosque remolliat artus' (*Metamorphoses*, iv, ll. 285–86).

58.   For further discussion of the enigmatic sequel *La Complainte* and its role in our interpretation of the *Champion*'s reception history, see Helen J. Swift, 'Martin Le Franc et son *livre qui se plaint*: une petite énigme à la cour de Philippe le Bon', in *L'écrit et le manuscrit à la fin du moyen âge*, ed. Tania Van Hemelryck and Céline Van Hoorebeeck (Turnhout: Brepols, 2006), pp. 329–42.

59.   Medieval writers including Nicole Oresme and Christine de Pizan reflected upon the semantic parameters of *homme*, regarding its equivalence (or otherwise) to Latin *homo*, which did include both sexes: see John Fyler, 'Man, Men, and Women in Chaucer's Poetry', in *The Olde Daunce: Love, Friendship, Sex, and Marriage in the Medieval World*, ed. Robert R. Edwards and Stephen Spector (Albany: State University of New York Press, 1991), pp. 154–76.

60.   'The ways in which man and woman are the same' (*Triomphe*, p. 11).

61.   'Je ne veux étudier davantage à montrer que nous pouvons estre homes, cela n'adjouste rien à nostre honneur, aussi n'enten-je pas m'en prévaloir, sinon entant que nous pouvons estre ce qu'ils sont, et ne peuent estre ce que nous sommes' (*Triomphe*, p. 11).

62.   Herodotus, *Histories*, iv, 114.1.

63.   Cf. my comments below about narrative voice and performativity.

64.   'An anonymous maid' (*Triomphe*, p. 3).

65.   'Ce que j'escry n'a autre but que la defense de la justice de vos querelles que le sexe a fait miennes' (*Triomphe*, p. 3).

66.   Some of these questions are explored in Swift, *Gender*.

7

Constructing Female Sanctity in Late Medieval Naples: The Funerary Monument of Queen Sancia of Majorca

Aislinn Loconte

On 21 January 1344, a year and a day after the death of her husband King Robert of Anjou, Queen Sancia of Majorca (1286–1345) entered the convent of Santa Croce di Palazzo in Naples. By this action, Sancia fulfilled a lifelong wish to enter the Franciscan order and when she died a year later, a monumental tomb was erected to hold her body in the convent church. This now lost monument commissioned by Queen Giovanna I of Anjou used a highly innovative iconographic design which recognized the roles that her grandmother Sancia assumed during her lifetime, as both an Angevin monarch and a devout Clarissan sister. The tomb presents an interesting case study through which to consider these positions, and to explore how a female patron used iconography to construct persuasive visual evidence supporting the case for Sancia's canonization. In particular, the imagery provides insight into the central role that devotion to the Eucharist and *imitatio Christi* played in Sancia's spirituality. This essay both analyzes the significance of these to Sancia and examines the ways that they connect her to the Franciscans. Indeed, her tomb represents an extraordinary departure from the long-standing iconography found on sepulchres in the late medieval kingdom of Naples as evident in the image on the sarcophagus which depicts Sancia seated amongst her fellow nuns at a banquet table (fig. 7.1). This scene is often interpreted as an unusual 'female Last Supper' yet such a limited reading of this imagery aims to characterize it within established and static categories and thus fails to consider how it intentionally blurs and subverts accepted boundaries surrounding gendered behaviour and representation.

Even though she held a strong desire to become a cloistered nun, Sancia of Majorca spent much of her life in a public role as queen of the kingdom of Naples, Sicily and Jerusalem, also known as the Regno.[1] In

1309, four years after her marriage, Robert of Anjou was crowned king and they came to Naples where Sancia assumed her position at the royal court. Their politically instrumental marriage linked the Angevin dynasty, which had ruled the Regno since 1266, with the House of Majorca, joining two of the most prominent powers in the late medieval Mediterranean. An influential figure at the Neapolitan court, Sancia took on an active position in governing the Regno, and by the 1330s she had assumed a significant role in mentoring Robert of Anjou's granddaughter and the heir to the throne, Giovanna of Anjou. Indeed, through her considerable success as a royal monarch she was able to use her role at court to promote her own religious and political ideas.

Throughout her lifetime Sancia petitioned the papacy for special permissions and privileges intended to facilitate and strengthen her own religious experience. The first evidence of this appears in 1312 when the pope gave his consent for her to have two Clarisses as her constant companions.[2] In addition to granting her permission to have her own Clarissan community with her at all times, Sancia was also given the right to enter the cloistered spaces of the Clares' houses. Even though this dispensation was offered to Sancia on subsequent occasions, her desire to live permanently within the walls of a convent was not satisfied and her persistent requests to the pope to cloister herself continued. This desire took the form of a dramatic plea in 1317 when she petitioned the pope for a divorce from her husband so she could enter a convent.[3] Unsurprisingly, Pope John XXII did not support her wishes and suggested instead that she pay greater attention to her earthly spouse.

Historically, the House of Majorca had been strong supporters of the order and both Sancia's parents gave generously to support the establishment of religious foundations in Perpignan and throughout the Majorcan territories. Similarly, the Angevin dynasty patronized and supported the order; in particular, promoting its close links to the brother of King Robert of Anjou and newly canonized Angevin saint, Louis of Toulouse.[4] While Sancia's interest in the order fits appropriately within the dynastic and religious concerns of both her birth family in Majorca and the Angevin dynasty in Naples into which she married, her continuation of this tradition and devotion to the order also stemmed from intensely personal religious concerns.

Sancia sought avenues through which to voice her support for the order, and particularly for the Spiritual Franciscans. An active correspondent with the papacy as well as a prolific patron of convents and monasteries in Naples and abroad, Sancia created a public role for herself in line with her private religious concerns. In the midst of the great debate of the early fourteenth century on the interpretation of apostolic poverty, Sancia emerged as a supporter of the Spiritual Franciscans. Championing literal poverty over theoretical observance, the Spirituals were declared heretical by Pope John XXII, yet they found Queen Sancia sympathetic to their cause.[5] Sancia forged a path which, at times, brought her into conflict with more conservative papal attitudes but was deeply engaged with Spiritual Franciscan concerns. Instrumental in the foundation and maintenance of many Franciscan religious institutions in the kingdom of Naples, her homeland of Majorca as well as the Holy Land, Sancia played a prominent role in promoting the interests of both the order's male and female branches.[6] In Naples alone she was a significant patron of numerous religious institutions, both those intended to house nobility, as well as foundations for penitent women such as former prostitutes.[7] Yet her desire to take the veil remained strong and in November 1343, following the death of King Robert, the pope finally granted permission for Sancia to cloister herself. As her new home, Sancia chose the final institution that she had founded, the convent of Santa Croce di Palazzo in Naples.

Sancia played an active role in the establishment and administration of the Clarissan convent of Santa Croce di Palazzo located outside the city walls to the north of Castel Nuovo. After receiving permission from Pope Benedict XII to found the convent she continued to actively petition the papacy for privileges for it. Specifically, she was concerned that Santa Croce follow the original rule of St Clare.[8] In 1338, in her first request to establish the convent, Sancia specifically asked to bring a group of Clarisses to Naples from Assisi, and in 1342 she succeeded in receiving confirmation from the Pope that the monastery could indeed follow the first rule of St Clare.[9] Sancia's promotion of the original rule of St Clare and her insistence that sisters from Assisi come and live at the new foundation in Naples indicate her desire to model the convent of Santa Croce di Palazzo after San Damiano the first house of the followers of Clare in Assisi.

Unfortunately, little survives today of the original religious complex; however, the written and visual descriptions of the organization of the religious buildings of Santa Croce di Palazzo seem to indicate a similar architectural plan to those of the Clarissan convents of the Nativity of Christ in Aix-en-Provence and Santa Chiara in Naples, both founded by Sancia of Majorca.[10] These institutions were double monasteries, consisting of a church and convent for the Clares, as well as a friary for the Franciscans who administered them. Thus, their architectural and administrative structure allowed the sisters to follow the original rule of St Clare, while being adequately supported by the male order living adjacent to them. After being admitted to the convent Sancia gained the pope's consent to leave Santa Croce di Palazzo to visit other convents and her active relationship with the foundations she had supported throughout her lifetime may have continued after she took the veil. Her long-desired life as a Clarissan sister however, was short, and Sancia died in Santa Croce di Palazzo on 28 July 1345.[11]

Sancia was initially buried in a simple, freestanding monument in the choir of the convent of Santa Croce di Palazzo, yet it was probably just

7.1   Tomb of Sancia of Majorca in Santa Croce di Palazzo, Naples.
Vatican City, Biblioteca Apostolica Vaticana, Vat. Lat. 9840, f. 59r

intended to be a temporary tomb. Only a few months after Sancia's death, the Regno fell into turmoil. In September 1345, Andrew of Hungary, the husband of the reigning queen, Giovanna I of Anjou, was murdered, and his brother, King Louis I of Hungary, invaded Naples to avenge his death, thus forcing Giovanna to flee Naples for Provence. Hence Sancia's body was kept in the provisional tomb in the choir of Santa Croce di Palazzo for almost seven years until 1352, when following her victorious return to the throne, Queen Giovanna I commissioned an elaborate double-sided monument for the convent church to receive Sancia's body. In size and grandeur this monument seems to have been much more in keeping with the long-standing Angevin tradition of monumental sepulchres.

The tomb is now lost, but it is known in part from two late eighteenth-century drawings which illustrate the sarcophagus of the monument and the two caryatids which supported the tomb chest (figs 7.1 and 7.2).[12] These illustrations demonstrate that the subject chosen for the two sides of the funerary chest was particularly appropriate given Sancia's history. Her two major roles in the Regno as queen and as a Clarissan sister were given equal prominence in the iconography of the tomb chest. On one side of the chest Sancia is shown in the centre of the scene, enthroned, wearing a crown

7.2   Tomb of Sancia of Majorca in Santa Croce di Palazzo, Naples.
Vatican City, Biblioteca Apostolica Vaticana, Vat. Lat. 9840, f. 58v

decorated with the fleur-de-lis, and holding the orb and sceptre (fig. 7.2). On either side of her, Franciscan nuns and friars kneel and pay her homage. The reverse side of the funerary chest represents Sancia sitting n the centre of a long table between eight Clares (fig. 7.1). The sisters around her are shown eating while Sancia solemnly stares outward with her hands raised in prayer. She is dressed in an identical habit to those of the sisters surrounding her and the only reference to her royal title is the crown placed under her feet.

In addition to the illustrations of the sarcophagus, two of the caryatids which supported the monument are also partially depicted. One of these, 'Charity', has been identified and is now held in the Musée des Beaux Arts in Lyon, but the whereabouts of other sculpture from the tomb remains unknown.[13] These female figures representing the Franciscan virtues of Charity and Poverty must have been well suited to the audience of the Clares who would have been able to view the monument from their choir.[14] Although we have little further evidence to indicate what the rest of the monument may have looked like, the location of the tomb can be more securely determined. Early descriptions of the church as well as a letter written by Queen Giovanna to Pope Clement IV indicate that the tomb was located behind the high altar.[15] Furthermore, below the drawing of the tomb chest supported by caryatids and depicting Sancia seated with her fellow nuns, is a note written in pencil: 'S. Croce. T. de. la R. Sancia da dentro il coro'. Thus it seems that the monument used a double sarcophagus sculpted on either side, and that this particular side of the chest faced the choir where it would have been seen by its primary beholders, the nuns of Santa Croce di Palazzo.

In 1352, when the tomb was unveiled in Santa Croce di Palazzo, the last major royal tomb to have been constructed in the Regno was the funerary monument of Sancia's husband, Robert of Anjou, in Santa Chiara. Giovanna I and Sancia of Majorca, who acted as her regent until 1345, together had commissioned this monumental tomb in 1344. The tomb was placed in the convent church of Santa Chiara separating the space of the high altar and the nuns' choir.[16] Both the architectural arrangement of the church and the placement of Robert's tomb behind the high altar, so that the nuns could see through it to the main church, were innovations which proved influential in the Regno. As the joint patron with Sancia of Robert's tomb, Giovanna would have known about the important concessions Sancia had initiated in Santa Chiara to give the nuns of the convent a more active role in viewing the Eucharist, notably by incorporating the grilles, through which they could see the high altar, into the design of Robert's tomb. This contextual evidence supports the documented location of Sancia's tomb behind the high altar and indicates that it was most likely that her sepulchre was placed behind the high altar of the convent church in a similar position to Robert of Anjou's tomb in Santa Chiara, with the image of Sancia as a Clarissan sister visible to only those in the choir of Santa Croce di Palazzo.[17]

The unfortunate destruction of the monument by the start of the nineteenth century and the relative lack of evidence documenting its location and form may account for the fact that early considerations of the monument do not move beyond mere descriptions of the tomb.[18] Since the 1990s scholars have considered the monument in greater depth, drawing useful links between the visual language of the tomb and well-known iconographic models used by the Angevin dynasty, as well as contextualizing the iconography within the atmosphere of Franciscan religiosity at the royal court.[19] While the subject matter of the sarcophagus owes much to the visual models of prior Angevin imagery and the religious ideals of the Spirituals, the two relief panels of the tomb sarcophagus also strongly support the intended function of the sepulchre. This monumental tomb commemorated Sancia as a Poor Clare and glorified her role as queen of the Regno, yet it also was intended to provide persuasive visual evidence in the campaign to have Sancia canonized.

The House of Anjou had traditionally claimed *beata stirps* or a royal legacy of sanctity. The canonization in 1298 of King Louis IX of France (1215–70), brother of King Charles I of Anjou, and Louis of Toulouse (1274–1297), son of King Charles II of Anjou, in 1317, had done much to cement this well-established tradition. The Angevin dynasty in Naples had long realized the potential benefits, spiritual as well as secular, which came from having members of the royal family proclaimed saints.[20] Furthermore, the development of a holy legacy would be greatly enhanced by the canonization of a recently deceased member of the family. Thus, in 1352, Queen Giovanna I of Anjou set about attempting to have Sancia of Majorca canonized. In a lengthy letter to Pope Clement VI. Giovanna outlined in detail the reasons why Sancia should be canonized.[21] She highlighted the numerous acts of charity that Sancia had performed during her lifetime and the tremendous dedication which her grandmother had held for the Franciscan order. As Giovanna explained to the pope, when Sancia's temporary tomb was opened in the choir of Santa Croce, in the presence of the archbishop of Naples and many royal dignitaries, religious and lay people, her body was discovered to be incorrupt. Indeed, Giovanna's formal request to have Sancia's body translated to her new tomb in an elaborate ceremony and the precautions that the queen instated to protect the monument from grave robbers, further demonstrates that, at least in Naples, Sancia was already being treated like a saint.[22] The visual evidence conveyed by the tomb, reinforced by her pious works as well as her incorrupt body, was intended to convince the pope of Sancia's candidacy for sainthood.

Development of support for Sancia's sanctity was further promoted by the iconography of the tomb which emphasized her religious piety and virtue. The successful campaign to have Louis of Toulouse canonized and the promotion of his cult must have stood as a potent model for Queen Giovanna I as she attempted to achieve the same recognition for her grandmother. Indeed, the large image of St Louis of Toulouse painted by Simone Martini and commissioned by King Robert of Anjou would have been a particularly suitable model (fig. 7.3). The large panel painting depicts the Angevin saint enthroned and wearing his Franciscan habit underneath his ecclesiastical robes. He is crowned by two angels while he simultaneously reaches out to place a crown upon the head of Robert of Anjou who kneels before him. This royal commission intended to promote the veneration of this newly canonized saint, can be linked to the image depicted on Sancia's tomb sarcophagus and representing her enthroned with Franciscan saints kneeling on either side of her. The iconic portrayal of St Louis is similar to the presentation of Sancia, who is also enthroned and is depicted both crowned and wearing her royal regalia. Like Louis, who gave up his throne in order to become a Franciscan, Sancia too long desired to give up her role at court for a religious life. Thus by using this image as a model for the depiction of Sancia on her tomb, their dynastic as well as spiritual links were strengthened. By clearly referencing the well-used iconography of the renowned and pious Angevin royal saint Louis of Toulouse, the image of Sancia on her tomb chest actively functioned to associate the queen with his powerful legacy while at the same time promoting her own virtuous character worthy of canonization.

7.3   Simone Martini, *St Louis of Toulouse Crowning Robert of Anjou*, 1317, Museo Nazionale di Capodimonte. Image courtesy of Luciano Pedicini

The image also recalls the iconography of the Madonna enthroned receiving devotees who pay her honour. The subject of the Madonna being honoured by supplicants who kneel before her was well known in Angevin imagery. Indeed, it had been adopted for the personal high-relief sculpture that Sancia had commissioned when she entered the convent of Santa Croce di Palazzo (fig. 7.4). This work depicts Sancia in the role of supplicant as she humbles herself before the Madonna and Christ. Upon entering the convent, Sancia took the name 'Suor Chiara', and in the relief, her namesake St Clare places a protective hand on Sancia's shoulder while the Madonna reaches out to touch her head and Christ raises his hand toward her in blessing. In the image on her tomb, Sancia is placed in the central role, seated on a large throne; she is represented as a Madonna-like queen as she receives homage from the friars and Clares who surround her.

By linking Sancia to the figure of the Madonna, emphasis is placed on the motherly role she cast for herself during her lifetime. Writing to Michael of Cesena, Minister General of the Franciscan Order in 1316, Sancia characterized her relationship to the order in distinctly maternal terms:

> Although I am not worthy on my own, nevertheless through the grace of God I can be called the true mother of the order of Blessed Francis in several ways, not only in word or writing, but also by the works I have performed continuously, as well as those I intend to do with his help all the days of my life.[23]

7.4   Tino di Camaino, *Madonna and Child with Queen Sancia, Saints and Angels*, c. 1335, Samuel H. Kress Collection, National Gallery of Art, Washington

The imagery of her tomb draws attention to her self-proclaimed position as a protector and advocate of the order, who through her commitment to their spiritual and material well-being enabled their pious works. Moreover, the image also suggests the important role she played as their benefactress through her support of the order, her position as their patron and her foundation of numerous houses for them. Sancia was not unique among pious women in late medieval Italy in offering maternal comfort and spiritual advice to the Franciscans.[24] Angela of Foligno, Elizabeth of Hungary and Margaret of Cortona are cast as 'spiritual mothers' to the Franciscan friars in the writings associated with them.[25] The centrality of their maternal roles to these accounts may have provided significant role models for Sancia during her lifetime. Subsequently, following her death, the similarity between her behaviour and well-known female Franciscan saints would have helped to build support for her sanctity.

While the front of the sarcophagus is linked to established iconographic representations of the Madonna enthroned and Angevin saints such as Louis of Toulouse, at first glance the other side of the sarcophagus seems rather unusual. This image, which depicts Sancia seated in the middle of a long table amongst her fellow Clares, has typically been described as an inventive Last Supper scene emphasizing the links between this scene and well-known depictions of this event from the life of Christ. While allusions to the Last Supper at once seem obvious, the complex iconography of the scene deserves further consideration.

The image is informed by eucharistic events from Christological narratives. Specifically, the image is linked to the 'Christ at Table' scenes which occur throughout the life of Christ. While not often depicted in the rest of the late medieval Italian peninsula, events such as the Communion of the Apostles, the Supper at Emmaus and Christ appearing to his disciples at supper were part of an established iconographic tradition in Naples. Indeed these scenes intended primarily for an audience of cloistered women, are represented in the fresco decoration of the Clarissan convent of Santa Maria Donna Regina commissioned by Sancia's mother-in-law, Maria of Hungary.[26] One of the earliest-known depictions of the scene of the Communion of the Apostles in the western tradition appeared in the fresco cycle in the nuns' choir of this church painted circa 1320.[27] This episode, along with the other scenes of 'Christ at Table' included within the monumental fresco programme, emphasized the theme of the Eucharist in the Passion narrative. The inventive iconography of these scenes intended for a primary audience of Clares would have set an important precedent for the similarly innovative and eucharistic imagery of Sancia's tomb sarcophagus.

Eucharistic imagery in the visual culture of the late medieval Regno can be linked to the political and religious interests of the Angevin dynasty in the location in the Holy Land where these events occurred, namely the Cenaculum on Mount Zion. The Last Supper, Communion of the Apostles and Christ appearing to his disciples at supper – all were thought to have occurred at this location which, even in the fourteenth century, was the site of long-contested religious and military control. Although King Charles I of Anjou had bought the title to the kingdom of Jerusalem and given the site to the Franciscans, by 1291 the order had been forced to leave the Holy Land for Cyprus. However, the Franciscans retained their claims to a number of religiously significant locations in the Holy Land and their interests gained the support of influential figures including the Angevins. In the early 1330s, with the support of the pope and in conjunction with her husband and the minister general of the Friars Minor, Sancia sought to secure a number of sites throughout the Holy Land as a possible residence for a group of Franciscan brothers. The bid was successful and by 1336 certain areas of particular religious importance had been secured for the Franciscans including the Cenaculum on Mount Zion.[28] Sancia seems to have played a significant role in the negotiations for the site and in the foundation of the house. She is recorded as giving funds to enclose the Cenaculum and the surrounding buildings and to endow a community of twelve friars who were installed at the site.[29]

Sancia's active campaign to gain control of the Cenaculum for the Franciscans, the supposed site of many events of eucharistic significance in the life of Christ, demonstrates the importance of the Eucharist as an element of her religious devotion.[30] Indeed, it seems particularly fitting that she dedicated the church of Santa Chiara to *corpus Christi* and that she ensured that the Clares, and she herself when she visited, could venerate the host during Mass from a privileged position. She dedicated the church where she was buried to the Holy Cross and many of the images of the queen that survive show her kneeling before the Crucifixion meditating on the suffering body of Christ. Moreover, in her letters to the Franciscans, she made numerous references to her desire to emulate Christ and claimed to have been divinely inspired in her writings and works through her contemplation of the blessed host as allowed by special papal dispensation in her private chapel in the royal palace. She wrote:

> On Thursday the eighteenth day of April, I entered the small chapel next to my chamber in the Castel Nuovo in Naples, where well through three candles before daybreak, with the door closed, alone with the body of Christ, which was upon the altar, I commended myself to him and afterward began to write as the Lord directed me, without any counsel, human or earthly…[31]

In her letter she writes of her desire to give herself entirely to Christ. Sancia's devotion to the Eucharist was not unusual and the importance of the Eucharist is found in other female saints' discussions of their own religious experiences as well as in the writings of their male biographers and chroniclers. From the founder of the female order of Franciscans, Clare of Assisi, to the penitent Angela of Foligno, there are many examples of eucharistic miracles involving women and these typically form a key part of the evidence supporting these women's sanctity.

A longing for a greater experience of Christ fuelled devotion to the Eucharist. It was through the Eucharist that one achieved communion with him and this came not solely through physical reception of the Sacrament but equally through contemplation of the consecrated host. As Sancia recalled in a letter to the Franciscans, she spent hours alone before the host in her private chapel preparing to commend herself to Christ. In such a manner, Sancia's contemplation of the body of Christ provided her with an occasion for a more profound knowledge of his human suffering. *Imitatio Christi*, the sense of becoming one with Christ, lay at the centre of eucharistic devotion. Indeed the host, which in the mystery of transubstantiation became the body of Christ, provided an appropriate medium through which this unity could be achieved. In the lives of holy women, their fulfilment of *imitatio Christi* provided convincing evidence of their sanctity. For instance, both Marie d'Oignies and Margaret of Cortona described their mystical experiences of the Crucifixion during which they did not just remember Christ on the Cross, or empathize with him but, rather, *became* Christ.[32] Deeply engaged in the theological ideas of the Franciscans, *imitatio Christi* was central to Sancia's religious experience. As Ronald Musto has demonstrated, the ethical imitation of Christ was a formative element in Neapolitan Franciscan spirituality of this period and it was promoted and aspired to by a range of heterodox individuals who were patronized by Sancia or whose works were openly discussed and upheld at the royal court in Naples.[33] While *imitatio Christi* typically provided an outlet for religious devotion, for Queen Sancia in Naples it was also linked to her personal, political and religious concern for the Spiritual Franciscans.

The imagery of Sancia of Majorca's tomb emphasizes her devotion to the Eucharist through a visual representation of *imitatio Christi*. The scene recalls established traditions for representing 'Christ at Table' scenes and, read as such, the image seems to portray a eucharistic banquet in which the nuns assume the roles of Christ's male apostles and Sancia plays the central role of Christ. This re-gendering of the roles of the male protagonists provided a visual exemplum in which Sancia and her fellow nuns fulfil their religious desires and act out their devotion to the Eucharist.[34] This appears in a similar manner, albeit in visual form, to the recorded events from female saints' lives, such as those discussed previously of Marie d'Oignies and Margaret of Cortona, whereby holy women also transgressed the boundaries of their sex to project themselves and their own religious experience with that of Christ. The imagery of Sancia's tomb sarcophagus emphasized the potential for slippage between gender identities through the performance and visual spectacle of subversive behaviours and appearances. In this vein, when the pursuit of holiness involved one assuming the role of Christ, it also problematized accepted gender roles while opening new possibilities for revisionist inventions in texts and images, such as the imagery on Sancia's tomb.

While there are many known textual accounts of late medieval holy women who took on the experience of Christ, visual depictions of *imitatio Christi*, such as that on the funerary monument of Sancia of Majorca, appear

7.5   Anonymous Pistoian painter, *Scenes from the Life of Saint Irene*, 1325–30.
Private collection. Image courtesy of Sotheby's Inc., New York © 2010

particularly remarkable. At the same time, illuminating comparisons can be drawn between the iconography of Sancia's tomb sarcophagus and an early fourteenth-century panel painting depicting the life of St Irene (fig. 7.5).[35] Although painted in Pistoia in the 1320s by an anonymous local painter, this panel was likely commissioned by a patron from the Regno. Its southern Italian origin hints that the panel, like the tomb of Sancia, may have been conceived with knowledge of iconographic traditions prevalent in the kingdom of Naples which emphasized the significance of the Eucharist.

Like the scene on Sancia's tomb, the upper level of this panel represents a group of figures seated behind a long table enjoying a banquet spread out in front of them. At the centre of the table is the crowned figure of St Irene who is accompanied by eleven female figures and a lone man. Larger in size than the other figures, St Irene is represented gazing straight ahead while the other figures around her eat and drink. Depicted above the scenes of her martyrdom which unfold in the lower zone of the panel, the scene occupies a notably large part of the panel. This eucharistic banquet seems to provide the saint with an opportunity for spiritual preparation before the events of her human suffering depicted below. The apparent parallels between the life of St

Irene and the Passion of Christ strengthen the visual evidence supporting her sanctity and furthermore point to how St Irene's representation upsets and transforms gender roles.

Venerated almost exclusively in southern Italy, the cult of St Irene commemorated a Byzantine princess who, after having been kept in a tower for much of her youth, rejected a secular marriage in order to follow the example of Christ. It is tempting to draw comparisons between this princess who desired a life of chastity and communion with Christ and the life of Queen Sancia of Majorca, also born into privilege but who longed for a cloistered life devoted to her spiritual bridegroom. While these similarities remain at best supposition, it does appear that the iconography of the tomb of Sancia of Majorca could have been inspired by a southern Italian tradition used in visual depictions of the lives of female saints. As a monument intended to provide visual evidence in support of Sancia's sanctity, the notable similarities between the scene on her tomb and that used to depict a female saint who was particularly venerated in the Regno could have lent strategic weight to the arguments for her canonization.

The depictions of eucharistic banquet scenes in the panel of St Irene and the tomb of Sancia of Majorca highlight the significance of food to the religious experience of both women. Food was a central motif in medieval spirituality both on a metaphorical and practical level. The religious significance of food was witnessed in the proliferation of food-related practices and devotions embraced by many late medieval women such as fasting, visions involving food and eucharistic devotion.[36] For holy women, food-related miracles, charitable acts of feeding and the practice of denying themselves the sustenance of earthly food were recounted in their *vitae* and provided important evidence of their sanctity.

The significance of the depictions of food in the image on Sancia's tomb sarcophagus can not be denied. Spread out before Sancia and the Clarissan sisters is a banquet of loaves of bread and plates of fish, interspersed with carafes and drinking vessels. The food and drink at their table symbolize the body and blood of Christ and his sacrificial Passion. However, they also allude to the food miracles performed by Christ during his lifetime such as the marriage feast at Cana and the miracle of the loaves and fishes. These food miracles, in which Christ's multiplication of resources allowed for the feeding of many, became a well known theme in the lives of female saints.

The fresco cycle from the church of Santa Maria Donna Regina depicting the Life of St Elizabeth of Hungary provides an important precedent in the visual culture of late medieval Naples.[37] During her lifetime, St Elizabeth performed a number of food-related miracles which are part of the twenty-five episodes represented in the fresco cycle. Both the 'Miracle of the Fish' in which she prayed for fish to feed a dying man, as well as the 'Miracle of the Flowers', when the bread she was carrying to feed the poor was transformed into flowers to avoid discovery by her husband, are depicted. The importance of food-related miracles in the life of St Elizabeth may have established a model for female devotion for the primary audience of the frescoes. It may also have set a precedent for later Franciscan imagery commissioned by the Angevins. The significance of food-related miracles is also found in a fresco from the church of Santa Chiara founded by Sancia of Majorca.[38] Here, the fresco of the 'Distribution of Bread' contains a never-before represented scene which highlights the particular significance of eucharistic-themed scenes to the Angevin dynasty. The fresco depicts Christ seated amongst his disciples with loaves of bread at his feet, Sts Francis and Clare are feeding his faithful. The entire image is placed against the heraldic device of the Angevin dynasty and framed with roundels containing the *Agnus Dei*. Within the fresco, dynastic and religious concerns converge to create a potent argument for the support of the Franciscan order championed by the ruling Angevin monarchs, Robert of Anjou and Sancia of Majorca. Yet the presence of this image within the decoration of the church and convent which she founded and dedicated to *corpus Christi* also alludes to Sancia's own particular spirituality as well as the centrality of food and food-related miracles to the Clares and other Franciscans in Naples.

For Sancia and her fellow Clares at Santa Croce di Palazzo, Clare of Assisi provided a powerful model of a female saint for whom food played a major part in her spiritual practice. Throughout her life Clare rejected ordinary food, preferring largely to fast and contemplate the holy food of the Eucharist. Yet while she herself restrained from consuming food, she actively sought to feed others. By serving others she cared for their physical and spiritual needs and her activities assumed a maternal character typical of Franciscan piety. Unsurprisingly, feeding miracles played a major part in her canonization and she is recorded as multiplying bread as well as oil for her fellow nuns to feed others.

These miracles emphasize the centrality of the Eucharist to Clare's piety and highlight the significance of *imitatio Christi* to her religious experience. As Catherine Mooney has argued, in her own writings Clare promoted the importance of contemplation and emulation of the human experience of Christ both to her own spirituality and as part of the guidance that she offered to other women.[39] It was not only Francis who modelled himself after Christ but also Clare who encouraged her female followers to make themselves *alteri Christi*. Through her food-related miracles she associated herself with the many eucharistic events from the life of Christ, thereby emphasizing her devotion to the body of Christ.

We have seen that Sancia clearly identified with the spiritual concerns of St Clare. She ensured that at Santa Croce di Palazzo the nuns were able to follow her original rule and when she entered the convent she took the name 'Suor Chiara', directly associating herself with the saint. This association was visually strengthened after her death by the representation on her tomb chest where she is linked with the renowned eucharistic piety of her namesake. On her funerary monument, like Clare, Sancia of Majorca is portrayed as feeding those around her. Sancia, as Sister Clare, sits amongst the nuns who consume the banquet in front of them while she herself abstains. Seated in the centre of the table she presides over this worldly feast whilst simultaneously engaging in a personal holy fast. She raises her hands in prayer and gazes in a frontal pose out beyond the bounty of the table. The image alludes to the multiplication miracles performed by St Clare, her emphasis on *imitatio Christi* as a outlet for religious devotion and the strength of her eucharistic piety; however, here the central role is not assumed by the saint herself but is filled by her namesake Sancia of Majorca.

As the inscription on her sepulchre emphasized for the audience in Naples, Sancia of Majorca had once been 'Lady Sancia [...] widow of the most fair lord Robert, King of Jerusalem and Sicily' yet now she was revered as 'the venerable Suor Chiara of Holy memory'.[40] The hagiographic portrait of Sancia in the tomb inscription does not mention her accomplishments as a royal ruler or as an extensive patron; rather, it describes her as a woman who gave up her wealth and privilege for a life of poverty following the example of St Francis. In the imagery of her tomb this straightforward textual portrait is enriched through allusions to existing Angevin iconography used for both royal rulers and saints. The intimate relationship which Sancia maintained throughout her lifetime with the Franciscan order is captured in the representation of her as enthroned queen and 'mother' to the order. Her lifelong role as a patron as well as devotee of the Clares is represented in the image of her as 'Suor Chiara'. Through the theme of *imitatio Christi* her personal devotion to the Eucharist, inspired by Clare and Francis, is prominently displayed, thus enhancing the aim of the tomb to construct persuasive visual evidence in support of Sancia of Majorca's sanctity.[41]

Notes

An earlier version of this paper was presented in the Early Modern Forum at the University of Oxford. I would like to thank Frank Henderson, Martin Kemp, Geraldine Johnson as well as the editors of this volume, Alison More and Elizabeth L'Estrange, for their astute suggestions and stimulating comments which strengthened this essay.

1.   Sancia of Majorca was born into the Majorcan royal family as the daughter of King James II and Queen Sclaramonda of Foix. The first historian to prepare an in-depth study of Sancia's life was Ronald Musto; see 'Queen Sancia of Naples (1286–1345) and the Spiritual Franciscans', in *Women of the Medieval World: Essays in Honor of John H. Mundy*, ed. Julius Kirshner and Suzanne F. Wemple (Oxford: Blackwell, 1985), pp. 179–214. More recent studies include Caroline Bruzelius, 'Queen Sancia of Mallorca and the Convent Church of Sta. Chiara in Naples', *Memoirs of the American Academy in Rome*, 40 (1995), 69–100; Matthew J. Clear, 'Piety and Patronage in the Mediterranean: Sancia of Majorca (1286–1345) Queen of Sicily, Provence and Jerusalem' (University of Sussex, PhD thesis, 2001) and Adrian Hoch, 'Sovereignty and Closure in Trecento Naples: Images of Queen Sancia, Alias "Sister Clare"', *Arte Medievale*, 10 (1996), 121–39; Mario Gaglione, 'Sancia d'Aragona-Majorca: da regina di Sicilia e Gerusalemme a monaca di Santa Croce', *Archivio Storico per la storia*

delle Donne, 1 (2004), 27–54; and Darleen Pryds, *Women of the Streets, Early Franciscan Women and Their Mendicant Vocation* (St. Bonaventure, NY: Franciscan Institute Publications, 2010).

2. Lucas Wadding, *Annales Minorum seu trium ordinum a S. Francesco institutorum auctore*, VI (Lyon: No Pub., 1626), p. 203.

3. Useful discussion of this request and the pope's response is found in Musto, 'Queen Sancia', p. 186.

4. The importance which Sancia placed on the Majorcan royal family's long-standing relationship with the order is outlined in her letter of 1334 to the Franciscans. See Musto, 'Queen Sancia', pp. 213–14.

5. The pope heavily criticized Sancia for her support of the Spiritual Franciscans and in the early 1330s two of her chaplains living in Santa Chiara, a religious institution she had founded, were tried for heresy. Sancia's support of the Spirituals is effectively demonstrated in Musto, 'Queen Sancia'. While Sancia's position seems clear, debate continues between scholars concerning the extent of her husband, King Robert of Anjou's, support of the Spirituals. For instance, see Samantha Kelly, *The New Solomon: Robert of Naples (1309–1343) and Fourteenth-Century Kingship* (Leiden: Brill, 2003); and Roberto Paciocco, 'Angioini and "Spirituali". I differenti piani cronologici e tematici di un problema', in *L'Etat Angevin: pouvoir, culture et société entre XIIIe et XIVe siècle* (Rome: Ecole française de Rome, 1998), pp. 253–87. Discussion of the Franciscan Spiritual controversy is found in David Burr, *The Spiritual Franciscans: From Protest to Persecution in the Century after Saint Francis* (University Park, PA: Pennsylvania State University Press, 2001).

6. For further discussion of Sancia's extensive patronage legacy see, Aislinn Loconte, 'Royal Women's Patronage of Art and Architecture in the Kingdom of Naples 1300–1450: From Maria of Hungary to Maria d'Enghien' (University of Oxford, DPhil thesis, 2004).

7. These include, amongst others; Santa Maria Annunziata, Santa Chiara and Santa Maria Egiziaca.

8. In 1253, shortly before her death, Clare wrote an official rule for the group of sisters that she had gathered around herself. In her decree she asserted that the sisters were to be supported by their male counterparts, the Franciscan brothers, who would minister to their religious needs. This rule was approved in 1253. In 1263 Urban IV issued a new rule which diminished the responsibilities of the friars in regards to the *cura monialium*. See Lezlie Knox, 'Audacious Nuns: Institutionalizing the Franciscan Order of Saint Clare', *Church History*, 69 (2000), 41–62; and Lezlie Knox, *Creating Clare of Assisi* (Leiden: Brill, 2008).

9. *Bullarium Franciscanum* ed. Conrado Eubel VI (Rome, 1898), n. 163. See also Mario Sensi, 'Clarisses entre spirituels et observants', in *Sainte Claire d'Assise et sa postérité, Actes du colloque international organisé á l'occasion du VIIIe centenaire de la naissance de sainte Claire: U.N.E.S.C.O., 29 septembre–1er octobre 1994*, ed. Geneviève Brunel-Lobrichon, Dominique Dinet, Jacqueline Gréal and Damien Vorreux (Nantes: Association Claire Aujourd'hui, 1995), pp. 101–18.

10. By the end of the eighteenth century, the convent and the monastery of Santa Croce di Palazzo had been destroyed, and by the mid-nineteenth century, the church was also demolished. See Mario Gaglione, 'Qualche ipotesi e molti dubbi su due Fondazione Angione a Napoli: S. Chiara e S. Croce di Palazzo', *Campania Sacra*, 33 (2002), 61–108.

11. Camillo Minieri-Riccio, *Notizie Storiche Tratte da 62 Registri Angioini Dell'archivio di Stato di Napoli* (Naples: R. Rinaldi & G. Sellitto, 1877), p. 47.

12. The tomb was destroyed when the church was torn down in the nineteenth century. The drawings were discovered by Tanja Michalsky in the Biblioteca Apostolica Vaticana (Vat. Lat. 9840, fols. 58v and 59r) and must have been executed by a collaborator of J.B.L.G. Seroux d'Agincourt, who published engravings of the tomb in *Histoire de l'art par les monumens, depuis sa décadence au IVe siècle jusqu'à son renouvellement au XIVe*, IV (Paris: Treuttel et Würtz, 1823), plate XXXI. See Tanja Michalsky, *Memoria und Repraesentation. Die Grabmäler des Königshauses Anjou in Italien* (Göttingen: Vandenhoeck & Ruprecht, 2000), pp. 121–23, 171–72, 342–45.

13. For discussion of the caryatid 'Charity' which is attributed to Pacio Bertini, see Francesco Aceto, 'Un'opera "ritrovata" di Pacio Bertini: il sepolcro di Sancia di Maiorca in Santa Croce a Napoli e la questione dell' "usus pauper"', *Prospettiva* 100 (2000), 26–35.

14. I follow Professor Aceto's suggestion that the second caryatid may represent 'Poverty'. Aceto, 'Un opera', p. 32.

15. 'Cronicon Suessanum (1103–1348)', in *Raccolta di varie croniche, diarj, ed altri opuscoli, così italiani, come latini, appartenenti alla storia de Regno di Napoli*, ed. A.A. Pelliccia (Naples, 1780–82), I, pp. 64–65; Pietro De Stefano, *Descrittione de i luoghi sacri della città di Napoli* (Naples: No Pub., 1560), f. 130r;

and Cesare D'Engenio, *Napoli Sacra* (Naples: No Pub., 1623), p. 557; for the letter of Giovanna I, see Matteo Camera, *Elucubrazioni storico-diplomatiche su Giovanna I, regina di Napoli e Carlo III di Durazzo* (Salerno: Tip. Nazionale, 1889), p. 160. A seventeenth-century plan including the church is discussed in Caroline Bruzelius, *The Stones of Naples: Church Building in Angevin Italy 1266–1343* (New Haven: Yale University Press, 2004), p. 150.

16.   Caroline Bruzelius, 'Hearing is Believing: Clarissan Architecture ca. 1213–1340', *Gesta*, 31 (1992), 83–91.

17.   This arrangement seems more plausible than the hypothesis suggested by Michalsky that the two illustrations could have been taken from a single side of the tomb. See Michalsky, 'Memoria', p. 344.

18.   For instance see, Elena Romano, *Saggio di iconografia dei Reali angioini di Napoli* (Naples: Fratelli Bergamo, 1920), pp. 56–57.

19.   Hoch, 'Sovereignty and Closure'; Michalsky, *Memoria*, pp. 121–23, 171–72, 344; and Aceto, 'Un opera'.

20.   Sancia had been particularly dedicated to the veneration of her newly canonized brother-in-law, Louis of Toulouse. In 1319, she travelled to Marseilles with Robert of Anjou to witness the translation of Louis' body into a new tomb. Together they commissioned reliquaries for the brain and arm of the saint, eventually bringing these back to Naples. The importance placed by the Angevins on a royal legacy of sanctity is discussed in Jean-Paul Boyer, 'La "Foi Monarchique": Royaume de Sicile et Provence', in *Le Forme delle Propaganda Politica nel Due e nel Trecento*, ed. Paolo Cammarosano (Rome: Ecole Française de Rome, 1993), pp. 85–110; and Gábor Klaniczay, *Holy Rulers and Blessed Princesses: Dynastic Cults in Medieval Central Europe* (Cambridge: Cambridge University Press, 2002).

21.   Camera, *Elucubrazioni storico-diplomatiche*, p. 160.

22.   The three keys to Sancia's casket were held by Giovanna I, the archbishop of Naples, and a Clarissan sister of Santa Croce di Palazzo. Camera, *Elucubrazioni storico-diplomatiche*, p. 160.

23.   Musto, 'Queen Sancia', p. 214. Specific discussion of her letters is found in Isabelle Heullant-Donat, 'En amont de l'observance. Les lettres de Sancia, reine de Naples, aux chapitres généraux et leur transmission dans l'historiographie du XIVe siècle', in *Identités franciscaines à l'âge des Réformes*, ed. Frédéric Meyer and Ludovic Viallet (Chambéry: Presses Universitaires Blaise Pascal, 2005), pp. 73–100; and Maria Teresa Dolso, *La 'Chronica XXIV Generalium' Il difficile percorso dell'umilità nella storia francescana* (Padua: Centro Studi Antoniani, 2003), pp. 221–33.

24.   St Francis spoke of himself as a mother and he encouraged his followers to be mothers to each other. Maternal imagery was also prevalent among female Franciscans; see Catherine M. Mooney, 'Imitatio Christi or Imitatio Mariae? Clare of Assisi and her Interpreters', in *Gendered Voices: Medieval Saints and their Interpreters*, ed. Catherine M. Mooney (Philadelphia: University of Pennsylvania Press, 1999), pp. 52–77.

25.   Caroline Walker Bynum, 'Women Mystics and Eucharistic Devotion', in *Fragmentation and Redemption: Essays on Gender and the Human Body in Medieval Religion* (New York: Zone Books, 1992), p. 138.

26.   Cathleen A. Fleck, '"Blessed the eyes that see those things you see": The Trecento Choir Frescoes at Santa Maria Donnaregina in Naples', *Zeitschrift für Kunstgeschichte*, 67 (2004), 201–24.

27.   Dominique Rigaux, *A la table du Seigneur: L'Eucharistie chez les primitifs italiens 1250–1497* (Paris: Cerf, 1989), pp. 59–67.

28.   The acquisitions of Sancia and Robert are outlined in the bull of Clement VI of 21 November 1343; see Wadding, *Annales Minorum*, VII, p. 260.

29.   Wadding, *Annales Minorum*, VII, p. 260.

30.   Her concern for the Eucharist recalls the religious devotion of her mother Sclaramonda of Foix, who had also demonstrated great dedication to the Franciscans, especially the female order. She too was granted the privilege of the constant company of Clarissan nuns and permission to venerate a consecrated host in her private chapel.

31.   Musto, 'Queen Sancia', p. 214.

32.   For Mary of Oignies, see *AASS*, June, v, pp. 551–52. For Margaret of Cortona see Giunta Bevegnati, *Legenda de vita et miraculis beatae Margaritae de Cortona*, ed. Fortunato Iozzelli (Grottaferrata: Ediciones Collegii S. Bonaventurae ad Claras Aquas, 1997).

33. Ronald Musto, 'Franciscan Joachimism at the Court of Naples, 1309–1345: A New Appraisal', *Archivium Franciscanum Historicum*, 90 (1997), 419–86.

34. The theme of disguising oneself in order to carry out pious works or cross-dressing in order to assume male roles appears in the lives of many holy women. Female saints could take on the physical characteristics of men as an outward sign of their links to the experience of Christ. See Andrée Hayum, 'A Renaissance Audience Considered: The Nuns at S. Apollonia and Castagno's Last Supper', *Art Bulletin*, 88 (2006), 243–66.

35. Discussion of the panel is found in Brendan Cassidy, 'A Byzantine Saint in Tuscany: A Proposal for the Solution of a Trecento Enigma', in *Arte Cristiana*, 83 (1995), 243–56; and Hayum 'A Renaissance Audience'. I thank Brendan Cassidy and Andrée Hayum for their suggestions on this panel.

36. See Caroline Walker Bynum, *Holy Feast and Holy Fast: The Religious Significance of Food to Medieval Women* (Berkeley: University of California Press, 1987).

37. The patron of the church and convent, Maria of Hungary, was the great-niece of St Elizabeth. For discussion of the frescoes see Cordelia Warr, 'The Golden Legend and the cycle of the Life of Saint Elizabeth of Thuringia-Hungary', in *The Church of Santa Maria Donna Regina: Art, Iconography and Patronage in Fourteenth-Century Naples*, ed. Janis Elliott and Cordelia Warr (Aldershot: Ashgate, 2004), pp. 155–74.

38. Ferdinando Bologna, *I pittori alla corte angioina di Napoli 1266–1414* (Rome: Ugo Bozzi, 1969), pp. 200–203.

39. Mooney, 'Imitatio Christi', pp. 52–77.

40. De Stefano, *Descrittione*, pp. 64–65.

41. Sancia was never canonized, although her sanctity was unofficially honoured by the Franciscans.

8

Deschi da parto and Topsy-Turvy Gender Relations in Fifteenth-Century Italian Households[1]

Elizabeth L'Estrange

In Tuscany in the fifteenth century large, round wooden trays, known as *deschi da parto*, were given between friends and families in anticipation or in celebration of the birth of a child. These birth trays were often painted on both sides and were used to bring food and drink into the chamber where the mother lay. Extant trays show that the decoration could vary considerably: from confinement scenes and images of baby boys (figs 8.1 and 8.2), to episodes from classical narrative such as the Judgement of Paris, and biblical stories like the Meeting of Solomon and Sheba.[2] Other trays were painted with images deriving from Petrarch's *Triumph* poems (begun in the 1340s), especially the *Triumph of Love* and the *Triumph of Chastity* (figs 8.3 and 8.4).[3] The dominant theme of the *Triumph of Love*, namely the way men and women have been driven to foolish acts because of an infatuation with their loved one, was part of the 'women-on-top' topos, which was exceedingly popular in the fifteenth and early sixteenth century in both texts and images.[4] In 'world-turned-upside-down' images such as the prints produced by the Housebook Master in Germany in 1485, women were depicted in dominating positions, and men were shown submitting to their power or obediently serving them.[5] On a birth tray from the Victoria and Albert Museum in London, Phyllis is shown riding Aristotle and Delilah cutting Samson's hair (fig. 8.3).[6]

It has long been noted that images of women dominating men or behaving in an 'unruly' fashion were intended to serve as examples to reinforce the established social and gender hierarchy in which men's place was legitimately 'on top'.[7] As such they have been considered *temporary* inversions, demonstrating the need for men and women to keep to their normalized gender roles. The use of such scenes on *deschi*, which, as we shall see, were often bought and given by men, yet intended for female viewers, suggests that there was a need to maintain order within the context of marriage, with the man at the

8.1   *Desco da parto*, Confinement scene, Florence,
mid-fifteenth century, Galleria Franchetti, Ca' d'Oro, Venice
© Cameraphoto arte, Venice

8.2   *Desco da parto*, Florence, Two boys making music
(reverse of fig. 8.1), mid-fifteenth century, Galleria Franchetti,
Ca' d'Oro © Cameraphoto arte, Venice

8.3 Workshop of Apollonio di Giovanni, *Desco da parto*, *Triumph of Love*, c. 1460, Victoria and Albert Museum, published by kind permission of the Board of Trustees of the V&A © V&A Images/Victoria and Albert Museum

8.4 Workshop of Apollonio di Giovanni, *Desco da parto*, *Triumph of Chastity* c. 1450–60, North Carolina Museum of Art, Raleigh, Gift of the Samuel H. Kress Foundation © Raleigh, North Carolina Museum of Art

head of his faithful, obedient wife. However, such an interpretation needs to be examined further. Natalie Zemon Davis argued in her now-seminal essay, 'Women on Top', that 'the image of the disorderly woman did not always function to keep women in their place. On the contrary, it was a multivalent image that could operate [...] to widen behavioural options for women within and even outside marriage'.[8] Furthermore, as Adrian Randolph has pointed out, *deschi*, as 'the only genre of painting explicitly addressed to a female spectatorship', constitute one way of exploring 'how visuality was structured by gender'.[9] This essay seeks to bring together Randolph's readings of *deschi*, which are grounded in postmodern visual theories, and Zemon Davis's idea of multivalency, to offer an historically specific interpretation of these trays. In particular it aims to pay close attention to both the topsy-turvy and the normalized imagery on *deschi* to examine how they functioned from the point of view of the women who received them as gifts. I will suggest that the images on *deschi* could have been interpreted by mothers as a *sustainable* allegory of their post-partum lying-in, and thus as an inversion of their normal gendered position in fifteenth-century society. Through this analysis, the potentially subversive and multivalent nature of late medieval gendered imagery can be revealed in greater detail.

Ideal Mothers: The World the Right Way Up

The confinement scenes that are depicted on birth trays, as elsewhere in late medieval manuscripts, panel paintings and frescoes, present an idealized image of childbirth. Not only is the outcome successful – both mother and child have survived – but sufficient provision is made for the mother and her guests.[10] On a mid-fifteenth-century tray now in the Ca' d'Oro museum in Venice, the mother is seated in bed and is greeted tenderly by a female visitor; another follows close behind with an offering of food. In the foreground, two female figures converse, and another three play with the child. On the right, another woman arrives with more provisions (fig. 8.1). This is very much a female space. Another tray made in Florence around 1400 again shows the mother as the focus of attention, sitting in an elaborate bed hung with curtains and dressed in stylish clothes.[11] She is attended by a dozen or so female visitors, two of whom are looking after the swaddled child in the foreground. The floral headbands and gold-embroidered clothes worn by the guests suggest wealth and taste, as does the supply of bowls, jugs and flowers being brought into the room.

It is likely that such scenes depict an idealized version of the actual practices surrounding childbearing and with which a wife or mother of the patrician classes would have been familiar.[12] As Jacqueline Marie Musacchio has shown in her in-depth study of the material culture of childbirth in Renaissance Italy, parallels can be drawn between the depictions of food, bedding and clothing on *deschi* and information about these preparations for childbirth recorded in contemporary inventories and accounts.[13] She argues that the images with which *deschi* were painted were therefore intended to appeal to female viewers as a means of assuaging any fears surrounding the birth.[14] Since it has been suggested that almost a fifth of 'the recorded deaths of young, married women in early fifteenth-century Florence were associated in some way with childbearing', such images would seem to encode a desired reality.[15] The confinement scenes on *deschi* thus provided a space in which a woman could envisage her own successful – and elaborate – childbearing, surrounded and supported by her female friends and relations. Women saw their maternal and civic role codified in a pleasant and luxurious way: this was the natural order of society. However, given the relative exclusion of lay women from the political, economic and social life of fifteenth-century Florence, seeing the function of such imagery simply as a comforting stimulus is problematic and warrants further investigation.

Deschi were usually purchased by or decorated at the behest of male, rather than female, patrons.[16] It was in the interests of husbands and the society in which they operated to provide their wives, daughters and daughters-in-law with a means to conceive sons and to bring them successfully to full term. This was particularly the case in late fourteenth- and fifteenth-century Florence since the city had fallen victim to recurring outbreaks of the plague. The resulting drastic decrease in the number of inhabitants led to 'an intense focus on renewing the population in a civic sense and renewing the family in a personal sense'.[17] Male children who would continue the patriline and secure the inheritance and wealth of Florentine families were more desirable than females, whose marriages could entail excessive dowry demands. The depiction of baby boys on the reverse of many *deschi*, such as those on the Ca' d'Oro tray (fig. 8.2) or that on a tray painted by Bartolomeo di Fruosino (Metropolitan Museum, New York), appears to be related to this desire for male children since the maternal imagination was held to be particularly susceptible to visual stimuli.[18] If a woman beheld or imagined deformed or horrific images during copulation or pregnancy there was a fear that this could affect the future appearance of the unborn child.[19] Similarly, presenting a woman with idealized, chubby and angelic boys would have been considered a way to help influence the sex of the child in the womb. As Geraldine Johnson has argued, terracotta reliefs of the Virgin and Child intended for the bed chambers of young wives and brides-to-be functioned in a similar way, by encouraging maternity and the conception of male children.[20]

The images on *deschi* sometimes also allude to other contemporary beliefs and practices thought to influence conception and birth. The Fruosino tray noted above shows the figure of a naked, urinating boy wearing a coral branch around his neck and 'an invocation for good health and successful childbirth' is inscribed around the edge.[21] Coral was used as an amulet to ward off evil and was often given to newborn infants to wear around their necks.[22] The two boys depicted on the reverse of the tray in the Ca' d'Oro also wear coral branches – one around his wrist, the other round his neck (fig. 8.2). The *verso* of another tray (c. 1427) which is now in Berlin and attributed to Masaccio, shows a small boy playing with a marten or weasel.[23] Representations of this animal, which was believed to conceive and give birth in a miraculous way, were often used as a talismanic device or symbol for women.[24]

In addition to offering protection to women and newborn children, *deschi da parto* also functioned as tangible links between families. Even if they appear to have been excluded from the birth chamber, men encouraged and exploited female gatherings around childbirth as a means 'to foster lineal and political ties'.[25] Through their wives, men presented gifts to other, sometimes more powerful, men and thereby ingratiated themselves with, or obtained obligations from, those in a higher social position. Thus, Musacchio notes that women 'may have received [...] gifts [like *deschi*], but they were determined by lineal, political, and social ties, and they were paid for by men'.[26] The pregnant woman or the new mother was a medium through which bonds between men were made and reinforced. Thus the confinement scenes and images of baby boys on *deschi da parto* functioned as way for men to guarantee the best outcome for a patriarchal society at the same time as they offered encouragement and protection for wives, mothers and the children themselves.

The question therefore arises of how to interpret the imagery on *deschi*, especially when this imagery appears to mock, in order to reinforce, traditional gender roles. In analyzing *deschi* as part of the visual culture aimed at lay women, Randolph has opposed the roundness, tactility and sociability inherent in birth trays to the ordered, geometric visual fields that Michael Baxandall argued structured the viewing of images in the Renaissance.[27] Through his concept of the 'period eye', Baxandall showed how princes, courtiers and merchants in fifteenth-century Italy were schooled in the reading and interpreting of paintings through their knowledge of religion, gestures, mathematics and Albertian perspective.[28] Therefore, for Randolph, in their shape and intended audience, the *deschi* offer an alternative viewing strategy to this masculine 'period eye', 'challeng[ing] scientific perspective's fixity' and embodying an 'inherent instability' and 'begg[ing] to be flipped'.[29] On the one hand, Randolph's interpretation seems to imply a binary gender opposition which echoes that of ancient and medieval medical and philosophical writers and emphasizes women's 'instability' and men's 'rationality'. On the other, given that in the lay patrician classes in fifteenth-century Italy men's and women's roles were strictly defined, it is important to consider how wives and mothers could have responded, from within their gendered positions, to the images offered to them on *deschi* by their male relatives. By looking at some examples of birth trays that depict the 'women-on-top' topos noted at the beginning of this essay, it is possible to nuance Randolph's claim further, suggesting how the *deschi*'s subversion of traditional form and perspective is mirrored in, or reinforced by, the subject matter that they depict. In doing so, I want to tease out the multiplicities of meanings that these trays might have embodied, and suggest that the upsetting of normalized gender roles that occurred during childbearing could be sustained through the continual viewing and re-viewing of these objects and the images they depict.

Men in the Service of Women: The World Turned Upside Down

Two examples of *deschi* from the workshop of Apollonio di Giovanni depict world-upside-down scenes from Petrarch's *Triumph of Love* (fig. 8.3) and the *Triumph of Chastity* (figs 8.4 and 8.5). The tray depicting the *Triumph of Love*, now in the Victoria and Albert Museum, dates from about 1460 and

8.5   Workshop of Apollonio di Giovanni, *Desco da parto*, Small boys playing with poppy seeds, c. 1450–60, North Carolina Museum of Art, Raleigh, Gift of the Samuel H. Kress Foundation © Raleigh, North Carolina Museum of Art (reverse of fig. 8.4)

represents specific details of Petrarch's poem.[30] Petrarch's text opens with a springtime dream vision, often used to begin medieval love-narratives.[31] The love-sick narrator describes an apparition of 'four steeds [...] whiter than whitest snow', pulling a 'fiery cart' on which rides 'a cruel youth / With bow in hand and arrows at his side'; 'his body was all bare' but 'on his shoulders he had two great wings / Of a thousand hues'.[32] Around this chariot is a throng of people, who, the narrator goes on to describe, have all been captured, slain or wounded by Love. Then ensues a whole list of men who were unable to resist the love of a woman, often leading to their downfall, including 'Caesar, whom in Egypt / Cleopatra bound'; and Hercules, who 'for all his strength' was captured by Love.[33] In the centre of the Victoria and Albert Museum birth tray is a golden cart pulled by two white horses (fig. 8.3). The cart is mounted by a globe on top of which stands the winged figure of Love, naked except for a quiver, and holding a bow and arrow. Below, at the corners of the cart, are small, winged cupid-like figures in the process of aiming their bows and arrows. One of these aims his arrow directly at a man dressed all in red, seated on the cart. The man's genitals are prominently defined by the tight-fitting clothes that he wears yet his hands are hidden behind his back, suggesting that is he has been tied up and disempowered by Love. Around the cart are a number of men and women conversing discreetly with each other and dressed in contemporary, fashionable, clothes. Although it is impossible to identify the conversing men and women with those particular historical figures listed by Petrarch at the beginning of the *Triumph of Love*, the two groups of figures in the foreground are identifiable as Phyllis riding Aristotle (left) and Delilah cutting Samson's hair (centre). These two groups serve to set the 'women on top' tone of this *desco*.

The story of the philosopher Aristotle allowing himself to be dominated by Phyllis, sometimes described as the mistress of his pupil Alexander the Great, does not actually appear in Petrarch's *Triumph of Love* but it does appear frequently on birth trays given this title.[34] As Jane Campbell Hutchinson notes, this apocryphal story probably first originated with the thirteenth-century cleric Jacques de Vitry who may have 'affixed the name of Aristotle to [the tale] in order to ridicule the philosopher whose current vogue was beginning to worry thirteenth century theologians'.[35] The tale was also included in the thirteenth-century misogynistic Latin text, the *Lamentations of Matheolus*, translated into French by Jehan Lefèvre in the fourteenth century. In the *Lamentations*, Phyllis is described as a 'hussy' who 'spurred [Aristotle] on like a female ass'. The result of Aristotle's infatuation with a woman and the satisfaction of his carnal desire was the complete reversal of the natural order of things: 'the governor was governed and the roles of the sexes reversed, for she was active and he passive [....]. What was normally underneath was on top, and confusion reigned'.[36] In this text as

8.6   Paolo Ucello, Interior of a marriage chest (*cassone*), The Battle of Greeks and Amazons before the Walls of Troy; Allegories of Faith and Justice; and Reclining Nude (detail), © Yale University Art Gallery, New Haven, Gallery Gift of the Associates in Fine Arts

well as in the image on the *desco*, the wise philosopher has been feminized. He is described as a female beast, a term which operates as a kind of double insult, and on the tray he is represented wearing a bridle and behaving like a subordinate animal. Furthermore, in allowing himself to be ridden he takes up the 'passive' position associated with women's sexuality in late medieval and early modern medical thought and which itself derived in no small way from the rediscovery of Aristotle's own ideas.[37] Here, it appears, gender – and even the 'science' on which it was based – was mutable, an idea also discernible in the tray's depiction of Samson and Delilah.

In the centre of the tray, just in front of the bridled Aristotle, lies the figure of Samson whom Petrarch described in the *Triumph of Love* as 'Stronger than he is wise' since he 'foolishly / Laid low his head upon a hostile lap'.[38] In this topsy-turvy image, the male figure is again feminized. Samson is depicted naked, languishing on his side with his head in the lap of Delilah. His eyes are shut and he appears blissfully unaware of the scissors she is about to use to cut off his hair and thus disarm him of his strength. The way Samson's left arm lies along his side draws the viewer's attention to the womanly curve of his hips and the roundedness of his belly. Furthermore, his slightly crossed legs not only hide his genitals but also assimilate that area of his body and his position in general to contemporary representations of naked women, such as the image of a reclining, nude lady painted inside a Florentine *cassone* (fig. 8.6). Samson's lack of genitalia, the external symbol of his masculinity, emphasizes his drunkenness and hence powerlessness in the hands of a woman. The feminized pubic area of Samson's body is in direct contrast to the phallic-like blades that Delilah holds in her hands and with which she will 'finish the job' of seduction by removing the hair from his head, thus emasculating him.

8.7   *Desco da parto, Triumph of Love*, fifteenth century, Victoria and Albert Museum, published by kind permission of the Board of Trustees of the V&A © V&A Images/ Victoria and Albert Museum

The same schema has been used on another *desco* also in the Victoria and Albert Museum to represent the *Triumph of Love* (fig. 8.7). Here, however, another 'woman-on-top' motif has been included, that of Virgil in the basket. Like the story of Phyllis and Aristotle, that of Virgil in the basket was apocryphal and not included in Petrarch's *Triumph of Love*. Nevertheless, it was another popular tale in 'power of women' stories. The legend told that the ancient poet Virgil fell in love with the daughter of the Roman emperor. She, having promised to bring him into her bedroom at night by raising him up in a basket, actually left him suspended half way up, where he became an object of public ridicule the following day.[39] The *desco* shows, in the background on the left-hand side, the poet Virgil suspended in a basket from a window while a female figure looks down on him from above. The stories of Aristotle, Samson and Virgil ostensibly had a didactic intent: to demonstrate, by inversion, how society should be ordered, and to keep women in their place.

A similarly didactic message about women's roles and responsibilities was probably the impetus behind the depiction of the *Triumph of Chastity* on a birth tray from about 1450–60, now in the North Carolina Museum of Art (figs 8.4 and 8.5). On this *desco* the figure of Chastity rides atop a chariot drawn by two unicorns, animals which, in the Middle Ages, were associated with virginity.[40] The winged figure of Love, the only male figure in the scene, also rides on the chariot; in contrast to the *Triumph of Love* tray, he is shown kneeling with his hands tied behind his back. His head and eyes are downcast, reminiscent of the submissive manner thought to be the ideal behaviour for women and the way in which they were often represented in late medieval art.[41] In the rest of the scene the women, dressed in rich and brocaded clothes, perhaps in allusion to the sumptuary laws designed to curb women's excesses, are engaged in conversations and take no notice of the disempowered figure of Love.[42] Here it is Chastity – in the sense of faithfulness in marriage – who dominates. This theme continues on the reverse of the tray, which is decorated with an image of two baby boys playing with poppy seeds (fig. 8.5). Poppy seeds were a symbol of fertility, and their inclusion on this birth tray along with the *Triumph of Chastity*, Musacchio notes, 'must have been intended as a warning to the pregnant woman to remain chaste in her marriage and ensure the paternity of her children'.[43] However, although such kinds of messages about women, their sexuality and their place in society were likely central to the commissioning of *deschi*, it would be naive to accept them as the sole interpretations.

Aristotelian philosophy equated women's physiology with lack of reason and passivity yet the image of Aristotle being ridden demonstrates, to use Judith Butler's term, the *performative* nature of gender.[44] That a man like Aristotle could take up a 'feminine' position and, conversely, a woman like Phyllis take up a 'masculine' one, was a continual source of anxiety in the Middle Ages, as popular stories about sex and gender deception and cross-dressing demonstrated.[45] Furthermore, it would be simplistic to assume that fidelity in marriage and the conception of male children are the only possible interpretations of the images of demure women, Chastity and baby boys on the North Carolina tray. If we read the topsy-turvy imagery as a fictional inversion which only served to reinforce the idealized, material norm represented by Chastity and comfortable confinement scenes, then we neglect to consider how pregnant women and new mothers, as well as their helpers, might have interpreted such imagery. More importantly, as art historians, we risk denying women any possibility of agency or independent response, subversive or otherwise, to the works of art they encountered. It is important, therefore, to explore how the different types of tray decoration analyzed thus far could have been understood, beyond its original didactic intent, by the woman who was the vehicle for such gifts as well as their principle viewer.

Women on Top: Childbearing and Gender Disruption

Following a birth, a new mother spent up to four weeks 'lying in'. In western Europe, this ritual of rest and recuperation crossed class and geographical boundaries and is documented for the late medieval and early modern periods both north and south of the Alps.[46] This time, in which the mother was enclosed in a warm, dark room and provided with special soups, food and wines, constitutes part of what Adrian Wilson has called the 'ceremony' of childbirth, that also included the baptism of the child and the churching of the new mother.[47] Understood from a medieval Christian and medical standpoint, the lying-in ceremony reinforced notions of the female sex's inferiority by insisting on the removal of the mother's impure body from the community until it was ritually purified by a priest. However, as Wilson and Zemon Davis have noted, the subjection women suffered in marriage 'might be temporarily reversed during the lying-in period, when the new mother could boss her husband around with impunity': this placed her firmly 'on top' in the household.[48] I would argue, therefore, that the inversion of gender roles that occurred during the lying-in period was mirrored by the images on *deschi*, making it possible to propose alternative meanings for the *Triumph of Love* and *Triumph of Chastity* images. From the woman's point of view, such images may have been understood as symbols of sustained gender subversions and inversions, rather than – or as well as – as examples that ultimately reinforced the norm. This interpretation thus corroborates Zemon Davis's notion that the 'image of the disorderly woman did not always function to keep women in their place'.[49] As we will see in the following section, the image of the 'orderly' woman may also have functioned in a similar way.

As noted above, the confinement scenes painted on *deschi* re-presented and reinforced the lying-in space in an idealized manner. Together with the images of baby boys they provided a means for a Florentine mother to envisage the presumably desired outcome of a pregnancy for all concerned: a successful (male) birth, numerous visitors, a well-furnished room, plenty of food and drink. Assuming that a mother interpreted her birth tray in such a way may appear to reinforce women's subjugation by suggesting that women were colluding in the upholding of the roles scripted for them by patriarchy. However, looking at such imagery from within those roles which, it was believed at the time, were ordained by nature and thus by God, the *deschi*'s confinement scenes offered a moment of subversion in which the woman was the centre of attention: the entire household revolved around the mother, the preparations for the birth and the care of the newborn. Furthermore, it was often the husband who, in a reversal of roles, was charged with the purchases necessary for the birth of a child, such as linens, sweetmeats and wine.[50] Satirical texts like the *Quinze joies de mariage* sometimes took the idea of the hen-pecked husband to the extreme: bossed about by his wife and her friends, it might still be down to him to summon the midwife and to make sure there was enough food and drink to entertain – and impress – the visitors.[51] Wilson has therefore argued that the seclusion of the woman during childbirth 'inverted the normal pattern of conjugal relations: the wife's bodily energies and sexuality now, for the space of "the month", belonged to her; what marriage had taken away from her, the ceremony of childbirth temporarily restored'.[52]

For the period of her lying-in, therefore, the expectations placed upon a young wife were momentarily suspended: she was no longer carrying a child, and her husband could not demand his right to the marital debt. A woman of a lower social status might also be absolved from household duties. To help her in her recovery, she was well looked after by other women and provided with nourishing food, all of which had to be paid for and organized by the husband himself, as the example of Ser Girolamo, who made special purchases of herbal remedies, fabrics and linens and food for his wife Caterina's pregnancy in 1473, makes clear.[53] With this in mind, the *deschi* and their images of powerful women or Chastity triumphant could have functioned as more than a means to keep women in their place. In their viewing and handling of the 'flippable' and tactile *deschi*, it is possible that women discerned a multivalency of meaning: warnings to fidelity, or the celebration of successful childbirth which ensured and maintained male kinship ties could be inverted or 'flipped' and re-read as positive signs of post-partum seclusion where the woman, her body, and her companions remain 'on top'.

It is, as I have argued elsewhere, problematic to use childbearing or maternity as a straightforward instance of subversion or resistance to patriarchy since these events serve the interests of men.[54] As Butler has argued in the context of contemporary gender studies, seeing childbearing as woman's 'natural' role carries the charge of essentialism, and ignores the appropriation of women's bodies for the 'exigencies of [patriarchal] kinship'.[55] In particular, the subjugation of women's bodies to the needs of patriarchy in fifteenth-century Florence cannot be denied. However, given the relatively few choices available to women at that time, it is important to acknowledge the possibilities for subversion *within* scripted gender roles rather than simply looking for cases of non-adherence to those roles, as Jennifer Borland also explores in this volume. Images of the bridled Aristotle, the disempowered Samson and Virgil suspended helplessly in his basket that illustrated the *Triumph of Love* theme, provide an analogy to the way men were required to serve women during and after the birth of a child. In images of the *Triumph of Chastity*, Chastity reigned supreme and could have been interpreted as an allusion to the suspension of the marital debt, in the wife's interests, during pregnancy and after childbirth.

Considering the social customs surrounding childbirth, the pressure placed on fifteenth-century Florentine women to procreate, and the dangers and complications associated with giving birth, it becomes evident that the objects, special foods and clothes, and arrangements for visitors not only celebrated patriarchal kinship but also conferred a great deal of care and attention on the child, mother and her companions. Furthermore, as practical objects used to bring food and drink into the room, *deschi* also functioned as what Musacchio has called 'maternal mediators', emphasizing and negotiating between the enclosed, female-dominated space of the birth chamber and the exterior, public, male, world.[56] The *Triumph* scenes on *deschi da parto*, should be considered, therefore, as more than just an admonition to chastity or fidelity; they should be seen as a way of restoring society's established gender hierarchies. Through their images and their mediating function, the trays alluded to and constituted an allegory of, the woman's lying-in and thus her position 'on top' in the household. Furthermore, the fact that *deschi* appear to have retained a place in households, as trays, wall decorations, and even game boards, suggests that their continual handling and re-viewing could have worked as a means to recall, and thus to sustain, the subversions they depict.[57] Received just before or after a birth, displayed in the home for years afterwards, *deschi* provided a continual reminder of the disruption of traditional gender roles that the social practices of childbearing entailed. Long after the lying-in month was over, then, female viewers could continue to enjoy the trays' depictions of celebrations centred on the new mother greeting her well-dressed visitors in an elaborate interior. In the *Triumph of Love* scenes, they saw Phyllis continually riding Aristotle, Samson forever disempowered by Delilah and Virgil hanging perpetually in his basket outside the window of his lover. In the *Triumph of Chastity*, they saw ladies forever conversing around the victorious figure of Chastity while Love remained bound and impotent.

Whether or not they saw themselves as subjugated to men in their need to produce healthy, male children for the repopulation of Florence and for the survival of their husband's family, it is likely that women in the fifteenth century approached their childbearing with a degree of uncertainty if not fear, given that it was a life-threatening experience. Such fear could be transformed into a sense of relief and happiness after a successful birth. Therefore, for pregnant women, women in labour, post-partum women and the lay women who assisted them, the images on *deschi* functioned simultaneously as reminders of their 'maternal' duties and their gendered positions within a demographically depleted Florence and as a reminder of the physical benefits that the post-partum ceremonials offered in which they remained 'on top'. They thus both provided and depicted a space for the projection of anxieties about the birth itself, for themselves, for the child and for the family at large. Therefore, to read the topsy-turvy iconography as continually unstable and subversive *as well as* prescriptive is less a reiteration of the instability of the female sex and more an acknowledgement of the instability of late medieval gender roles. To interrogate the apparently non-subversive images of confinement from the same point of view reveals further the multivalency of signs and their potential for interpretation. It is, more importantly, also to read these representations from the point of view of the mothers themselves.

Notes

1. This essay develops some material first discussed in my book, *Holy Motherhood: Gender, Dynasty and Visual Culture in the Later Middle Ages* (Manchester: Manchester University Press, 2008).

2. For details and pictures of the variety of themes found on *deschi da parto* see Jacqueline Marie Musacchio, *The Art and Ritual of Childbirth in Renaissance Italy* (New Haven and London: Yale, 1999), especially pp. 66–70. Many of these themes are also found on painted *cassone* (wedding chests) that were used to transport the bride's possessions from her parents' house to that of her husband. For a major study of *cassone* in the context of gender studies, see Cristelle L. Baskins, *Cassone Painting, Humanism, and Gender in Early Modern Italy* (Cambridge and New York: Cambridge University Press, 1998). See also the exhibition catalogue, *Love and Marriage in Renaissance Florence: The Courtauld Wedding Chests* (London: Courtauld Gallery, 2009).

3. During his life, Petrarch composed six *Triumphs*, of Love, Chastity, Death, Fame, Time and Eternity. The exact dating of these poems is a matter of debate.

4. The origins of the 'woman on top' motif did not originate with Petrarch and representations of the powerful or dominant woman are found in texts like the thirteenth-century Latin *Lamentations of Matheolus*, translated into French in the fourteenth century by Jehan Lefèvre; and Boccaccio's *Il Corbaccio* (c. 1355). See Natalie Zemon Davis, 'Women on Top', in her *Society and Culture in Early-Modern France* (London: Duckworth, 1975), pp. 124–25.

5. See Yvonne Bleyerveld, 'Powerful Men, Foolish Women: The Popularity of the "Power of Women" Topos in Art', in *Women of Distinction: Margaret of York–Margaret of Austria*, ed. Dagmar Eichberger (Leuven: Brepols, 2005), pp. 167–75.

6. The story of Phyllis and Aristotle does not actually appear in Petrarch's original poems. See pp. 136–37.

7. See Zemon Davis, 'Women on Top'.

8. Zemon Davis, 'Women on Top', p. 131.

9. Adrian W.B. Randolph, 'Gendering the Period Eye: *Deschi da parto* and Renaissance Visual Culture', *Art History*, 27 (2004), 538–62 (p. 542); see also his essay, 'Renaissance Household Goddesses: Fertility, Politics, and the Gendering of Spectatorship', in *The Material Culture of Sex, Marriage and Procreation in Premodern Europe*, ed. Anne L. McClaren and Karen Rosoff Encarnación (New York: Palgrave, 2001), pp. 163–89.

10. On the generic nature of such images, which usually depict the births of saints and heroic figures, see L'Estrange, *Holy Motherhood*, pp. 1–43.

11. Florence, Alberto Brusci Collection: see the reproduction in Musacchio, *Art and Ritual*, fig. 34.

12. Information about the management of childbearing in the fifteenth century is relatively scarce but it can be inferred from extant visual and written records that women were primarily cared for by other women during childbirth. However, as Monica Green has argued, there was not as clear a gendering of women's healthcare as might be assumed. See her book, *Making Women's Medicine Masculine: The Rise of Male Authority in Premodern Gynaecology* (Oxford: Oxford University Press, 2008).

13. Musacchio, *Art and Ritual*, especially Chapter 2; for a parallel study of images of childbearing and the material culture of childbirth in northern Europe, see L'Estrange, *Holy Motherhood*.

14. Musacchio, *Art and Ritual*, pp. 28, 33.

15. On mortality rates see David Herlihy and Christiane Klapisch-Zuber, *Tuscans and their Families: A Study of the Florentine Catasto of 1427* (New Haven and London: Yale University Press, 1985), p. 277.

16. Musacchio, *Art and Ritual*, p. 46.

17. Musacchio, *Art and Ritual*, p. 32.

18. Bartolomeo di Fruosino, *Desco da parto*, c. 1427, New York, Metropolitan Museum of Art, no. L.1995.17; reproduced in Musacchio, *Art and Ritual*, figs 1–2. For other examples, see Musacchio, *Art and Ritual*, esp. pp. 131–33.

19. Geraldine A. Johnson, 'Beautiful Brides and Model Mothers: the Devotional and Talismanic Functions of Early Modern Marian Reliefs', in *The Material Culture of Sex*, pp. 135–61 (p. 151).

20. See Johnson, 'Beautiful Brides', pp. 142, 147–52.

21. Musacchio, *Art and Ritual*, p. 1.

22. See Musacchio, *Art and Ritual*, pp. 131–32; and John Cherry, 'Healing through Faith: The Continuation of Medieval Attitudes to Jewellery into the Renaissance', *Renaissance Studies*, 15 (2001), 154–71 (p. 155).

23. Masaccio, *Desco da parto*, c. 1427, Gemäldegalerie, Staatliche Museen zu Berlin; reproduced in Musacchio, *Art and Ritual*, fig. 132.

24. Jacqueline Marie Musacchio, 'Weasels and Pregnancy in Renaissance Italy', *Renaissance Studies*, 15 (2001), 172–87.

25. Musacchio, *Art and Ritual*, p. 46; and see also Christiane Klapisch-Zuber, *Women, Family and Ritual in Renaissance Italy*, trans. Lydia G. Cochrane (Chicago: University of Chicago Press, 1987), esp. pp. 213–46.

26. Musacchio, *Art and Ritual*, p. 46.

27. Michael Baxandall, *Painting and Experience in Fifteenth-Century Italy: A Primer in the Social History of Pictorial Style* (Oxford: Oxford University Press, 1972; repr. 1986).

28. Baxandall, *Painting and Experience*, pp. 38–39.

29. Randolph, 'Gendering the Period Eye', pp. 550, 548. Baxandall's period eye has come in for criticism because of its lack of attention to gender. In addition to Randolph work on this, see also Paolo Berdini, 'Women under the Gaze: A Renaissance Genealogy', *Art History*, 21 (1998), 565–90. For a reassessment of the 'period eye' in relation to female viewers and manuscript illuminations of childbearing, see L'Estrange, *Holy Motherhood*, esp. pp. 25–43.

30. However, as Dorothy C. Shorr notes, it is possible that this and other representations of Petrarch's *Triumphs* were also influenced by fourteenth-century *trionfo* street pageants. See Dorothy C. Shorr, 'Some Notes on the Iconography of Petrarch's Triumph of Fame', *The Art Bulletin*, 20 (1938), 100–107 (p. 100). To my knowledge, the only complete English edition of Petrarch's *Triumphs* was published by Ernest Hatch Wilkins, *The Triumphs of Petrarch* (Chicago: University of Chicago Press, 1962). The Italian and an English translation (used here) is also available online: <http://petrarch.petersadlon.com/trionfi.html> [accessed 2 July 2010]. Roman numerals in citations refer to the division of the books in the online edition.

31. Famous examples of the dream vision in relation to love include Guillaume de Lorris and Jean de Meung's *Romance of the Rose* and Chaucer's *Legend of Good Women* and *Book of the Duchess*.

32. Petrarch, I, *Love*, ll. 22–27: the original section reads 'quattro destrier vie più che neve bianchi; / sovr'un carro di foco un garzon crudo / con arco in man e con saette a' fianchi; / nulla temea, però non maglia o scudo, / ma sugli omeri avea sol due grand'ali / di color mille, tutto l'altro ignudo'.

33. Petrarch, *Love*, II, ll. 89–90. 'vien primo è Cesar, che 'n Egitto / Cleopatra legò tra' fiori e l'erba'; Colui ch'è seco è quel possente e forte Ercole, ch'Amor prese'. The poem goes on to detail women, such as Hypsipyle (I, ll. 133–34), who were also overcome by love, although such stories, presumably because they did not entail an upsetting of social order, do not appear to have become part of this topsy-turvy iconography.

34. Other examples include a tray from c. 1453–55 by the workshop of Apollonio di Giovanni and Marco del Buono belonging to the National Gallery, London (NG3898), but on loan to the Victoria

and Albert Museum; and a tray from c. 1450–70 also in the Victoria and Albert Museum (Museum no. 398–1890).

35. Jane Campbell Hutchinson, 'The Housebook Master and the Folly of the Wise Man', *The Art Bulletin*, 48 (1966), 73–78 (p. 75).

36. See the extracts from Jehan Lefevre's translation of the *Lamentations of Matheolus* in *Woman Defamed and Woman Defended: An Anthology of Medieval Texts*, ed. Alcuin Blamires (Oxford: Clarendon Press, 1992), pp. 177–97 (p. 180).

37. Aristotle's writings on physiology began to be studied in the twelfth century with the result that women's role in the process of procreation was often reduced to 'a place for it to occur'. Aristotle's ideas were, however, not always accepted without question, and were studied alongside those of Galen, who attributed a more active role to women in reproduction. For extracts of original texts see Blamires, *Woman Defamed*, pp. 39–43; see also Joan Cadden, *Meanings of Sex Difference in the Middle Ages: Medicine, Science and Culture* (Cambridge: Cambridge University Press, 1993).

38. Petrarch, *Love*, III, ll. 124–25. 'Poco dinanzi a lei vedi Sansone, / vie più forte che saggio, che per ciance / in grembo a la nemica il capo pone.'

39. For the origin and development of this legend, see John Webster Spargo, *Virgil the Necromancer: Studies in Virgilian Legends* (Cambridge, MA: Harvard University Press, 1934), pp. 136–97.

40. The idea that a unicorn could only be captured by a virgin, in whose lap he would lay his head, comes from the medieval bestiary and was depicted in manuscripts, tapestries and ivories. See for instance Richard de Fournival, *Le Bestiaire d'amour et la réponse du bestiaire*, ed. and trans. Gabriel Bianciotto (Paris: Champion, 2009).

41. Conduct manuals advised women on how to behave and how to carry themselves in public, not casting their gaze too widely. On conduct manuals see *Medieval Conduct*, ed. Kathleen Ashley and Robert L.A. Clark (London and Minneapolis: University of Minnesota Press, 2001); see also Kim M. Philips, 'Bodily Walls, Windows, and Doors: The Politics of Gesture in Late Fifteenth-Century English Books for Women', in *Medieval Women: Texts and Contexts in Late Medieval Britain: Essays for Felicity Riddy*, ed. Jocelyn Wogan-Browne et al. (Turnhout: Brepols, 2000), pp. 185–98. For an interpretation of this representation of women see the essay by Berdini cited above.

42. As Musacchio notes (*Art and Ritual*, p. 55), sumptuary laws and maternity were closely intertwined: 'By controlling excessive feminine display, and relegating women to the role of childbearing, the governing men hoped these laws would help decrease expenses and increase the population.'

43. Musacchio, *Art and Ritual*, p. 55.

44. Judith Butler, *Gender Trouble: Feminism and the Subversion of Identity* (New York: Routledge, 1990; repr. 1999).

45. For example, the story of Pope Joan, included in Boccaccio's *De mulieribus claris*, who, through dressing as a man, rose to become pope, demonstrates anxiety about the possibilities for women to usurp men's roles. Joan's downfall comes when she gives birth in the middle of a procession, thus suggesting an inevitable link not only between women and their 'natural' roles, but also their inconstancy. See Giovanni Boccaccio, *Famous Women*, trans. Virginia Brown (Cambridge, MA and London: Harvard University Press, 2003), pp. 215–17.

46. In addition to Musacchio, see Adrian Wilson, 'The Ceremony of Childbirth and its Interpretation', in *Women as Mothers in Pre-Industrial England: Essays in Memory of Dorothy McLaren*, ed. Valerie Fildes (London: Routledge, 1990), pp. 68–107; and L'Estrange, *Holy Motherhood*, pp. 76–109.

47. Wilson, 'Ceremony'. See also Paula M. Rieder, *On the Purification of Women: Churching in Northern France, 1100–1500* (New York: Palgrave Macmillan, 2006).

48. Zemon Davis, 'Women on Top', p. 145; see also Wilson, 'Ceremony', p. 86.

49. Zemon Davis, 'Women on Top', p. 131.

50. Musacchio, *Art and Ritual*, pp. 36–42.

51. The *Quinze joies de mariage* was published anonymously in France in the fifteenth century and parodied the fifteen joys of the Virgin Mary; see *The Fifteen Joys of Marriage*, trans. Brent A. Pitts (New York: Peter Lang, 1985).

52. Wilson, 'Ceremony', p. 87.

53. Musacchio, *Art and Ritual*, pp. 36–42.

54. I explore the subversive limits of maternity in relation to late medieval visual culture in *Holy Motherhood*, pp. 25–43.

55. See Butler, *Gender Trouble*, p. 115. Butler's critique is centred on Julia Kristeva's conception of maternity, see esp. pp. 101–104.

56. See Musacchio, *Art and Ritual*, pp. 125–47.

57. Musacchio, *Art and Ritual*, pp. 63–65.

9

Fashioning Female Humanist Scholarship: Self-representation in Laura Cereta's Letters

Jennifer Cavalli

Studies of female Italian humanists have followed a similar approach to those of their male counterparts, focusing on the success and influence of individuals and the ways in which those exposed to humanist learning contributed to their communities. Concentrating on exemplary figures, such as Isotta Nogarola (1418–66), Cassandra Fedele (1465?–1558) and Laura Cereta (1469–99), their brief periods of literary activity and the men in their lives who promoted and supported their learning, these studies have shown the opportunities and limitations of humanist learning for women and the conditions in which educated women worked.[1] The goals that humanists, both men and women, were promoting – eloquence, honour, glory – assumed access to social and political power, and although women had influence in these realms, they lacked the official power of men to act. One of these female humanists, Laura Cereta, manipulated the boundaries of gender and incorporated her social and cultural role as a woman with her intellectual authority, thereby creating a space in which to think about female scholarship. In her letters, she argues that she is at once an individual accomplished in study and a woman who attends to domestic responsibilities. This essay explores the ways in which Cereta integrated both of these qualities in her letters, altering masculine humanist style to thereby carve out a role for herself as a learned woman.[2] It also argues that Cereta's peculiar expression of humanist themes can be attributed, at least partially, to the deliberate blending of two worlds: the world of literary men, to which she was trying to gain acceptance, and the cultural world of the convent, where she was first educated, and to which she thus already belonged. Cereta sought entry into one community, adapted humanist ideals to another and wrote for both, crafting her self-image along the way.

Letters became increasingly important for fifteenth-century humanist writers, especially within the private prose genre and in autobiographical work. Popularized by Petrarch, the humanist private letter was a means to promote oneself and display personality.[3] Cereta's letters, which she edited and dedicated to Cardinal Ascanio Maria Sforza in 1488, follow the primary conventions of the humanistic epistolary genre.[4] They are addressed to both men and women and discuss personal and public matters, give advice on marriage, address the benefits of liberal studies, include narratives of her life, and even tackle friendship. In her essay 'Humanism and Feminism in Laura Cereta's Public Letters', Diana Robin draws attention to both the novelty of this theme for a woman, and the way in which her approach to the topic differs from that of male humanists, writing that Cereta 'focuses her generalisations less on the bond between friends and more on the genesis of the tensions and conflicts that pull at the fabric of such relationships'.[5] In her letters Cereta expresses pride in her personal intellectual capabilities and represents herself as a unique individual, incorporating her likes and dislikes, her feelings and motivations. Cereta is direct about her desire to immortalize her name through her writings, just as Petrarch had done for himself. Writing to her cousin Bernardino di Leno, she describes her efforts toward this end:

> Thus, after the fruits of my study ripened and the golden grain fell from the stalk, I began to gather the harvest with my rustic pen, so that it could safely and quickly be transported to faraway peoples of the world.[6]

Further stressing the importance of recognition and fame, Cereta writes to her maternal uncle, Lodovico di Leno,

> [...] at this point I believe that public acclaim has built a solid enough foundation for my immortality, and in this way an initial reservoir for my glory has been established: I, for example, who was a young girl to the wonderment and perturbation of everyone until now, may perhaps emerge as an exceptional woman. Indeed, this glitter of eloquence, which feeds the hunger and dryness located deep within discordant lies, is faint. Nonetheless, some attention still is paid to the acquiring of mental powers and the most penetrating minds are seasoned with the fiery food of virtue. A public acknowledgement of one's fame is, in the order of things, quite important.[7]

Yet, she worries that her efforts at acquiring fame, now hampered by the duties of domestic leisure and lack of public standing, will result in a personal history of the 'simplest piece of weaving'.[8] Cereta's anxiety about the fate of her own history testifies to her awareness of her unstable presence in the male-dominated sphere of secular letters. Nevertheless, she is determined to transform herself as a woman and a scholar. Unlike her celebrated contemporary Cassandra Fedele, who wrote that she was 'armed with distaff and needle' as her ('woman's') weapons, Laura Cereta, used both 'pen' and 'needle' – what Diana Robin describes as 'the emblems that separate male and female space in the Renaissance ideology of gender' – outwardly blurring male and female spheres. [9]

Cereta's brief writing career, spanning the years 1485–88, was supported and promoted by her father, Silvester Cereta, an attorney and local magistrate in Brescia. In 1476, when she was seven, Cereta's father sent her for primary schooling at a local convent, where she 'was entrusted to a woman highly esteemed for both her counsel and sanctity'.[10] She returned home two years later and her father sent her back to her 'instructress in liberal studies'.[11] Her father was therefore instrumental in securing an early audience for her writing by taking a keen interest in her education. Cereta also found support, and an addressee, in her husband Peter Serina, whom she married at age fifteen. Serina died after only eighteen months of marriage, but his extended business trips provided Cereta with regular opportunities to compose letters. In the letters both before and after her husband's death, Cereta stresses the importance of her individual effort in attaining knowledge.[12] Writing to Giovanni Oliver, Cereta reminds the professor of grammar and rhetoric that,

> Education is a thing highly esteemed – and this is something learned men certainly know. I've obtained whatever plumage I do have from strong wings – this I do not deny. But finally I progressed beyond the stage of being a chick and my skill at flying has become so good that the great forest of Mt Ida might find me worthy of adopting.[13]

It is diligent study, she implies, that has contributed most to the knowledge she demonstrates in her writing. Cereta relates her diligence in study to the discipline she first acquired while learning the art of embroidery while at the convent. In her letter to Nazaria Olympica, she recalls,

> My hand, obedient enough after a brief period of time, committed the rudiments of my new learning to thread and fabric. There was in fact no embroidery stitch so elegant or difficult that I could not master it, once I discerned its fine point through delicate and gentle probings. In this way a mind quite helpless and quite deficient in knowledge was able to raise itself up, once it was inspired, to those gentle breezes of hope.[14]

Cereta's experience at the convent was formative in inspiring a desire for knowledge. Moreover, it was her teacher at the convent who first suggested that Cereta pass her sleepless nights with embroidery, something she traded in for study in later years. This is perhaps the reason for her frequent incorporation of embroidery imagery throughout her letters.

Cereta's self-fashioning as a dedicated scholar is seen most clearly in her rejection of praise for exceptionality. Her abilities derive from hard work, as would be the case with any other individual, male or female. Although she is admittedly 'naturally suited' for study, she emphasizes, 'I spent seven years so that I would be able to purchase this priceless dowry for myself for who would not go into debt to buy this most luxurious jewel?'[15] For Cereta, the differences between male and female social roles do not have an impact on the ability and equality of the mind, since 'Nature has granted to all enough of her bounty; she opens to all the gates of choice, and through these gates, reason sends legates to the will, for it is through reason that these legates can transmit their desires'.[16]

Cereta uses her roles as daughter, wife and widow to communicate her own experience and individuality, presenting her achievement in learning through her daily life, not as something separate from it. The context of Cereta's early education in a convent, and her continuing ties to the mixed community of lay and religious women, may help to explain her perspective. Early education in a convent was considered an extension of familial education. In her case study of two Quattrocento Florentine convent schools, Sharon Strocchia argues that convent learning was situated within a larger framework of moral formation, or what she calls 'learning the virtues'.[17] With its main aim the moral formation of the individual, Strocchia argues that on the one hand, 'learning the virtues' limited girls' education, especially in contrast to the expansion of the curriculum generally taught to boys under the influence of humanism, yet 'at the same time this conservative moral education forwarded the creation of a distinctive female culture that united family, community, and convent life'.[18] Cereta's pairing of embroidery and study, one leading to the other as a natural extension, suggests that there was not a clear division between the formal education of reading and writing and corporate approaches to learning for girls. Her continued pairing of domestic and intellectual pursuits reflects the lingering influence of this early female community on her self-formation.

Forced to attend to domestic responsibilities at an early age, Cereta studied and wrote during the night and early mornings. Recalling this transition from having the leisure to study Seneca and Cicero to taking on domestic responsibilities, she writes,

> But when scarcely a year had gone by, I assumed the responsibility for almost all of the household duties myself. Thus it was my lot to grow old when I was not far from childhood. Even so, I attended lectures on mathematics during the days I had free from toil, and I did not neglect those profitable occasions when, unable to sleep, I devoured the mellifluous-voiced prophets of the Old Testament and figures from the New Testament too.[19]

These time constraints were, in short, related to the tension between study and being a wife and a daughter. Time is something that Cereta is forced to negotiate, trading and stealing:

> Time is a terrible scarce commodity for those of us who spend our skills and labour equally on our families and our own work. But by staying up all night,

I become a thief of time, sequestering a space from the rest of the day, so that after working by lamplight for much of the night, I can go back to work in the morning.[20]

She eulogizes 'those days when my mind was free from pain and I devoted all my time, which went by so quickly, to literature [...] '.[21]

Cereta's incorporation of domestic roles and study in her writing is especially important in light of the ways in which male writers tended to portray learned women. To account for the presence of women in an educational programme designed to develop eloquent and distinguished citizens and rulers, male humanists drew attention to the existence of socially-accepted masculine characteristics rather than feminine characteristics in learned women.[22] Male correspondents celebrated learned women in terms of an 'abstract intellectual ideal (warrior-maiden, *virilis animi*, grieving spouse majestic in suffering), or in terms of a social ideal (chastity, obedience, modesty, constancy, beauty)'.[23] The use of Amazonian imagery is one example of male writers' reliance on martial and political tropes – themes rooted in the masculine realm – to reinforce the abnormality of a female scholar. The use of a mythological comparison attempts to excuse what society would have seen as a refusal of the proper female characteristics: chastity, silence, piety and obedience. It also demonstrates the strength of liberal studies and humanists' own merit in promoting them, since women who diligently took up humanist study were able to transcend the characteristics traditionally believed to have plagued women, such as an overabundance of emotion, or passion, which was in turn linked to a diminished intellect.

Male writers, however, were not the only ones to find such themes useful. In her examination of Renaissance feminism, Constance Jordan reveals the extent to which female writers also incorporated the theme of the virile woman.[24] When it suits her argument, Cereta frames her position of learnedness in terms of war and mythological imagery. This occurs most often in letters in which she responds to perceived attacks. Writing to her cousin, Bernardino di Leno after such an occasion, she states,

Since the Amazon's name is now extinct, and those women who bore arms have returned their weapons and bows to the temple of Bellona, I have completely transferred my passion for feminine things to the love of literature.[25]

In another letter, one which takes on the character of a formal invective, Cereta warns her detractors,

[...] I shall strive in a war of vengeance against the notorious abuse of those who fill everything with noise, since armed with such abuse, certain insane and infamous men bark and bare their teeth in vicious wrath at the republic of women, so worthy of veneration.[26]

These passages demonstrate Cereta's flexibility and willingness to use whatever imagery conveys her point best. In a position of self-defence, she opts for metaphors of battle traditionally associated with men. This underscores her rejection of the notion that writing is a male activity. Moreover, she implies that she, as a scholar, is entitled to draw upon all possible examples from the literature she studies, not just those that pertain to women.

Male humanists often singled out learned women according to the 'illustrious women' tradition of which Boccaccio's catalogue *Concerning Famous Women* (1361–62) is perhaps the most famous example, and which served as a model for the many catalogues of illustrious women that followed.[27] For example, Quirini commented in a letter to Isotta Nogarola, 'And should we not greatly rejoice that you can be named among those admittedly few but certainly famous women [of the past], when we see that the ancients gloried in the learning of such outstanding women?'[28] Guarino Guarini, the esteemed humanist educator from Verona, received compositions from Isotta and her sister Ginevra. In his return letter of praise, Guarini issues a collective identity for the sisters, emphasizing their status as virgins and their spiritual connection to the catalogue of famous classical women.[29] Such an identity, as Lisa Jardine has argued, shifts the focus from any measurable, or real contribution Isotta and Ginevra make to their immediate environment, treating them instead as emblems or ornaments, not real women. This is a situation Cereta wants to avoid. She regularly reminds her readers that idealization and praise for exceptionality by men undermines her daily efforts. She will not allow her work to be dismissed by being singled out. For Cereta, learning was women's legitimate inheritance. In her letter to Bibolo Semproni, Cereta is 'impelled to show what great glory that noble lineage which I carry in my own breast has won for virtue and literature – a lineage that knowledge, the bearer of honours, has exalted in every age. For the possession of this lineage is legitimate and sure, and it has come all the way down to me from the perpetual continuance of a more enduring race'.[30] This 'enduring race' is a community of past and present women possessing knowledge. Therefore, when Cereta argues that she should not be singled out – 'I, who in the light of the well-deserved fame of other women, am indeed only the smallest little mouse' – she is mostly referring to this specific community of learnedness, not necessarily to women in general.[31]

Cereta's tactic of distinguishing herself is the most direct among fifteenth-century female humanists, yet it may not be all strategy. Her letters demonstrate that she had an integrated view of her response and approach to study from an early age, which was conditioned by the mutual influence and fluidity of humanist and female monastic ideals on notions of female learning and virtue.[32] Although she is conscious of the particular balance she must strike between her (feminine) domestic responsibilities and her study, she does not present the two as separate, competing realms. They have never been separate for Cereta, but rather always pursued in tandem from the very beginning of her schooling. For Cereta, 'nature imparts one freedom to all human beings equally – to learn. But the question of my exceptionality remains. And here choice alone, since it is the arbiter of character, is the distinguishing factor'.[33] If Cereta allows for a choice, it is not one *between* realms of activity, but rather one concerning the life and activity of the mind. She contrasts her position, having chosen the life of an active mind, with the laziness of other women, explaining that,

> Virtue is something that we ourselves acquire; nor can those women who become dull-witted through laziness and the sludge of low pleasures ascend to the understanding of difficult things. But for those women who believe that study, hard work, and vigilance will bring them sure praise, the road to attaining knowledge is broad.[34]

Study, she claims, is to be used to create an enlightened and virtuous self.[35] Cereta uses every free minute to study, as 'you grow weak with the sickness of debilitating leisure'.[36] Like other learned women, she has *chosen* studies, while other women choose 'the styling of their hair, the elegance of their clothes, the pearls and other jewellery they wear on their fingers'.[37] Cereta likens the 'gabbling and babbling women' to 'scarecrows hung up in the garden to get rid of sparrows',[38] but then counters the image, writing,

> Human error causes us to be ashamed and disgusted that those women who are themselves caught in a tangle of doubt have given up hope of attaining knowledge of the humane arts, when they could easily acquire such knowledge with skill and virtue.[39]

The women to whom she refers have not dedicated themselves to a higher good, yet all women remain able:

> But those women for whom the quest for the good represents a higher value restrain their young spirits and ponder better plans. They harden their bodies with sobriety and toil, they control their tongues, they carefully monitor what they hear, they ready their minds for all-night vigils, and they rouse their minds for the contemplation of probity in the case of harmful literature. For knowledge is not given as a gift but by study. For a mind free, keen, and unyielding in the face of hard work always rises to the good, and the desire for learning grows in depth and breadth.[40]

Cereta has devoted herself to nurturing the desire to learn and working around the obstacles of her domestic role. She does not, however, indicate that she believes she must overcome her sex to represent 'a higher value'. In this respect – that of the mind – she sees herself as no different from male scholars. The primary obstacle for Cereta is negotiating time to pursue the rewards that accompany learning: knowledge, virtue and ultimately, fame.

The autobiographical aspects of Cereta's letters with which we are dealing owe their expression largely to the autobiographical ethos Petrarch forged through his *Epistola posteritati*.[41] Karl Enenkel explores this development in his essay 'Self-representation in Neo-Latin Humanism', explaining the challenges facing Petrarch in the following manner:

> How does the ethos of the 'classical' Latin Poet; the belief in glory, fame, and immortality via literature go together with the obligatory Christian values of humility (*humilitas*), of the dispraise of the transitory world (*contemptus mundi*)? [...] The concepts of *humilitas* and *contemptus mundi* inevitably bring about the danger that writing an autobiography would be considered an act of vanity (*vanitas*), of immodesty or even impiety. Thus, it was of crucial importance to the autobiographer to avoid such an impression and to subject his mode of presentation to the demands of *humilitas* and the *contemptus mundi*.[42]

This situation shifts by the fifteenth century to a general acceptance of 'the author's pride in his intellectual qualities,' and away from the 'sphere of negative moral evaluation'.[43] This is not necessarily the case, however, for female writers. In many respects, Cereta inherits a feminized version of Petrarch's problem. For example, how does a woman claim desire for worldly fame and still maintain *feminine* modesty and piety, much less Christian humility? If Cereta addresses these questions, she does so under the umbrella of 'virtue'. What exactly she means by 'virtue', however, is ambiguous. She places no conditions on her usage of 'virtue', attaching it to the benefits of secular learning and religious devotion in a similar manner. Furthermore, she credits virtue with any honour she may receive. In a letter to Agostino Emilio, she writes,

> Do be aware, though, that you are going to see a little woman who is humble in both her appearance and dress, since I am more concerned with letters than adornment, having committed myself to the care of virtue, which can indeed confer honour on me not only during my lifetime but when I am dead.[44]

Since Cereta is responding to the praises of her addressee, it may be argued that she is following established humanist form in deflecting praise. There is, however, another viable reading of 'virtue' in this passage. While Cereta is linking study with virtue – typical of humanist writing – she juxtaposes her humble and modest demeanour with women whose concern for adornment leaves them less virtuous. Thus, the traditional female ideal of modesty is linked with active study.

The humanist perception of *virtus* has been described by scholars as a 'consciousness of personal distinction [...], [a] desire for public acknowledgement [...]'.[45] Some male humanists bypass the absence of a public role for women by focusing on 'right living' and securing 'virtue'. In theory, a curriculum consisting of history, moral philosophy, rhetoric and poetry would endow virtue on all who studied them. Girls who received the same humanist education as boys were expected to have literary skills comparable to their male counterparts who were being prepared for civic participation. The benefits of such study, however, were justified in a manner that coincided with a woman's social roles as wife, mother and daughter. In his letter to Battista Malatesta of Montefeltro (1423), Leonardo Bruni defined 'genuine learning' as the combination of literary skill and knowledge. Bruni does not impose a mythological characterization on the woman he addresses, but he does account for the fact that his addressee is a female by making mention of the type of knowledge that a woman should make her first priority. He insists that a woman's first priority should be sacred letters, followed by moral philosophy. This emphasis does not result in a diversion from the humanist curriculum. She, like her male counterpart, should read the historians, orators and poets. However, the moral lessons most pertinent to Bruni's female addressee were those examples of 'womanly modesty and goodness' and 'the finest patterns of the wifely arts', in addition to 'what their doctrines are concerning continence, temperance, modesty, justice, courage [and] liberality'.[46] By tailoring the benefits of liberal studies according to gender, humanists like Bruni reinforced perceived differences between men and women and reasserted gender order.

There is no evidence in Cereta's letters that would suggest her acknowledgement of Bruni's division of benefits and moral lessons along gender lines. For Cereta, it is not 'feminine' virtue that she sees herself acquiring. It is the humanist virtue and honour that comes through knowledge and wisdom, and the promise of glory that this will bring. Perhaps one reason for this is because although she does not outwardly distinguish between them, Cereta has two communities to which she is writing – one to which she hopes to gain entry, and one to which she already belongs. Continued interaction – both physical and literary – with a mixed community of religious and lay women suggests an additional audience for Cereta's displays of learning.

In her essay 'The Convent Muses: The Secular Writing of Italian Nuns, 1450–1650', Elissa Weaver surveys non-religious writing by nuns which reveals familiarity with, and at times mastery of, genres and literary forms being practised by leading humanist figures.[47] Weaver attributes the continuation of studies and writing inside the convent to increasing literacy levels, but also, and more importantly, to 'internal pressures' from the community. The community to which Weaver refers extends beyond the convent walls to the lay women with whom nuns regularly interacted – the external community which was never completely separate, and which she refers to as a 'feminine sub-culture'. Weaver's notion of a 'feminine sub-culture' is a space wherein female relatives, friends and benefactors met regularly, sharing 'interests that were often different from the interests of men,' a culture that indeed 'seems to have defined itself in some ways in opposition to the world of men'.[48] Two of Cereta's letters mention visits to the monasteries Santa Chiara and Ursine and four of her letters are to religious women, one of whom is her younger sister. Albert Rabil describes the purpose of these visits as being for 'intellectual discussions' and Diana Robin describes Cereta as having participated 'in at least one informal learned academy at the monastery of S. Chiara near Brescia'.[49] While there is some question over whether or not one of her religious addressees, Santa Pelegrina, is an actual person, the newly elected abbess of Santa Chiara, Veneranda, to whom Cereta writes, is real. The letter offers congratulations, advice and encouragement. In this community, one that is woman-centred, Cereta could follow the principle of the active life. Although she does not specifically adapt humanist notions through feminized expressions as she does in many of her other letters, the intellectual exchange implies a dynamic flow of influence between the secular and religious worlds for women, fostering a space that was neither purely sacred nor worldly.

Perhaps another reason Cereta does not recognize a gendered split in the benefits of liberal study is that she does not see her learning as a threat to her social role as a woman. She does not rebuff her domestic life, but rather incorporates it into her identity as a scholar. In so doing, she takes up another traditional humanist theme: the active life versus the contemplative life. In pursuing this theme, Cereta composes letters to two female figures, Sister Deodata di Leno and Europa Solitaria, arguing opposite sides of the issue. This allows her to follow humanist precedent in displaying her knowledge of both sides of the debate, ultimately coming down on the side of the active life. In her promotion of the active life, Cereta counsels Europa Solitaria that, 'Too much freedom from responsibility dishonours your womanly respect'.[50] Thus, Cereta's praise of the active life relates to how the figure of Europa can benefit others around her by staying active in her community as a woman. She expresses the same sentiment in the prologue to her collection, dedicated to Cardinal Ascanio Maria Sforza, writing,

Since men receive an education in literature and other studies, however, so that they may benefit from the example of their forebears, the most elect men of diverse orders have said publicly that education has been wasted on me because it has benefited only me and not others.[51]

To Cereta, this is an unfair assessment of her capabilities. Although she is 'a girl still unknown', her learning is for the benefit not just of herself, but of others. In this particular letter, she presents herself as a potential benefit to her dedicatee, to whom she will 'bring forth small (though I hope adequate) gifts from the secret places of my mind – a greater discovery, which, under your auspices, will cause new amazement to draw many people throughout the world to the greenness of my glory for centuries to come'.[52] Being a woman does not keep Cereta from participating in the distribution of fame.

Cereta's exchange with Brother Thomas of Milan exposes the potential for tension between the virtue pursued by humanist writers, which was classical in orientation, and the humility of Christian virtue. In her response to a letter from Brother Thomas, Cereta observes,

> Your letter seemed to reproach me because, although I have filled so many margins and now so many books with secular writing, I have neglected to write even a short commentary on a sacred topic, as though nothing to do with the subject of Christian nobility could be impassioned.[53]

If there is a conflict between the virtue to which she refers in her writings and Christian virtue, Cereta does not seem to see it. Her letter continues,

> Although you have criticized me with serious intent and knowledgeable too, still what you say seems hostile and hard for me to hear. But the argument is not equal to the subject at hand; nor is the basis for your accusation anything that would make me uncomfortable – as though I were a plaintiff in a case with no defence.[54]

As we see in this passage, there is no reason for Cereta to see herself as anything but a good Christian. Her piety speaks for itself, which is her message to Brother Thomas in a second letter:

> As I prepare a mirror of my mind for death, I always hold up to my mind the teaching of our Saviour. And though vain criticism may sometimes cause me to be distracted, still I rise up again from misfortune more determined than before with the help of God, and I think nothing of the usefulness of the body, for which the smallest plot of land will suffice. For my faith is contented in itself, and with it I am carried to God under the sail of humility.[55]

Coming through in her responses to Brother Thomas is Cereta's notion of virtue as universal and resistant to qualification. She believes in the humanist precept that the contemplation of moral lessons increases an individual's virtue, that the virtue acquired through study applies to all aspects of life, spiritual and worldly, male and female.

In her last letter to Brother Thomas, which Cereta includes in the collection dedicated to Cardinal Ascanio Maria Sforza in 1488, she abruptly announces that she is giving up her 'plan to seek fame through human letters, lest my mind, bereft, unhappy, and unaware of the future should seek happiness through diligence', citing a longing for 'a life more free from anxiety'.[56] We do not know exactly why Cereta ceased to write. The year of her collection is also the year of her father's death, perhaps rendering her effort to secure a social identity as a female scholar too vulnerable to sustain criticism. Although this last letter to Brother Thomas was written before her father's death, she alludes to weariness as one of the causes for her decision, explaining, 'What is more, since too great a concern for knowledge raises the suspicion that one leads a prodigal life, our all-night sessions of study ought not to continue, as if we were born solely for the sake of literature'.[57]

Laura Cereta exemplifies the goals of the humanist educational programme: cultivation of virtue, study as a means of withstanding the blows of fortune, creating value from one's experiences, the desire for fame and belief in the active life. This last goal proved the most difficult to achieve. How could Cereta, within the confines of female social roles, pursue an active life through study without posing a challenge to the existing socio-political power structure? For men, the *studia humanitatis* segued into enlightened and moral civic participation to the benefit of the larger community. Without similar licence to act, how did Cereta justify her engagement in a programme which, when enacted, primarily served to reinforce the socio-political power of men?

On the one hand, Cereta targets her pursuit of humanist virtue in its most classical sense – the active life – to a community composed solely of women. Offering advice, consolation, encouragement and serving as an example of righteous and virtuous living were all things women could do for each other at any point in their lives. This approach applies to both the *respublicum mulierum*, to which she refers in her letters, and to the mixed female community of convent culture. On the other hand, Cereta manipulates the humanist preference for an active life by situating it in the realm of the mind. In this way, Cereta can argue natural equality and ability without overtly challenging her social and cultural position as a woman. It is here also, in the realm of study and contemplation, that activities and virtue are able to resist the categories male and female. Thus, although she has no express public role, her learning still benefits others through her virtuous pursuit of a 'higher good,' bringing fame to her and those associated with her.

Through her letters, Cereta crafts an image of learnedness – thus virtue – anchored to her domestic role as daughter, wife and widow. For Cereta, the challenge is not how to 'overcome her sex', it is how to create a space in which her daily experiences as a woman with domestic tasks *and* as a scholar will be recognized as legitimate and valuable, a balancing act she begins early in her education. She rebuffs suggestions that she is exceptional and other attempts of correspondents to idealize her, directing their attention back to her sustained diligence in study and reminding them of the lengths to which she must go to find time for it. She juxtaposes the imagery of embroidery – the traditional realm of female activity – with that of war and self-defence, the traditional realm of male activity. She attributes any fame she may acquire to the virtue inherent in active study, thus maintaining female modesty, and yet implies that she indeed deserves fame based on her efforts. She alternates between 'pen' and 'needle', common emblems of gender ideology, depending on which tactic best suits her argument and illustrates her literary skill. Furthermore, Cereta refutes any suggestion that she is not simultaneously a dedicated student of classical literature *and* a pious Christian by repeatedly promoting herself as both an accomplished scholar who expresses pride in her intellectual ability *and* a humble and dutiful woman. Her letters attempt to join together the two communities that have influenced and conditioned the self-image she expresses: the community of letters dominated by men and the community of women – lay and religious – to which she regularly returns, in the flesh and in words. While most of her life is spent in the latter, in her mind and letters she is part of both, never fully joined, yet never fully separate.

Notes

1. For an overview of early work on women and learning see Melinda K. Blade, *Education of Italian Renaissance Women* (Mesquite: Ida House Inc., 1983) and the essays in *Beyond Their Sex: Learned Women of the European Past*, ed. Patricia H. Labalme (New York: New York University Press, 1980), especially Margaret King's essay, 'Book-Lined Cells: Women and Humanism in the Early Italian Renaissance', pp. 66–90. Also see Lisa Jardine, 'Women Humanists: Education for What?', in *Feminism and Renaissance Studies*, ed. Lorna Hutson (Oxford: Oxford University Press, 1999), pp. 48–81. Critical editions of female humanist writings include *Her Immaculate Hand: Selected Works By and About the Women Humanists of Quattrocento Italy*, ed. Albert Rabil and Margaret King (Binghamton, NY: Medieval and Renaissance Texts and Studies, 1983); *Laura Cereta: Collected Letters of a Renaissance Feminist*, ed. Diana Robin (Chicago: University of Chicago Press, 1997), upon which this essay draws; and Isotta Nogarola, *Complete Writings: Letterbook, Dialogue on Adam and Eve, Orations*, ed. Margaret King and Diana Robin (Chicago: University of Chicago Press, 2004). For an examination of factors that increased the potential for a girl to receive a humanist education, see Holt Parker, 'Women and Humanism: Nine Factors for the Woman Learning', *Viator*, 35 (2004), 581–616, and 'The Magnificence of Learned Women', *Viator*, 38 (2007), 265–89.

2. On Cereta, see Albert Rabil, *Laura Cereta: Quattrocento Humanist* (Binghamton, NY: Medieval and Renaissance Texts and Studies, 1981); and Diana Robin, 'Humanism and Feminism in Laura Cereta's Public Letters', in *Women in Italian Renaissance Culture and Society*, ed. Letizia Panizza (Oxford: European Humanities Research Centre, 2000), pp. 368–83, and 'Woman, Space, and Renaissance Discourse', in *Sex and Gender in Medieval and Renaissance Texts: The Latin Tradition*, ed. Barbara K. Gold, Paul Allen Miller, and Charles Platter (New York: State University of New York Press, 1997), pp. 165–88.

3. On Petrarch's influence, see Karl Enenkel, 'In Search of Fame: Self-Representation in Neo-Latin Humanism', in *Medieval and Renaissance Humanism: Rhetoric, Representation, and Reform*, ed. Stephen Gersh and Bert Roest (Boston: Brill, 2003), pp. 93–114. See also Margaret King, 'Petrarch, the Self-Conscious Self, and the First Women Humanists', *Journal of Medieval and Early Modern Studies*, 35 (2005), 537–58, where King argues that the model of subjectivity in Petrarch's letters can be seen especially in the works of female humanist writings.

4. Eighty-four extant letters, which include a prologue and epilogue addressed to her dedicatee, were sent to Cardinal Ascanio Maria Sforza.

5. Robin, 'Humanism and Feminism', p. 371.

6. Cereta, *Collected Letters*, p. 51.

7. Cereta, *Collected Letters*, pp. 49–50.

8. Robin's note in *Collected Letters*, p. 24, explains this reference: 'It is noteworthy that she introduces the figure of needlework here (*simplicissime texta*, a simple woven fabric), which in her letters will be a recurrent metaphor for writing, the self-fashioning that she does in her autobiographical letters, and for the creative act itself'.

9. See King and Rabil, *Her Immaculate Hand*, p. 77; and Robin, 'Women, Space and Renaissance Discourse', p. 179.

10. Cereta, *Collected Letters*, p. 25.

11. Cereta, *Collected Letters*, p. 27. Robin draws attention to Cereta's references to being instructed by a woman, commenting that it 'makes it difficult to dismiss this early evidence that there were in fact learned women who taught Latin in the mid- to late Quattrocento', p. 27, note 22.

12. Roughly half of Cereta's letters are dated before Serina's death.

13. Cereta, *Collected Letters*, p. 57.

14. Cereta, *Collected Letters*, pp. 25–26.

15. Cereta, *Collected Letters*, p. 51.

16. Cereta, *Collected Letters*, p. 79.

17. Sharon Strocchia, 'Learning the Virtues: Convent Schools and Female Culture in Renaissance Florence', in *Women's Education in Early Modern Europe: A History, 1500–1800*, ed. Barbara Whitehead (New York: Garland Publishing, 1999), pp. 3–46.

18. Cereta, *Collected Letters*, p. 19.

19. Cereta, *Collected Letters*, p. 27.

20. Cereta, *Collected Letters*, pp. 31–32.

21. Cereta, *Collected Letters*, p. 24.

22. The limitations of the tendency of (male) authors to measure women's success by their ability to 'become' men or to take on masculine characteristics are also discussed by Alison More and Helen Swift in their contributions to this volume.

23. Jardine, 'Women Humanists', p. 68.

24. Constance Jordan, *Renaissance Feminism: Literary Texts and Political Models* (Ithaca: Cornell University Press, 1990), p. 8.

25. Cereta, *Collected Letters*, p. 51.

26. Cereta, *Collected Letters*, p. 80.

27. Boccaccio's 106 short biographies were closely modelled on Petrarch's *On Illustrious Men*, and were confined to historical and mythological women found in ancient literary sources. Regardless of their moral stature, Boccaccio presents the women in his catalogue through the male tradition, and focused on deeds, both positive and negative.

28. King and Rabil, *Her Immaculate Hand*, p. 113.

29. Jardine, 'Women Humanists', p. 53.

30. Cereta, *Collected Letters*, p. 75.

31. Cereta, *Collected Letters*, p. 80.

32. Robin notes in 'Humanism and Feminism' that Cereta, having been born into the urban upper-middle class, would have 'assumed attributes of both Christian piety and humanist learning', p. 369. What is not fully addressed, and what this essay suggests, is the formative and gendered impact of these attributes on Cereta's approach to humanist studies.

33. Cereta, *Collected Letters*, pp. 78–79.

34. Cereta, *Collected Letters*, p. 82.

35. Bert Roest comments on the ideology Cereta is expressing, observing, 'The individual must create his own essential value from himself by developing his inherent qualities to the full by immersing himself in the *studia humanitatis*', in his essay 'Rhetoric and Recourse in Humanist Pedagogical Discourse', in *Medieval and Renaissance Humanism: Rhetoric, Representation, and Reform*, ed. Stephen Gersh and Bert Roest (Boston: Brill, 2003), p. 129.

36. Cereta, *Collected Letters*, p. 75.

37. Cereta, *Collected Letters*, p. 79.

38. Cereta, *Collected Letters*, p. 82.

39. Cereta, *Collected Letters*, p. 82.

40. Cereta, *Collected Letters*, p. 82.

41. Robin points to Cereta's reliance on early humanists such as Petrarch, Salutati and Lorenzo Valla in her introduction to the *Collected Letters*. See especially p. 17 and her comparison of Cereta's letter to Deodata di Leno and Petrarch's 'Ascent of Mount Ventoux', pp. 13, 114–23.

42. Enenkel, 'In Search of Fame', pp. 100–101.

43. Enenkel, 'In Search of Fame', pp. 101, 93.

44. Cereta, *Collected Letters*, p. 83.

45. William Harrison Woodward, *Vittorino da Feltre and Other Humanist Educators* (New York: Teachers College Press, 1963), p. 186.

46. Leonardo Bruni, 'On the Study of Literature', in *The Humanism of Leonardo Bruni: Selected Texts*, ed. Gordon Griffiths, James Hankins, David Thompson (Binghamton, NY: Medieval and Renaissance Texts and Studies, 1987), pp. 240–51 (p. 242).

47. Elissa Weaver, 'The Convent Muses: The Secular Writing of Italian Nuns, 1450–1650', in *Women and Faith: Catholic Religious Life in Italy from Late Antiquity to the Present*, ed. Lucetta Scaraffia and Gabriella Zarri (Cambridge, MA: Harvard University Press, 1999), pp. 129–43.

48. See Weaver, *Convent Theatre in Early Modern Italy: Spiritual Fun and Learning for Women* (Cambridge: Cambridge University Press, 2002), p. 3. Weaver is building upon Craig Monson's argument for convents as a 'women's sphere' in *Disembodied Voices: Music and Culture in an Early Modern Italian Convent* (Berkeley: University of California Press, 1995). In her essay '"Women talking about the things of God": A Late Medieval Sub-culture', in *Women and Literature in Britain 1150–1500*, ed. Carol M. Meale (Cambridge: Cambridge University Press, 1993), pp. 104–27, Felicity Riddy argues for a female sub-culture based on a shared literary culture among nuns and laywomen which formed a cultural space of reading and discussion able to exert influence on expressions by both female and male writers.

49. Albert Rabil, 'Laura Cereta', in *Italian Women Writers: A Bio-Bibliographical Sourcebook*, ed. Rinaldina Russell (Westport, Connecticut: Greenwood Press, 1994), pp. 67–75; Robin, 'Humanism and Feminism', p. 370. In *Collected Letters* the letters mentioning visits to monasteries appear in the appendix, separate from Cereta's compiled letterbook, and seem to suggest the presence of women and men, yet presumably presided over by the abbess. They are addressed to Fra Lodovico de la Turre and Clemenzo Longolio (pp. 176, 178). Along with Santa Pelegrina, most scholars agree that Europa Solitaria, Bibolo Semproni and Lucilia Vernacula are fictional. For discussion of an extended list of potential imaginary correspondents, see King, 'Petrarch, the Self-Conscious Self', pp. 551–52.

50. Cereta, *Collected Letters*, p. 26.

51. Cereta, *Collected Letters*, p. 39.

52. Cereta, *Collected Letters*, p. 45.

53. Cereta, *Collected Letters*, p. 104.

54. Cereta, *Collected Letters*, p. 104.

55. Cereta, *Collected Letters*, p. 108.

56. Cereta, *Collected Letters*, pp. 112–13.

57. Cereta, *Collected Letters*, p. 112.

10

Mightier than the Sword: Reading, Writing and Noble Masculinity in the Early Sixteenth Century

Fiona S. Dunlop

The standard model of the development of secular aristocratic masculinity presupposes a neat transition from a warrior masculinity characteristic of most of the medieval period to a courtier masculinity of the early modern period.[1] After the Norman Conquest, great noblemen held land directly from the crown in return for military service, so that in an important sense their military prowess justified reserving the primary source of wealth for themselves and power of the time.[2] A turning point came with the advent of the Tudors and the end of the Wars of the Roses which instituted a period of 'crisis' for the greater nobility as their traditional roles and sources of power were gradually eroded.[3] Aristocrats were increasingly dependent on the crown for advancement through the award of offices in the king's gift, yet increasingly in competition with men of undistinguished birth, but who had administrative talent for these offices. Particularly under Elizabeth, aristocratic identity became contingent on a new set of signs, in the form of the ritualized behaviour of the court, self-consciously enacted in the view of a well-informed courtly audience.[4]

This model is in many ways useful – particularly in that it stresses the historicity of gendered aristocratic identities. The idea of what a nobleman is alters over time, in response to changing social and political influences. Nevertheless, such a model assumes that there is only one aristocratic masculinity, a unified identity shared by all aristocratic men, regardless of age, region and status; and it ignores the fact that often aristocrats clung tenaciously to traditional components of aristocratic identity, regardless of how well they sat with the times. So we find nobles participating in tournaments right up to the 1620s, despite the fact that the warfare of that period no longer bore any relation to the ritualized conflicts of the tourney.[5] Moreover it ignores the self-consciousness of aristocratic identities which results in nobles picking up and dropping different traits of aristocratic identity in order to articulate different political messages at different times. In his study of the courtesy literature of Elizabeth's court, Frank Whigham describes the behaviours and gestures it taught as a kind of rhetoric, which allowed nobles to perform an aristocratic identity by deploying different 'tropes' of behaviour.[6]

This essay discusses an early sixteenth-century poem that shows the uncomfortable process involved in refashioning a noble identity for new times – consciously putting off old tropes of aristocratic masculinity and putting on new ones. The verse text 'He that made this hous for contemplacion' can be seen as a strategic manoeuvre by Henry Algernon Percy, fifth earl of Northumberland, in a wider campaign to ensure his family's continued access to noble privileges. This little-known moralizing poem was added to the manuscript now known as London, British Library, Royal 18.D.ii between 1516 and 1526, and probably at the instigation of the fifth earl of Northumberland.[7]

The manuscript itself is an object which expresses a powerful sense of aristocratic identity. It appears to have come into the possession of the Percy family on the marriage of Maud Herbert to the fourth earl of Northumberland (c. 1476) when it contained only Lydgate's *Troy Book* and *The Siege of Thebes*. The fourth earl added his arms while his son, the fifth earl, was probably responsible for the addition of many items in the early sixteenth century: more Lydgate texts including an account of the reigns of the English kings; a verse history of the Percy family; an account by Skelton of the fourth earl's death in 1489 on the king's business; and the Tudor-Percy emblem which symbolically depicts the Percy family basking in royal favour, in the form of beams of light. The manuscript attests therefore to the Percys' dynastic alliances, aristocratic lineage and loyal service to the crown.

The poem 'He that made this hous for contemplacion' belongs, in the manuscript, to a group of didactic verse which seems intended for the education of young noblemen. Generically, these works sit comfortably within the extensive literature of aristocratic education which survives from the later medieval and early modern periods.[8] This material, usually referred to as 'mirrors for princes', is concerned with the formation of a noble masculinity fit for the exercise of rule and governance.[9] Often works were addressed directly to young heirs to the throne, though they might be more widely disseminated amongst the nobility. The best known examples of princely mirrors in later medieval England were the *Secretum secretorum*, a mid-twelfth-century Latin translation of a tenth-century Arabic work the Latin text of which claimed to be a letter from Aristotle to his young charge Alexander.[10] At least thirteen independent translations into English are known dating from the fourteenth to sixteenth centuries.[11] The text offers counsel on how to cultivate kingly virtues and suppress vice, how to deal with counsellors and servants, how to exercise justice and mercy and how to regulate the royal body. The fact that this large body of texts should exist at all from the later medieval period is testament to the way in which the formation of aristocratic masculinities was becoming bound up with textuality: the role of such works was to help produce the right sort of kings, princes and noblemen.

'He that made this hous for contemplacion' is a particularly interesting example of such a text, first because it seems to have existed in two different contexts: in the manuscript and (according to the poem's rubric) as inscriptions 'in the rouf of my lorde percy closett at Lekyngfelde'.[12] From this, it would appear that the fifth earl's son and heir, Lord Henry Percy, was the primary audience for the work – he had to look at it every day, written up in his private room in the manor house at Leconfield in Yorkshire, one of the earl's favourite residences. Much of the moralizing verse of the manuscript is identified as inscriptional verse from various rooms in the manors at Wressle and Leconfield.[13] The inclusion of the educational verses in the manuscript may have had a practical purpose, as Alexandra Gillespie suggests, of keeping valuable precepts always before the eye of the young man even when he was not in his own closet, in line with Erasmian principles on the inculcation of knowledge. However, it is perhaps unlikely that such a large manuscript with its costly illumination, and its self-conscious engagement with the history and role of the Percy family, would have been suitable for the intensive use of young Percy alone. The manuscript is more likely to have been used in the context of the convivial life of the Northumberland household. In the evenings, nobles and their servants of gentle condition would gather in their lord's chamber and pass their time pleasantly with activities such as singing, dancing, music and chess – but they would also listen to texts being read aloud, and then use what they had heard as matter for discussion and debate.[14] Medieval references to reading of this kind in households and colleges mention chronicles, romances and princely mirrors as likely focuses for this sociable activity – exactly the kind of mixture of texts in the Percy manuscript.

If 'He that made this hous' was intended to teach young Henry Percy how to be an aristocratic man, then the first curious feature to note is its odd reluctance to offer an unambiguous programme for him to follow. The text is literally ambivalent because it is written in the form of a debate between two distinct voices who offer very different views on what the appropriate behaviours for a young man should be.

The first voice advocates an aristocratic masculinity, the central trope of which is learning and study. We are meant to identify his line of argument with the earl because, as the first voice reports, the earl has provided a physical space in his household for his son to pursue literate practices:

He that made this hous for contemplacion
Myndyde specially exercyse of lernynge and vertuus occupation.
And adolescencia whiche thynthithe hymself wyse
Shall know himself better by vertuus exercyse.[15]

The term 'closett' designates a space intended for religious devotions or study, pursuits which necessitated privacy.[16] It is not entirely clear from the poem's list of activities whether we should imagine Henry Percy reading texts to himself silently, writing, being read to or being instructed by others. References to nobles reading in the context of their household indicate that aristocrats might consider themselves to be 'reading' as they listened to others read aloud and as they discussed the text afterward.[17] Such group reading might take place in closets and private rooms in a more intimate atmosphere, as well as in more public settings. There is less extant evidence for aristocratic men writing, in the sense of using pen and ink themselves, and this is mostly in the form of marginal annotation by readers in manuscripts and printed books, since even personal letters tended to be written down by a scribe.[18]

However, the word 'contemplacion' used in the Percy poem certainly seems to indicate the kind of intensive meditational reading so often recommended to and practised by noblewomen of the later medieval period.[19] The term 'exercyse' has similar overtones, being used to describe both training and practice in physical activities like the use of arms, and the kind of moral and spiritual disciplining encouraged for religious and pious individuals in the secular life.[20] In Henry Percy's closet, devotional life elides with intellectual endeavour, since the habits of 'contemplacion' envisaged for the young man also encompass 'lernynge'. They are presented as character-building activities in the sense that they will help him acquire (presumably moral) virtues, and a degree of self-knowledge.

Evidence from the later medieval period suggests that private devotions were seen as a fundamental part of the education of young male aristocrats. Nicholas Orme, for example, has drawn attention to two plans drawn up to regulate the daily lives of young aristocrats: a set of ordinances drawn up in 1473 for the household and upbringing of Edward, son of Edward IV; and another dating to around 1435, designed for John Mowbray, duke of Norfolk, a ward of Henry VI.[21] Both indicate that religious observance was to be a regular and indeed substantial part of the young man's day. There is evidence of similar planning by adult lay men to create space in the day for religious observances.[22] It is likely that many adult noblemen took part in the round of religious observance which was such an important feature of the daily life of the majority of noble households.[23]

But no matter how conventional it might have been for young nobles to practise what Goldberg has called the 'conspicuous devotion' characteristic of aristocratic life, the second voice of 'He that made this hous' vigorously criticizes noble masculinity whose defining activity is learning, study and contemplation.[24] On one level, the second speaker asserts that youth is the natural time for leisure and pleasure, rather than for hard work which may 'breke his brayne'.[25] But a thoroughly worked out essentialist model of what it means to be a young man stands behind his view. The humoural theory prevalent in the later Middle Ages saw the young male body as driven by an excess of blood.[26] In this system of thought, the humours determined not only physical characteristics but aspects of personality and psychology, so the sanguine temperament characteristic of young men was held to endow them with a propensity to traits such as lust and anger. The second voice of 'He that made this hous' draws on this conception of young males in declaring that they are naturally inclined to 'play', to 'sensualite' and to 'sport'.[27] These are for the second speaker the tropes of youthful maleness, and the implication is that these activities – with their overtones of illicit sexual pleasure – are thoroughly natural. The pursuit of virtue (recommended by the earl and his avatar in the poem) is by this reasoning deeply unnatural. The first speaker is put in the position of having to justify the pursuit of holiness and hard work otherwise associated with the old. He argues that young men have to overcome their natural tendencies to sinful pleasures, because they may otherwise be unable to change in old age or have to suffer the consequences of their evil actions.

As Burrow has observed, in his studies of the medieval proverb 'Young saint, old devil', other morally didactic works of the later medieval period include similar debates about the nature of young men and old men.[28] References to the idea that young men are naturally inclined to vice are made most often by those who claim to be concerned about the spiritual dangers such views hold, and who then proceed, like 'He that made this hous for contemplacion', to argue against them and to endorse as the best kind of masculinity one where the young man overcomes his youthful nature and makes himself prematurely 'old' in terms of his habits, lifestyle and attitudes. While the notion of a school of thought actively promoting youthful vice may of course be a fiction, or simply an occasion for the writer to present a corrected view of youthful masculinity, such texts nonetheless create the sense of a conflict between different models of youthful masculinity. Moreover, by continually invoking the image of the naturally vicious young male body, even if only to discredit it, the texts paradoxically perpetuate it. The otherness of the young male body is perhaps necessary to conceptualize the mature, virtuous male body.

The debate between the first and second speakers in 'He that made this hous' about the suitableness of learning and virtue to the young man also has a political dimension. Medieval political theory, inspired by Aristotelian traditions, saw moral virtues as vital to kings and nobles, since they bespoke a capacity for governance.[29] As John Trevisa's fourteenth-century translation of *De regimine principum* put it, 'For he that wole be wise and kunnynge to gouerne and rule oþer schal be wise and konnynge to gouerne and to rule hymself'.[30] Some of these virtues – like wisdom and foresight – were directly related to the business of ruling; but in the more general sense the noble's capacity to discipline his own moral being and his physical body was taken as an indicator of his ability to wield political power.

Political literature of the medieval period places a particular onus on aristocratic men to display a capacity for virtue on the grounds that virtue justifies their elite status as rulers and governors in different kinds of polities. In turn, then, it is vital for young aristocratic men to discipline their naturally unruly bodies in order to make the transition to an adult masculinity which will justify them taking up roles of authority over others. The political literature of the reign of Richard II is a good example of how the political symbolism of youth and age might be deployed. In this political discourse, Richard's opponents attack his kingship by emphasizing how Richard has failed to achieve a disciplined adult masculinity. Despite having reached the age of maturity, Richard is constantly described in terms of his youth, which stands for political incompetence.[31]

The earl of Northumberland's verses invite us to imagine the young, well-disciplined, Henry Percy working away at the pursuit of virtue, with all the materials provided by a careful aristocratic father. The closing lines of 'He that made this hous' reinforce this picture by underscoring the earl's intentions for the work: 'his trust is that he shalbe had in remebraunce / ffor his faithfull goode mynde towards youthes goode gouernaunce'.[32] Such an image of the studious son may be completely fictional, but it is clearly one which helped to create aristocratic capital for the earl and his family. Why should the earl of Northumberland in particular be at such pains to build images of his son as the self-disciplining young noble devoted to study and virtue? Mervyn E. James has described the fifth earl's unhappiness at being excluded by Henry VII and Henry VIII from offices which he saw as rightfully his, especially that of Lieutenant of the North.[33] He can be seen as pursuing strategies at the beginning of the sixteenth century intended to convince Henry VIII that he and his son were in fact the only proper nobles capable of subduing the rebellious north. One might assume in this context that the earl would cultivate the ideology of a warrior masculinity in order to press his claims. In contrast, the earl appears to have taken some trouble to establish a reputation for the arts of peace, rather than those of war. Ruth Larsen has argued that the fifth earl's whole way of life at Wressle and Leconfield was carefully gauged to show the magnificence appropriate to a ruler of the north.[34] The earl was careful, however, not to invest in the appearance of military strength through large numbers of retainers, which, in any case, was carefully controlled by legislation. Instead he took care to project images of a well-ordered household through his investment in manuscripts containing household ordinances.[35] As Alexandra Gillespie has pointed out, the manuscript miscellanies associated with the Percy family were at work 'sustaining traditional ideas about noble service to the monarch' in terms of the military service owed by aristocrats to their king.[36] However, items like 'He that made this hous' modify the concept of service and the idea of what it means to be a nobleman for tactical reasons. The earl can be seen encouraging his son to adopt a masculinity based on the disciplining regimes of learning and piety, rather than those of arms, because this is a much more palatable noble masculinity to a crown highly sensitive to the threat posed by a martial aristocracy and the 'overmighty subject'.[37]

Again, we might assume that given its conventional association with aristocratic status, the advocacy of study, learning and devotion in 'He that made this hous for contemplacion' would be fairly unproblematic. Yet the poem continues to express anxieties about these activities as ways to perform adult and noble masculinity. After attempting to associate the period of youth with a 'natural' propensity to vice, the second voice invokes a status-related anxiety about literacy by cunningly eliding study and devotion with the literacy characteristic of those who have to work for a living:

Where plente is what nedith travayle
For hym that hathe litill lernynge doth well.[38]

Literacy is here presented as a pragmatic accomplishment, useful only to those who lack noble wealth. Work is opposed to leisure as the 'tropes' of widely different social groups. The medieval aristocratic lifestyle was distinguished by opportunities for leisure, including the rituals of dining, music, literature, discussion, and hunting and hawking.[39] By designating the activity of learning as 'travayle' the second voice associates it with painful exertion, just as Hoccleve associated writing with painful physical labour in his efforts to construct a masculine identity.[40] However, the second voice makes the connection between learning and labour in order to stigmatize literate practices so far as aristocratic men are concerned, since it would be disparaging for them to undertake the labour otherwise characteristic of the peasant. The second voice sounds, in other words, as if he is expressing the anxieties of an aristocrat wishing to preserve the traditional distinctions between status groups.

In response to this strain of argument, the first voice of the poem also plays on anxieties about maintaining the distinctions between noble and non-noble men, but turns the argument around. According to him, the fact that non-nobles possess learning poses a serious threat to aristocratic men, since learning, not military prowess, now wins privileged positions. In the first place, this speaker claims that 'To nobilnes a great lac it is / That a poore man hath that he dothe mysse'.[41] Noblemen ought to be able to demonstrate their innate superiority over other social groups: this is after all what justifies their privileges. If the non-noble can demonstrate some kind of excellence which the aristocrat cannot, then this undermines a social system which distributes the good things of life unequally, to the benefit of a noble elite. The first voice claims that this process is already underway:

He that hathe litill yet by lernynge may
Cum to greate honoures we se euery day.

And honoure by cunnynge is of more magnificens
And for lack of lernynge it is of les experiens.[42]

Poor men are already obtaining 'greate honoures' on the basis of their learning, learning which qualifies them for offices under the crown and other positions of governance because it gives them the qualities fitting for such roles. A nobleman needs to pursue scholarship because, in combination with other noble accomplishments, it will ensure he is better qualified for 'honoures' than the man from a humble background:

Honowres yf they be yeuyn aright
Sholde be yeuyn to noblenes whiche hathe aforesight
As nobleness withoute cunnynge ys dyssolate
So cunnynge withoute maners is reprobate.[43]

The nobleman here is represented as possessing a natural advantage over his low-born competitor for honours in the form of 'maners', the bearing and social accomplishments which in this account seem to be acquired by the aristocrat at birth. So long as the nobleman takes care to develop 'aforesight', the noble wisdom and prudence presented as the fruits of education, he ought to have a superior claim to remunerative positions of trust.

As well as defining noble masculinity by opposing it to non-noble masculinity, and considering the threat to noble privilege by the learned of non-aristocratic birth, there is the shadow of a further kind of opposition here: between the learned and virtuous aristocratic man and the unlearned and vicious one. As the first speaker of the poem says:

As golde makithe the precius stone more oriente
So cunnynge with vertu makithe nobilnes more excellent.[44]

The young Henry Percy certainly had to compete for royal patronage with the rising men of the middling sort, but even in the meritocratic world of royal administration relatively few men achieved lasting aristocratic status for their families.[45] The real competition was still to be found in other aristocratic families. Therefore, Henry Percy's job was essentially to use the rhetoric of aristocratic masculinity to argue that he showed a superior kind of noble existence, which merited advancement in service to the crown.

'He that made this hous for contemplacion' builds an argument for a noble masculinity where learning and piety are key activities, and it presents Lord Henry Percy as the prime example of one who has been brought up so as to attain this masculine identity. This is not to say that learning and piety were altogether new or unusual practices for noblemen, but the fifth earl chose to stress these as the foundations of a better kind of noble masculinity in order to claim high offices under the crown. The poem contains a covert challenge to the monarch in its assertion that 'yf they [honours] be yeuyn aright' they should be awarded to learned nobles. Since young Percy demonstrates the right sort of qualities, offices should then come to him as a matter of course – if the king rewards merit as he should do.

The fifth earl was in one sense successful in his campaign for offices in royal service. His son was awarded the wardenship of the East and Middle Marches along with other marks of royal favour after the fifth earl's death. But the new sixth earl was not an astute operator who might have capitalized on this position. Showing a remarkable lack of noble prudence and foresight, he squandered his money, quarrelled with his wife and died childless and poor, leaving the remainder of the Percy estates to the crown.[46] Ironically, he was unable to live up to the image of noble masculinity constructed for him by his father.

The poem 'He that made this hous for contemplacion' shows how concepts of noble masculinity were open to renegotiation in response to historical and social change. The fifth earl of Northumberland was not a radical: he had a traditional aristocratic priority to preserve the power and influence of his noble family, steering a careful course between the banks and shoals of his times. Yet he was utterly pragmatic in how this goal was to be achieved, and able to recourse to a new set of signs to signal his and his son's superior aristocratic claims to honours from the crown. The earl understood the advantages of a noble masculinity symbolized in acts of learning and devotion. These activities stand for the discipline and control of one's own noble body which bespeak an ability to discipline and control others. They justify the possession and acquisition of privileges in the face of social competition from other status groups. Moreover, they show a tacit commitment to a non-military masculinity, so avoiding even the appearance of a threat to royal power.

As a discussion of what it means to be noble, the poem draws on a discourse of masculinity and power from the later medieval period which persists into the early modern period. Despite the fact that many of the ideas it raises are conventional, it does not give a sense of aristocrats slipping seamlessly from one kind of masculinity to another, but having to negotiate carefully the boundaries between different kinds of masculine identities: youth and maturity; aristocratic and non-aristocratic; and different modes of aristocratic identity.

Notes

1. For the historiography of the concept of nobility, see David Crouch, *The Birth of Nobility: Constructing Aristocracy in England and France, 900–1300* (Harlow: Pearson Longman, 2005).

2. Chris Given-Wilson, *The English Nobility in the Late Middle Ages: The Fourteenth-Century Political Community* (London: Routledge and Kegan Paul, 1987), pp. 1–25.

3. Lawrence Stone, *The Crisis of the Aristocracy, 1558–1641* (Oxford: Clarendon Press, 1965).

4. Frank Whigham, *Ambition and Privilege: The Social Tropes of Elizabethan Courtesy Theory* (Berkeley, Los Angeles and London: University of California Press, 1984).

5. John S.A. Adamson, 'Chivalry and Political Culture in Caroline England', in *Culture and Politics in Early Stuart England*, ed. Kevin Sharpe and Peter Lake (Houndmills: Macmillan, 1994), pp. 161–98.

6. Whigham, *Ambition and Privilege*, pp. 33–62.

7. The manuscript is described in George F. Warner and Julius P. Gilson, *Catalogue of the Western Manuscripts in the Old Royal and King's Collections*, 4 vols (London: Trustees of the British Library, 1921), ii, 308–10. The text has been transcribed in Ewald Flügel, 'Kleinere Mitteilungen aus Handschriften', *Anglia*, 14 (1892), 463–501 (pp. 482–85). On the date of the additions, see Linne R. Mooney, 'Lydgate's *Kings of England* and Another Verse Chronicle of the Kings', *Viator*, 20 (1989), 255–89.

8. Anthony S.G. Edwards, 'Middle English Inscriptional Verse Texts', in *Texts and their Contexts: Papers from the Early Book Society*, ed. John Scattergood and Julia Boffey (Dublin: Four Courts Press, 1997), pp. 26–43 (pp. 29–30).

9. Nicholas Orme, *From Childhood to Chivalry: The Education of the English Kings and Aristocracy, 1066–1530* (London and New York: Methuen, 1984), pp. 81–111; Richard F. Green, *Poets and Princepleasers: Literature and the English Court in the Late Middle Ages* (Toronto: University of Toronto Press, 1980), pp. 135–67; Judith Ferster, *Fictions of Advice: The Literature and Politics of Counsel in Late Medieval England* (Philadelphia: University of Pennsylvania Press, 1996); John L. Watts, *Henry VI and the Politics of Kingship* (Cambridge: Cambridge University Press, 1996), pp. 16–38.

10. Orme, *From Childhood to Chivalry*, pp. 88–89, 95.

11. *Lydgate and Burgh's Secrees of Old Philisoffres*, ed. Robert Steele, EETS, e.s., 66 (London: Kegan Paul, Trench, Trübner, 1894); *Three Prose Versions of the* Secreta secretorum, ed. Robert Steele, EETS, e.s., 74 (London: Kegan Paul, Trench, Trübner, 1898); *Secretum secretorum: Nine English Versions*, ed. Mahmoud A. Manzalaoui, EETS, o.s., 276 (Oxford: Oxford University Press, 1977).

12. Flügel, 'Kleinere Mitteilungen', p. 482.

13. Ruins of some of the buildings survive, but none of the interior decoration.

14. Joyce Coleman, *Public Reading and the Reading Public in Late Medieval England and France* (Cambridge: Cambridge University Press, 1996), pp. 128–40.

15. Flügel, 'Kleinere Mitteilungen', p. 482.

16. Mark Girouard, *Life in the English Country House* (New Haven and London: Yale University Press, 1978), p. 56. See also Andrew Taylor, 'Into His Secret Chamber: Reading and Privacy in Late Medieval England', in *The Practice and Representation of Reading in England*, ed. James Raven, Helen Small and Naomi Tadmor (Cambridge: Cambridge University Press, 1996), pp. 41–61.

17. Coleman, *Public Reading*, pp. 128–40.

18. Jeremy P. Goldberg, *Medieval England: A Social History 1250–1550* (London: Arnold, 2004), p. 269. On medieval letters, see Sarah Rhiannon Williams, 'English Vernacular Letters c. 1400–c. 1600: Language, Literacy and Culture' (Unpublished PhD thesis, University of York, 2001).

19. For convenient overviews of the rise of private devotional reading in the fifteenth century, see Taylor, 'Into His Secret Chamber', pp. 43–46; Gerald Harriss, *Shaping the Nation: England 1360–1461* (Oxford: Oxford University Press, 2005), pp. 368–76; Paul Strohm, 'Reading and Writing', in *A Social History of England, 1200–1500*, ed. Rosemary Horrox and W. Mark Ormrod (Cambridge: Cambridge University Press, 2006), pp. 454–72; Jennifer Bryan, *Looking Inward: Devotional Reading and the Private Self in Late Medieval England* (Philadelphia: University of Pennsylvania Press, 2008). On women as practitioners of devotional reading see for instance Jocelyn Wogan-Browne, *Saints' Lives and Women's Literary Culture* (Oxford: Oxford University Press, 2001); C. Annette Grisé, 'Women's Devotional Reading in Late Medieval England and the Gendered Reader', *Medium Aevum*, 71 (2002), 209–23; Rebecca Krug, *Reading Families: Women's Literate Practice in Late Medieval England* (Ithaca and London, 2002); *Reading and Literacy in the Middle Ages and Renaissance*, ed. Ian F. Moulton (Turnhout: Brepols, 2004); Mary C. Erler, *Women, Reading and Piety in Late Medieval England* (Cambridge: Cambridge University Press, 2006).

20. *Middle English Dictionary*, ed. Hans Kurath and Robert E. Lewis, 118 fascicles (Ann Arbor, MI: University of Michigan Press, 1953–2001), *q.v.* 'exercise, -ice (n.)'.

21. Nicholas Orme, 'The Education of Edward V', *Bulletin of the Institute of Historical Research*, 57 (1984), 119–30.

22. William A. Pantin, 'Instructions for a Devout and Literate Layman', in *Medieval Learning and Literature*, ed. Jonathan J.G. Alexander and Margaret T. Gibson (Oxford: Oxford University Press, 1976), pp. 398–422.

23. R.A. Kate Mertes, 'The Household as a Religious Community', in *People, Politics and Community in the Later Middle Ages*, ed. Joel Rosenthal and Colin Richmond (Gloucester: Sutton, 1987), pp. 123–39; Christopher M. Woolgar, *The Great Household in Late Medieval England* (New Haven and London: Yale University Press, 1999), pp. 83–110, 176–79.

24. Goldberg, *Medieval England*, pp. 121–22.

25. Flügel, 'Kleinere Mitteilungen', p. 483.

26. Carole Rawcliffe, *Medicine and Society in Later Medieval England* (Stroud: Alan Sutton, 1995), pp. 29–40.

27. Flügel, 'Kleinere Mitteilungen', p. 482.

28. John A. Burrow, '"Young Saint, Old Devil": Reflections on a Medieval Proverb', *Review of English Studies*, 30 (1979), 385–96; idem, *The Ages of Man: A Study in Medieval Writing and Thought* (Oxford: Clarendon Press, 1986), pp. 148–50.

29. Greg Walker, *Plays of Persuasion: Drama and Politics at the Court of Henry VIII* (Cambridge: Cambridge University Press, 1991), pp. 60–101; John Scattergood, 'Skelton's *Magnyfycence* and the Tudor Royal Household', *Medieval English Theatre*, 15 (1993), 21–48.

30. Aegidius Romanus, *The Governance of Kings and Princes: John Trevisa's Middle English Translation of the* De regimine principum *of Aegidius Romanus*, ed. David C. Fowler, Charles F. Briggs and Paul G. Remley, Garland Medieval Texts 19 (New York and London: Routledge, 1997), p. 8, ll. 8–10.

31. Nigel Saul, 'Richard II and the Vocabulary of Kingship', *English Historical Review*, 110 (1995), 854–77; W. Mark Ormrod, 'Coming to Kingship: Boy Kings and the Passage to Power in the Fourteenth Century', in *Rites of Passage: Cultures of Transition in Fourteenth-Century England*, ed. Nicola F. McDonald and W. Mark Ormrod (Woodbridge: Boydell, 2004), pp. 31–49; Christopher Fletcher, 'Manhood and Politics in the Reign of Richard II', *Past and Present*, 189 (2005), 3–39.

32. Flügel, 'Kleinere Mitteilungen', p. 485.

33. Mervyn E. James, *A Tudor Magnate and the Tudor State: Henry Fifth Earl of Northumberland* (York: St Anthony's Press, 1966).

34. Ruth M. Larsen, 'Expressions of Nobility: Conspicuous Consumption and Segregation in the Household of the Fifth Earl of Northumberland' (unpublished MA dissertation, University of York, 1998).

35. The so-called First Northumberland Household Book (Alnwick, MS 99) was subsequently printed in *The Regulations and Establishment of the Houshold* [sic] *of Henry Algernon Percy, Fifth Earl of Northumberland*, ed. Thomas Percy (London: William Pickering, 1827) and in *The Antiquarian Repertory*, ed. Francis Grose, 4 vols (London: Faulder and Son, 1807), IV, 9–344. On the Second Northumberland Household Book (Oxford, Bodleian Library, MS Eng. hist. b. 208), see Dorothy M. Barratt, 'A Second Northumberland Household Book', *Bodleian Library Record*, 8 (1968), 93–98; Ian Lancashire, 'Orders for Twelfth Day and Night *circa* 1515 in the Second Northumberland Household Book', *English Literary Renaissance*, 10 (1980), 7–45.

36. Alexandra Gillespie, 'These proverbs yet do last': Lydgate, the Fifth Earl of Northumberland, and Tudor Miscellanies from Print to Manuscript', *Yearbook of English Studies*, 33 (2003), 215–32 (p. 229).

37. George W. Bernard, *The Power of the Early Tudor Nobility: A Study of the Fourth and Fifth Earls of Shrewsbury* (Brighton: Harvester, 1985); Helen Miller, *Henry VIII and the English Nobility* (Oxford: Blackwell, 1986); *The Tudor Nobility*, ed. George W. Bernard (Manchester: Manchester University Press, 1992).

38. Flügel, 'Kleinere Mitteilungen', p. 483.

39. *Middle English Dictionary*, q.v. 'travail (n.)'.

40. Isabel Davis, *Writing Masculinity in the Later Middle Ages* (Cambridge: Cambridge University Press, 2007), pp. 144–53.

41.   Flügel, 'Kleinere Mitteilungen', p. 483.

42.   Flügel, 'Kleinere Mitteilungen', p. 483.

43.   Flügel, 'Kleinere Mitteilungen', p. 483.

44.   Flügel, 'Kleinere Mitteilungen', p. 483.

45.   Philippa Maddern, 'Social Mobility', in *A Social History of England*, pp. 113–33 (pp. 130–32).

46.   James, *Tudor Magnate*; Richard W. Hoyle, 'Henry Percy, Sixth Earl of Northumberland, and the Fall of the House of Percy, 1527–1537', in *The Tudor Nobility*, pp. 180–209.

Bibliography

Manuscripts

Brussels, Royal Library, MS 7776-7781

London, British Library, Royal 18.D.ii

Munich, Bayerische Staatsbibliothek, Clm. 1133

Paris, Bibliothèque nationale, fonds latin, 5574

Electronic Sources

Petrarch's *Trionfi*: http://petrarch.petersadlon.com/trionfi.html

Halmii Codices Latini Monacenses: http://webserver.erwin-rauner.de/halm/vsign_saec.asp?provenienz=Bened

Printed Primary Sources

Aegidius Romanus, *The Governance of Kings and Princes: John Trevisa's Middle English Translation of the* De regimine principum *of Aegidius Romanus*, ed. David C. Fowler, Charles F. Briggs and Paul G. Remley, Garland Medieval Texts 19 (London and New York: Routledge, 1997)

Ælfric, *Ælfric's Lives of Saints*, ed. Walter W. Skeat, EETS, o.s. 76, 82, 94, 114 (London: Oxford University Press, 1881–1900; repr. in 2 vols, 1966)

—— , *Angelsachsische Homilien und Heiligenleben*, ed. Bruno Assmann (Kassel: G.H. Wigand, 1889; repr. Darmstadt: G.H. Wigand, 1964), pp. 199–207

Aldhelm: The Prose Works, trans. Michael Lapidge and Michael Herren (Ipswich: D.S. Brewer, 1979)

Aldhelmi Malmesbiriensis Prosa De Virginitate: Cum Glosa Latina Atque Anglosaxonica, ed. Scott Gwara, 2 vols (Turnhout: Brepols Publishers, 2001)

Ambrose, 'Letter No. 25', in *Saint Ambrose: Letters*, trans. M.M. Beyenke (New York: Fathers of the Church, 1954), p. 132

Anne de France, *Les Enseignements d'Anne de France, suivis de l'Histoire du siège de Brest*, ed. Tatiana Clavier and Éliane Viennot (Saint-Etienne: Publications de l'Université de Saint-Etienne, 2006)

Augustine, 'City of God', in *A Select Library of Nicene and Post-Nicene Fathers of the Christian Church*, ed. Philip Schaff and Henry Wace, 14 vols (Buffalo: The Christian Literature Company, 1887), II, pp. 1–511

Bede, *Historia ecclesiastica gentis Anglorum: Bede's Ecclesiastical History of the English People*, ed. and trans. Bertram Colgrave and Roger A.B. Mynors (Oxford: Clarendon Press, 1969)

Bevegnati, Giunta, *Legenda de vita et miraculis beatae Margaritae de Cortona*, ed. Fortunato Iozzelli (Grottaferrata: Ediciones Collegii S. Bonaventurae ad Claras Aquas, 1997)

Boccaccio, Giovanni, *Famous Women*, trans. Virginia Brown (Cambridge, MA and London: Harvard University Press, 2003)

Bonaventure, *De triplici via incendium amoris Fontes Christiani*, no. 14 (Freiburg: Herder, 1993)

Bruni, Leonardo, 'On the Study of Literature', in *The Humanism of Leonardo Bruni: Selected Texts*, ed. Gordon Griffiths, James Hankins and David Thompson (Binghamton, NY: Medieval and Renaissance Texts and Studies, 1987), pp. 240–51

Bullarium Franciscanum, ed. Conrado Eubel and Johannes H. Sbaralea, 7 vols (Rome: Quaracci, 1759–1904)

Cereta, Laura, *Collected Letters of a Renaissance Feminist*, ed. and trans. Diana Robin (Chicago: University of Chicago Press, 1997)

Christine de Pizan, *La Città delle dame*, ed. Patrizia Caraffi (Milan: Luni, 1997)

Chronica Villariensis monasterii, ed. Georg Waitz, *Monumenta Germaniae Historica, Scriptores*, 29 vols (Hanover: Hahn, 1826–94), XXV, pp. 192–235

'De b. Goberto confessor, Ordinis Cisterciensis, in abbatia Villariensi in Brabantia' *AASS*, Aug. IV, pp. 370–95

'De b. Nicolao fratre converso Ordinis Cisterciensis Villarii in Brabantia', *AASS*, Nov. IV, pp. 277–79

Dufour, Antoine, *Les Vies des femmes célèbres*, ed. G. Jeanneau (Geneva: Droz, 1970)

Duvivier, Charles Albert, *La Querelle des Avesnes et des Dampierre, jusqu'à la mort de Jean d'Avesnes, 1257*, 2 vols (Brussels: C. Muquardt/Paris: Alphonse Picard, 1894)

Gislebertus of Mons, *Chronicon Hanoniense. Chronicle of Hainaut*, trans. and ed. Laura Napran (Woodbridge: Boydell, 2005)

Goswin of Bossut, 'De b. Arnulfo monacho, Ordinis Cisterc. Villiarii in Brabantia', *AASS*, Iun. V, pp. 606–31

——— , 'De *Vita* Abundus van Hoei', ed. A.M. Frenken, *Cîteaux*, 10 (1959), 5–33

Isidore of Seville, 'Etymologiarum', *PL* 82, cc. 74–760

Jacques de Vitry, 'De b. Maria Oigniacensi in Namurcensi Belgii diocesii', *AASS*, Iun. IV, pp. 630–84

Jerome, 'Against Jovinian' in *A Select Library of Nicene and Post-Nicene Fathers of the Christian Church*, ed. by Philip Schaff and Henry Wace (Buffalo: The Christian Literature Company, 1887), VI, pp. 346–416

———, 'Vita Malchi monachi cativi,' *PL* 23, cc. 55–62

Le Franc, Martin, *Le Champion des dames*, ed. Robert Deschaux (Paris: Champion, 1999)

Lydgate and Burgh's Secrees of Old Philisoffres, ed. Robert Steele, EETS, e.s., 66 (London: Kegan Paul, Trench, Trübner, 1894)

Mouskes, Philippe, *Chronique rimée de Philippe Mouskes, évêque de Tournai au 13e siècle. Publiée pour la première fois avec des préliminaires, un commentaire, et des appendices*, ed. Baron de Reiffenberg, 2 vols (Brussels: M. Hayez, 1836)

Ovid, *Metamorphoses*, ed. Richard J. Tarrant (Oxford: Oxford University Press, 2004)

'Passio S. Margaretae', in *Sanctuarium seu Vitae Sanctorum*, ed. Boninus Mombritius, 2 vols (Paris: Fontemoing et Socios, 1910), II, pp. 190–96

Percy, Henry Algernon, *The Regulations and Establishment of the Houshold [sic] of Henry Algernon Percy, Fifth Earl of Northumberland*, ed. Thomas Percy (London: William Pickering, 1827)

[Pierre de Brinon], *Le Triomphe des dames* (Rouen: Jean Osmont, 1599)

Policraticus, *Policraticus: Of the Frivolities of Courtiers and the Footprints of Philosophers* ed. Cary J. Nederman (Cambridge: Cambridge University Press, 1990)

Secretum secretorum: Nine English Versions, ed. Mahmoud A. Manzalaoui, EETS, o.s., 276 (Oxford: Oxford University Press, 1977)

Severius, 'Commentarius in artem Donati', in *Grammatici Latini*, ed. Heinrich Keil, 7 vols (Leipzig: B.G. Teubner, 1864), IV, pp. 403–48

Speculum Virginum, ed. Jutta Seyfarth, *Corpus Christianorum Continuatio Mediaevalis* 5 (Turnhout: Brepols, 1990)

Sulpicius Severus, *Vie de saint Martin*, ed. and trans. Jacques Fontaine, Sources Chrétiennes 133 (Paris: Les Editions du Cerf, 1967)

Tertullian, 'On the Apparel of Women', in *The Ante-Nicene Fathers*, ed. Alexander Roberts and James Donaldson, 10 vols (Peabody, MA: Hendrickson Publishers, 1994), IV, pp. 14–25

The Fifteen Joys of Marriage, trans. Brent A. Pitts (New York: Peter Lang, 1985)

The Old English Lives of St. Margaret, ed. Mary Clayton and Hugh Magennis (Cambridge and New York: Cambridge University Press, 1994)

Thomas de Cantimpré, 'De s. Christina mirabili virgine vita', *AASS*, Iul. V, pp. 637–60

———, 'De s. Lutgarde virgine, sanctimoniali Ordinis Cisterciensis, Aquiriae in Brabantia', *AASS*, Iun. III, pp. 231–63

Three Prose Versions of the Secreta secretorum, ed. Robert Steele, EETS, e.s., 74 (London: Kegan Paul, Trench, Trübner, 1898)

'*Vita* domni Werrici, prioris de Alna', in *Catalogus Codicum Hagiographicorum Bibliothecae Regiae Bruxellensis*, 2 vols (Brussels: Typis Polleunis, Ceuterick and Lefébure, 1886), I, pp. 445–63

Wadding, Lucas, *Annales Minorum seu trium ordinum a S. Francesco institutorum auctore*, VI (Lyon: No Pub., 1626)

William of St. Thierry, et al., 'Vita prima sancti Bernardi', *PL* 185, cc. 225–368

Printed Secondary Sources

Abou-El-Haj, Barbara Fay, *The Medieval Cult of Saints: Formations and Transformations* (Cambridge and New York: Cambridge University Press, 1994)

Aceto, Francesco, 'Un'opera "ritrovata" di Pacio Bertini: il sepolcro di Sancia di Maiorca in Santa Croce a Napoli e la questione dell'"usus pauper"', *Prospettiva*, 100 (2000), 27–35

Adamson, John S.A., 'Chivalry and Political Culture in Caroline England', in *Culture and Politics in Early Stuart England*, ed. Kevin Sharpe and Peter Lake (Houndmills: Macmillan, 1994), pp. 161–98

Aers, David, and Lynn Staley, *The Powers of the Holy: Religion, Politics, and Gender in Late Medieval Culture* (Pennsylvania: Pennsylvania State Press, 1996)

Alexander, Jonathan J.G., *Medieval Illuminators and Their Methods of Work* (New Haven: Yale University Press, 1992)

———— , and M.T. Gibson, eds, *Medieval Learning and Literature* (Oxford: Oxford University Press, 1976)

Angelos, Mark, 'Urban Women, Investment, and the Commercial Revolution of the Middle Ages', in *Women in Medieval Western European Culture*, ed. Linda E. Mitchell (New York: Garland Publishing, 1999), pp. 257–72

Ariès, Philippe, and André Béjin, eds, *Western Sexuality: Practice and Precept in Past and Present Times*, trans. Anthony Forster (Oxford: Basil Blackwell, 1985)

Armour, Ellen T., and Susan St. Ville, eds, *Bodily Citations: Religion and Judith Butler* (New York: Columbia University Press, 2006)

Armstrong, Michael S., and Peter Jackson, 'Job and Jacob in the Old English *Life of Malchus*', *Notes and Queries*, 49 (2002), pp. 10–12

Arnold, John, 'The Labour of Continence: Masculinity and Clerical Virginity', in *Medieval Virginities*, ed. Anke Bernau, Ruth Evans and Sarah Salih (Cardiff: University of Wales Press, 2003), pp. 102–18

Ashley, Kathleen, and Robert L.A. Clark, *Medieval Conduct* (London and Minneapolis: University of Minnesota Press, 2001)

Aspegren, Kerstin, *The Male Woman: A Feminine Ideal in the Early Church* (Stockholm: Almqvist and Wiksell International, 1990)

Barratt, Dorothy M., 'A Second Northumberland Household Book', *Bodleian Library Record*, 8 (1968), 93–98

Baskins, Cristelle L., *Cassone Painting, Humanism, and Gender in Early Modern Italy* (Cambridge and New York: Cambridge University Press, 1998)

Baxandall, Michael, *Painting and Experience in Fifteenth-Century Italy: A Primer in the Social History of Pictorial Style* (Oxford: Oxford University Press, 1972; repr. 1986)

Beach, Alison I., *Women as Scribes: Book Production and Monastic Reform in Twelfth-Century Bavaria* (Cambridge: Cambridge University Press, 2004)

Beer, Gillian, 'Representing Women, Re-Presenting the Past', in *The Feminist Reader*, ed. Catherine Belsey and Jane Moore (London: Blackwell, 1989), pp. 77–90

Bennett, Judith, and Amy Froide, *Singlewomen in the European Past, 1250–1800* (Philadelphia: University of Pennsylvania Press, 1999)

Berdini, Paolo, 'Women under the Gaze: A Renaissance Genealogy', *Art History*, 21 (1998), 565–90

Bernard, George W., *The Power of the Early Tudor Nobility: A Study of the Fourth and Fifth Earls of Shrewsbury* (Brighton: Harvester Press, 1985)

———— , *The Tudor Nobility* (Manchester: Manchester University Press, 1992)

Bernau, Anke, Ruth Evans, and Sarah Salih, eds, *Medieval Virginities* (Cardiff: University of Wales Press, 2003)

Biddick, Kathleen, 'Genders, Bodies, Borders: Technologies of the Visible', *Speculum*, 68 (1993), 389–418

Biernoff, Suzannah, *Sight and Embodiment in the Middle Ages* (New York: Palgrave Macmillan, 2002)

Biggs, Frederick M., 'Ælfric as Historian: His Use of Alcuin's *Laudationes* and Sulpicius' *Dialogues* in his Two Lives of Martin', in *Holy Men and Holy Women: Old English Prose Saints' Lives and their Contexts*, ed. Paul E. Szarmach (Albany: State of New York University Press, 1996), pp. 289–316

Blade, Melinda K., *Education of Italian Renaissance Women* (Mesquite: Ida House Inc., 1983)

Blamires, Alcuin, ed., *Woman Defamed and Woman Defended: An Anthology of Medieval Texts* (Oxford: Clarendon Press, 1992)

Bleyerveld, Yvonne, 'Powerful Men, Foolish Women: The Popularity of the "Power of Women" Topos in Art', in *Women of Distinction: Margaret of York-Margaret of Austria*, ed. Dagmar Eichberger (Leuven: Brepols, 2005), pp. 167–75

Blumenfeld-Kosinski, Renate and Timea Klara Szell, eds, *Images of Sainthood in Medieval Europe* (Ithaca: Cornell University Press, 1991)

Bologna, Ferdinando, *I pittori alla corte angioina di Napoli 1266–1414* (Rome: Ugo Bozzi, 1969)

Boone, Marc, 'Urban Space and Political Conflict in Late Medieval Flanders', *Journal of Interdisciplinary History*, 32 (2002), 621–40

Boyer, Jean-Paul, 'La "Foi Monarchique": Royaume de Sicile et Provence', in *Le Forme delle Propaganda Politica nel due a nel Trecento*, ed. Philippe Contamine (Rome: Ecole française de Rome, 1993), pp. 85–110

Boydston, Jeanne, 'Gender as a Question of Historical Analysis', *Gender and History*, 20 (2008), 558–83

Bradley, Harriet, *Gender* (Cambridge: Polity, 2007)

Breitenstein, Renée-Claude, 'La rhétorique encomiastique dans les éloges collectifs de femmes imprimés de la première Renaissance française (1495–1555)' (unpublished doctoral thesis, McGill University, 2008)

Brown, Cynthia J., 'Le mécénat d'Anne de Bretagne et la politique du livre', in *Patronnes et mécènes en France à la Renaissance*, ed. Kathleen Wilson-Chevalier (St Etienne: University of St Etienne Press, 2007), pp. 195–224

———, *The Queen's Library: Image-Making at the Court of Anne of Brittany, 1477–1514* (Philadelphia and Oxford: University of Pennsylvania Press, 2011)

Brown-Grant, Rosalind, 'Writing Beyond Gender: Christine de Pizan's Linguistic Strategies in the Defence of Women', in *Contexts and Continuities: Proceedings of the IVth International Colloquium on Christine de Pizan (Glasgow 21–27 July 2000), Published in Honour of Liliane Dulac*, ed. Angus J. Kennedy et al., 3 vols (Glasgow: University of Glasgow Press, 2002), I, pp. 155–69

———, *French Romance of the Later Middle Ages: Gender, Morality, and Desire* (Oxford: Oxford University Press, 2008)

Bruzelius, Caroline, 'Hearing is Believing: Clarissan Architecture ca. 1213–1340', *Gesta*, 31 (1992), 83–91

———, *The Stones of Naples: Church Building in Angevin Italy 1266–1343* (New Haven: Yale University Press, 2004)

———, 'Queen Sancia of Mallorca and the Convent Church of Sta. Chiara in Naples', *Memoirs of the American Academy in Rome*, 40 (1995), 69–100

Bryan, Jennifer, *Looking Inward: Devotional Reading and the Private Self in Late Medieval England* (Philadelphia: University of Pennsylvania Press, 2007)

Bubenicek, Michelle, *Quand les femmes gouvernent: droit et politique au XIVe siècle, Yolande de France* (Paris: Ecole des Chartes, 2002)

Bucher, François, *The Pamplona Bibles: A Facsimile Compiled from Two Picture Bibles with Martyrologies Commissioned by King Sancho El Fuerte of Navarra (1194–1234): Amiens Manuscript Latin 108 and Harburg Ms. 1, 2, Lat. 4° 15* (New Haven: Yale University Press, 1971)

Bugge, John, *Virginitas: An Essay in the History of a Medieval Ideal* (The Hague: Martinus Nijhoff, 1975)

Bullough, Vern L., and James Brundage, eds, *Sexual Practices and the Medieval Church* (New York: Prometheus Books, 1982)

Burr, David, *The Spiritual Franciscans: From Protest to Persecution in the Century after Saint Francis* (University Park: Pennsylvania State University Press, 2001)

Burrow, John A., '"Young Saint, Old Devil": Reflections on a Medieval Proverb', *Review of English Studies*, 30 (1979), 385–96

———, *The Ages of Man: A Study in Medieval Writing and Thought* (Oxford: Clarendon Press, 1986)

Butler, Judith, *Gender Trouble: Feminism and the Subversion of Identity* (London and New York: Routledge, 1990; repr. 1999)

——— , *Bodies that Matter: On the Discursive Limits of 'Sex'* (London and New York: Routledge, 1993)

——— , *Undoing Gender* (London and New York: Routledge, 2004)

Bynum, Caroline Walker, *Jesus as Mother: Studies in the Spirituality of the High Middle Ages* (Berkeley: University of California Press, 1982)

——— , *Holy Feast and Holy Fast: The Religious Significance of Food to Medieval Women* (Berkeley and Los Angeles: University of California Press, 1986)

——— , '"…And Woman His Humanity": Female Imagery in the Religious Writing of the Later Middle Ages', in *Gender and Religion: On the Complexity of Symbols*, ed. Caroline Walker Bynum, Steven Harrell and Paula Richman (Boston: Beacon Press, 1986), 257–88

——— , *Fragmentation and Redemption: Essays on Gender and the Human Body in Medieval Religion* (New York: Zone Books, 1992)

Cadden, Joan, *Meanings of Sex Difference in the Middle Ages: Medicine, Science and Culture* (Cambridge: Cambridge University Press, 1993)

Camera, Matteo, *Elucubrazioni storico-diplomatiche su Giovanna I, regina di Napoli e Carlo III di Durazzo* (Salerno: Tip. Nazionale, 1889)

Camille, Michael, 'Obscenity under Erasure: Censorship in Medieval Illuminated Manuscripts', in *Obscenity: Social Control and Artistic Creation in the European Middle Ages*, ed. Jan M. Ziolkowski (Leiden and Boston: Brill, 1998), pp. 139–54

Campbell, Emma and Robert Mills, eds, *Troubled Vision: Gender, Sexuality and Sight in Medieval Text and Image* (Basingstoke: Macmillan Palgrave, 2004)

Carlson, Cindy L., and Angela Jane Weisl, eds, *Constructions of Widowhood and Virginity in the Middle Ages* (New York: St. Martin's Press, 1999)

Carrasco, Magdalena Elizabeth, 'Spirituality in Context: The Romanesque Illustrated Life of St. Radegund of Poitiers (Poitiers, Bibl. Mun., Ms 250)', *Art Bulletin*, 72 (1990), 414–35

Carubia, Josephine, Lorraine Dowler and Bonj Szczygiel, eds, *Landscape and Gender: Renegotiating Morality and Space* (London: Routledge, 2005)

Cassidy, Brendan, 'A Byzantine Saint in Tuscany: A Proposal for the Solution of a Trecento Enigma', *Arte Cristiana*, 83 (1995), 243–56

Castelli, Elizabeth, '"I Will Make Mary Male": Pieties of the Body and Gender Transformation of Christian Women in Late Antiquity', in *Body Guards: The Cultural Politics of Gender Ambiguity*, ed. Julia Epstein and Krista Straub (London and New York: Routledge, 1991), pp. 29–49

Caviness, Madeleine H., 'Patron or Matron? A Capetian Bride and a *Vade Mecum* for her Marriage Bed', *Speculum*, 68 (1993), 333–62

Cazelles, Brigitte, *The Lady as Saint: A Collection of French Hagiographic Romances of the Thirteenth Century* (Philadelphia: University of Pennsylvania Press, 1991)

Cherry, John, 'Healing through Faith: The Continuation of Medieval Attitudes to Jewellery into the Renaissance', *Renaissance Studies*, 15 (2001), 154–71

Clear, Matthew J., 'Piety and Patronage in the Mediterranean: Sancia of Majorca (1286–1345) Queen of Sicily, Provence and Jerusalem' (unpublished PhD thesis, University of Sussex, 2001)

Clover, Carol J., *Men, Women, and Chain Saws: Gender in the Modern Horror Film* (Princeton: Princeton University Press, 1992)

Coakley, John, *Women, Men and Spiritual Power: Female Saints and Their Male Interpreters* (New York: Columbia University Press, 2006)

Cohen, Jeffrey Jerome, *Medieval Identity Machines* (Minneapolis: University of Minnesota Press, 2003)

Coleman, Joyce, *Public Reading and the Reading Public in Late Medieval England and France* (Cambridge: Cambridge University Press, 1996), pp. 128–40

Collette, Carolyn P., *Species, Phantasms, and Images: Vision and Medieval Psychology in the Canterbury Tales* (Ann Arbor: University of Michigan Press, 2001)

Collins, Patricia Hill, *Black Feminist Thought: Consciousness and the Politics of Empowerment* (New York: Routledge, 1990; repr. 2000)

Connell, R.W., *Masculinities* (Cambridge: Polity Press, 1995)

——— , 'The Social Organization of Masculinity', in *The Masculinities Reader*, ed. Stephen M. Whitehall and Frank J. Barrett (Cambridge: Polity, 2001), pp. 30–51

Corona, Gabriella, 'Saint Basil in Anglo-Saxon Exeter', *Notes and Queries*, 49 (2002), 316–20

Cownie, Emma, 'The Cult of St. Edmund in the Eleventh and Twelfth Centuries – The Language and Communication of a Medieval Saint's Cult', *Neuphilologische Mitteilungen*, 99 (1998), 177–97

Crouch, David, *The Birth of Nobility: Constructing Aristocracy in England and France, 900–1300* (Harlow: Pearson Longman, 2005)

Cullum, Patricia H., and Katherine J. Lewis, eds, *Holiness and Masculinity in the Middle Ages* (Cardiff: University of Wales Press, 2004)

Cutler, Anthony, *The Hand of the Master: Craftsmanship, Ivory, and Society in Byzantium (9th–11th Centuries)* (Princeton: Princeton University Press, 1994)

Dalby, Marcia A., 'The Good Shepherd and the Soldier of God: Old English Homilies on St. Martin of Tours', *Neuphilologishe Mitteilungen*, 85 (1984), 422–34

Damico, Helen, and Alexandra Hennessy Olsen, eds, *New Readings on Women in Old English Literature* (Bloomington: Indiana University Press, 1990)

Davis, Isabel, *Writing Masculinity in the Later Middle Ages* (Cambridge: Cambridge University Press, 2007)

Davis, Natalie Zemon, *Society and Culture in Early-Modern France* (London: Duckworth, 1975)

De Cant, Geneviève, *Jeanne et Marguerite de Constantinople: Comtesses de Flandre et de Hainaut au XIIIe siècle* (Brussels: Editions Racine, 1995)

Delepierre, Octave, *Précis analytique des documents que renferme le Dépôt des Archives de la Flandre-occidentale à Bruges. Premier volume. Inventaire des pièces concernant la ville de Bruges, qui reposent aux archives générales du département du Nord à Lille. Année 1089 a 1359* (Bruges: Vandecasteele-Werbrouck, 1840)

D'Engenio, Cesare, *Napoli Sacra* (Naples: No Pub., 1623)

Dempsey, George T., 'Aldhelm of Malmesbury's Social Theology: The Barbaric Heroic Ideal Christianised', *Peritia*, 15 (2001), 58–80

De Stefano, Pietro, *Descrittione de i luoghi sacri della città di Napoli* (Naples: No Pub., 1560)

Dolso, Maria Teresa, *La 'Chronica XXIV Generalium'. Il difficile percorso dell'umilità nella storia francescana* (Padua: Centro Studi Antoniani, 2003)

Dor, Juliette, Lesley Johnson and Jocelyn Wogan-Browne, eds, *New Trends in Feminine Spirituality: The Holy Women of Liège and Their Impact* (Turnhout: Brepols, 1999)

Driver, Martha W., 'Mirrors of a Collective Past: Re-Considering Images of Medieval Women', in *Women and the Book: Assessing the Visual Evidence*, ed. Lesley Smith and Jane H.M. Taylor (London: The British Library and Toronto University Press, 1997), pp. 75–93

Dubois, Henri, *Les Foires de Chalons et le commerce dans la vallée de la Saône à la fin du Moyen Age: vers 1280–vers 1430* (Paris: Publications de la Sorbonne, 1976)

Dulac, Liliane, 'Un mythe didactique chez Christine de Pizan: Sémiramis ou la veuve héroïque (du *De mulieribus claris* de Boccace à la *Cité des Dames*)', in *Mélanges de philologie romane offerts à Charles Camproux*, 2 vols (Montpellier: Centre d'Estudis Occitans, 1978), I, pp. 315–43

Dumolyn, Jan, 'Nobles, Patricians and Officers: The Making of a Regional Political Elite in Late Medieval Flanders', *Journal of Social History*, 40 (2006), 431–52

Earenfight, Theresa, ed., *Queenship and Political Power in Medieval and Early Modern Spain* (Aldershot: Ashgate, 2005)

Edwards, Anthony S.G., 'Middle English Inscriptional Verse Texts', in *Texts and their Contexts: Papers from the Early Book Society*, ed. John Scattergood and Julia Boffey (Dublin: Four Courts Press, 1997), pp. 26–43

Elliott, Dyan, *Spiritual Marriage: Sexual Abstinence in Medieval Wedlock* (Princeton: Princeton University Press, 1993)

———, *Fallen Bodies: Pollution, Sexuality and Demonology in the Middle Ages* (Philadelphia: University of Pennsylvania Press, 1999)

———, 'Tertullian, the Angelic Life, and the Bride of Christ', in *Gender and Difference in the Middle Ages*, ed. Sharon Farmer and Carol Braun Pasternack (Minneapolis and London: University of Minnesota Press, 2003), pp. 16–33

Enenkel, Karl, 'In Search of Fame: Self-Representation in Neo-Latin Humanism', in *Medieval and Renaissance Humanism: Rhetoric, Representation, and Reform*, ed. Stephan Gersh and Bert Roest (Boston: Brill, 2003), pp. 73–114

Erler, Mary C., *Women, Reading and Piety in Late Medieval England* (Cambridge: Cambridge University Press, 2006)

—— , and Maryanne Kowalski, *Gendering the Master Narrative: Women and Power in the Middle Ages* (Ithaca: Cornell University Press, 2003)

Evans, Ruth, and Lesley Johnson, eds, *Feminist Readings in Middle English Literature: The Wife of Bath and All her Sect* (London: Routledge, 1994)

Evergates, Theodore, ed., *Aristocratic Women in Medieval France* (Philadelphia: University of Pennsylvania Press, 1999)

Falmagne, Thomas, *Un Texte en contexte: 'Les Flores Paradisi' et le milieu culturel de Villers en Brabant dans la première moitié du 13e* (Turnhout: Brepols, 2001)

Farmer, Sharon, and Carol Braun Pasternack, eds, *Gender and Difference the Middle Ages* (Minneapolis and London: University of Minnesota Press, 2003)

—— , and Barbara H. Rosenwein, eds, *Monks, Nuns, Saints and Outcasts: Religion in Medieval Society. Essays in Honour of Lester K. Little* (Ithaca and London: Cornell University Press, 2000)

Fenster, Thelma, 'Possible Odds: Christine de Pizan and the Paradoxes of Woman', in *Contexts and Continuities: Proceedings of the IVth International Colloquium on Christine de Pizan (Glasgow 21–27 July 2000), Published in Honour of Liliane Dulac,* ed. Angus J. Kennedy et al., 3 vols (Glasgow: University of Glasgow Press, 2002), II, pp. 355–66

Ferster, Judith, *Fictions of Advice: The Literature and Politics of Counsel in Late Medieval England* (Philadelphia: University of Pennsylvania Press, 1996)

Fetterley, Judith, *The Resisting Reader: A Feminist Approach to American Fiction* (Bloomington: Indiana University Press, 1978)

Fleck, Cathleen A., '"Blessed the eyes that see those things you see": The Trecento Choir Frescoes at Santa Maria Donnaregina in Naples', *Zeitschrift für Kunstgeschichte*, 67 (2004), 201–24

Fletcher, Christopher, 'Manhood and Politics in the Reign of Richard II', *Past and Present*, 189 (2005), 3–39

Flügel, Ewald, 'Kleinere Mitteilungen aus Handschriften', *Anglia*, 14 (1892), 463–501

Forey, Alan, 'The Military Orders and the Conversion of Muslims in the Twelfth and Thirteenth Centuries', *Journal of Medieval History*, 28 (2002), 1–22

Foucault, Michel, 'The Battle for Chastity', in *Western Sexuality: Practice and Precept in Past and Present Times*, ed. Philippe Ariès and André Béjin, trans. Anthony Forster (Oxford: Basil Blackwell, 1985), pp. 14–25

Fyler, John, 'Man, Men, and Women in Chaucer's Poetry', in *The Olde Daunce: Love, Friendship, Sex, and Marriage in the Medieval World*, ed. Robert R. Edwards and Stephen Spector (Albany: State University of New York Press, 1991), pp. 154–76

Gaglione, Mario, 'Qualche ipotesi e molti dubbi su due Fondazione Angione a Napoli: S. Chiara e S. Croce di Palazzo', *Campania Sacra*, 33 (2002), 61–108

—— , 'Sancia d'Aragona-Majorca: da regina di Sicilia e Gerusalemme a monaca di Santa Croce', *Archivio Storico per la storia delle Donne*, 1 (2004), 27–54

Gaites, Judith, 'Ælfric's Longer *Life of Saint Martin* and its Latin Sources: A Study in Narrative Technique', *Leeds Studies in English*, 13 (1982), 23–41

Garber, Marjorie, *Vice Versa: Bisexuality and the Eroticism of Everyday Life* (London: Penguin, 1995)

Gillespie, Alexandra, 'These proverbs yet do last': Lydgate, the Fifth Earl of Northumberland, and Tudor Miscellanies from Print to Manuscript', *Yearbook of English Studies*, 33 (2003), 215–32

Girouard, Mark, *Life in the English Country House* (New Haven and London: Yale University Press, 1978)

Given-Wilson, Chris, *The English Nobility in the Late Middle Ages: The Fourteenth-Century Political Community* (London: Routledge and Kegan Paul, 1987)

Glissen, John, 'Le privilège de masculinité dans le droit coutumier de la Belgique et du nord de la France', *Revue du Nord*, 43 (1961), 201–16

Godden, Malcolm R., 'Ælfric's Saints' Lives and the Problem of Miracles', *Leeds Studies in English*, 16 (1985), 83–100

Godefroy, Frédéric, *Dictionnaire de l'ancienne langue française et de tous ses dialectes du IXe au XVe siècle* (Paris: Vieweg, 1881–1902)

Goldberg, Jeremy P., *Medieval England: A Social History 1250–1550* (London: Arnold, 2004)

Grabar, André, *Christian Iconography: A Study of Its Origins* (Princeton: Princeton University Press, 1968)

Gray, Floyd, *Gender, Rhetoric and Print Culture in French Renaissance Writing* (Cambridge: Cambridge University Press, 2000)

Green, Monica, *Making Women's Medicine Masculine: The Rise of Male Authority in Premodern Gynaecology* (Oxford: Oxford University Press, 2008)

_____ , 'Gendering the History of Women's Healthcare', *Gender and History*, 20 (2008), 487–518

Green, Richard F., *Poets and Princepleasers: Literature and the English Court in the Late Middle Ages* (Toronto: University of Toronto Press, 1980)

Grisé, C. Annette, 'Women's Devotional Reading in Late Medieval England and the Gendered Reader', *Medium Aevum*, 71 (2002), 209–23

Grose, F., ed., *The Antiquarian Repertory*, 4 vols (London: Faulder and Son, 1807)

Grundmann, Herbert, *Religious Movements in the Middle Ages*, trans. Steven Rowan (Notre Dame: Notre Dame University Press, 1995)

Hadley, Dawn M., ed., *Masculinity in Medieval Europe* (London: Longman, 1999)

Hahn, Cynthia J., *Portrayed on the Heart: Narrative Effect in Pictorial Lives of Saints from the Tenth through the Thirteenth Century* (Berkeley: University of California Press, 2001)

Hamburger, Jeffrey, *Nuns as Artists: The Visual Culture of a Medieval Convent* (Berkeley: University of California Press, 1997)

_____ , *The Visual and the Visionary: Art and Female Spirituality in Late Medieval Germany* (New York: Zone Books, 1998)

Harriss, Gerald, *Shaping the Nation: England 1360–1461* (Oxford: Oxford University Press, 2005)

Hayum, André, 'A Renaissance Audience Considered: The Nuns at S. Apollonia and Castagno's *Last Supper*', *Art Bulletin*, 88 (2006), 243–66

Heene, Katrien, 'Deliberate Self-Harm and Gender in Medieval Saints' Lives', *Hagiographica*, 6 (1999), 213–33

Hemmerle, Josef, ed., *Das Bistum Augsburg I: Die Benediktinerabtei Benediktbeuern, Germania Sacra* (Berlin and New York: Walter de Gruyter, 1991)

Heullant-Donat, Isabelle, 'En amont de l'observance. Les lettres de Sancia, reine de Naples, aux chapitres généraux et leur transmission dans l'historiographie du XIVe siècle', in *Identités franciscaines à l'âge des Réformes*, ed. Frédéric Meyer and Ludovic Viallet (Chambéry: Presses Universitaires Blaise Pascal, 2005), pp. 73–100

Hoch, Adrian, 'Sovereignty and Closure in Trecento Naples: Images of Queen Sancia, Alias "Sister Clare"', *Arte Medievale*, 10 (1996), 121–39

Hollywood, Amy, *Sensible Ecstasy: Mysticism, Sexual Difference, and the Demands of History* (Chicago: University of Chicago Press, 2002)

Horner, Shari, 'The Violence of Exegesis: Reading the Bodies of Ælfric's Female Saints', in *Violence Against Women in Medieval Texts*, ed. Anna Roberts (Gainesville: University Press of Florida, 1998), pp. 22–43

Horrox, Rosemary, and W. Mark Ormrod, eds, *A Social History of England, 1200–1500* (Cambridge: Cambridge University Press, 2006)

Hotchkiss, Valerie, *Clothes Make the Man: Female Cross Dressing in Medieval Europe* (New York and London: Garland Publishing, 1996)

Howell, Martha, 'The Gender of Europe's Commercial Economy, 1200–1700', *Gender and History*, 20 (2008), 519–38

Huntington, Joanna, 'Edward the Celibate, Edward the Saint: Virginity in the Construction of Edward the Confessor', in *Medieval Virginities*, ed. Anke Bernau, Ruth Evans and Sarah Salih (Cardiff: University of Wales Press, 2003), pp. 119–39

Hutchinson, Jane Campbell, 'The Housebook Master and the Folly of the Wise Man', *Art Bulletin*, 48 (1966), 73–78

Irvine, Martin, 'Abelard and (Re)Writing the Male Body: Castration, Identity, and Remasculinization', in *Becoming Male in the Middle Ages*, ed. Jeffrey Jerome Cohen and Bonnie Wheeler (London: Garland Publishing, 1997), pp. 87–106

James, Mervyn E., *A Tudor Magnate and the Tudor State: Henry Fifth Earl of Northumberland* (York: St Anthony's Press, 1966)

Jardine, Lisa, 'Women Humanists: Education for What?', in *Feminism and Renaissance Studies*, ed. Lorna Hutson (Oxford: Oxford University Press, 1999), pp. 48–81

Johnson, Geraldine A., 'Beautiful Brides and Model Mothers: The Devotional and Talismanic Functions of Early Modern Marian Reliefs', in *The Material Culture of Sex, Marriage and Procreation in Premodern Europe*, ed. Anne L. McClaren and Karen Rosoff Encarnación (New York: Palgrave, 2001), pp. 135–61

Jordan, Constance, *Renaissance Feminism: Literary Texts and Political Models* (Ithaca: Cornell University Press, 1990)

Jordan, Erin, *Women, Power, and Religious Patronage in the Middle Ages* (New York: Palgrave-Macmillan, 2006)

Jordanova, Ludmilla, *History in Practice* (London: Edwards Arnold, 2000)

Kaeuper, Richard W., ed., *Violence in Medieval Society* (Woodbridge: Boydell Press, 2000)

Karras, Ruth M., 'Holy Harlots: Prostitute Saints in Medieval Legend', *Journal of the History of Sexuality*, 1 (1990), 3–32

_____ , *From Boys to Men: Formations of Masculinity in Late Medieval Europe* (Philadelphia: University of Pennsylvania Press, 2003)

_____ , 'Thomas Aquinas's Chastity Belt', in *Gender and Christianity in Medieval Europe*, ed. Lisa M. Bitel and Felice Lifshitz (Philadelphia: University of Pennsylvania Press, 2008), 52–67

Kay, Sarah, 'The Sublime Body of the Martyr: Violence in Early Romance Saints' Lives', in *Violence in Medieval Society*, ed. Richard W. Kaeuper (Woodbridge: Boydell Press, 2000), pp. 3–20

_____ , 'Original Skin: Flaying, Reading, and Thinking in the Legend of Saint Bartholomew and Other Works', *Journal of Medieval and Early Modern Studies*, 36 (2006), 35–73

Kelly, Kathleen Coyne, and Marina Leslie, eds, *Menacing Virgins: Representing Virginity in the Middle Ages and Renaissance* (London: London: Associated University Presses, 1999)

Kelly, Samantha, *The New Solomon: Robert of Naples (1309–1343) and Fourteenth-Century Kingship* (Leiden: Brill, 2003)

King, Margaret, *Women of the Renaissance* (Chicago: University of Chicago Press, 1991)

_____ , 'Petrarch, the Self-Conscious Self, and the First Women Humanists', *Journal of Medieval and Early Modern Studies*, 35 (2005), 537–58

_____ , and Albert Rabil, Jr., eds, *Her Immaculate Hand: Selected Works By and About the Women Humanists of Quattrocento Italy* (Binghamton, NY: Medieval and Renaissance Texts and Studies, 1983)

Kittell, Ellen E., 'Guardianship over Women in Medieval Flanders: A Reappraisal', *Journal of Social History*, 31 (1998), 897–930

_____ , 'Women, Audience, and Public Acts in Medieval Flanders,' *Journal of Women's History*, 10 (1998), 74–96

_____ , and Kurt Queller, '"Whether Man or Woman": Gender Inclusivity in the Town Ordinances of Medieval Douai', *Journal of Medieval and Early Modern Studies*, 30 (2000), 63–100

Klaniczay, Gábor, *Holy Rulers and Blessed Princesses: Dynastic Cults in Medieval Central Europe* (Cambridge: Cambridge University Press, 2002)

Klapisch-Zuber, Christiane, *Women, Family and Ritual in Renaissance Italy*, trans. Lydia G. Cochrane (Chicago: University of Chicago Press, 1987)

Knox, Lezlie, 'Audacious Nuns: Institutionalizing the Franciscan Order of Saint Clare', *Church History*, 69 (2000), 41–62

—— , *Creating Clare of Assisi* (Leiden: Brill, 2008)

Kolsky, Stephen, *The Ghost of Boccaccio* (Turnhout: Brepols, 2005)

Korieh, Chima J., and Philomina E. Okeke-Ihejirika, eds, *Gendering Global Transformations: Gender, Culture, Race, and Identity* (London: Routledge, 2008)

Kuefler, Mathew, *The Manly Eunuch: Masculinity, Gender Ambiguity and Christian Ideology in Late Antiquity* (Chicago and London: University of Chicago Press, 2001)

—— , 'Male Friendship and the Suspicion of Sodomy in Twelfth-Century France', in *Gender and Difference in the Middle Ages*, ed. Sharon Farmer and Carol Braun Pasternack (Minneapolis and London: University of Minnesota Press, 2003), pp. 145–81

Krug, Rebecca, *Reading Families: Women's Literate Practice in Late Medieval England* (Ithaca and London: Cornell University Press, 2002)

Kruger, Steven F., 'Becoming Christian, Becoming Male', in *Becoming Male in the Middle Ages*, ed. Jeffrey Jerome Cohen and Bonnie Wheeler (London: Garland Publishing, 1997), pp. 21–41

Kurath, Hans, and Robert E. Lewis, eds, *Middle English Dictionary*, 118 fascicles (Ann Arbor, MI: University of Michigan Press, 1953–2001)

Labande, Edmond-René, 'Les filles d'Aliénor d'Aquitaine: étude comparative', *Cahiers de civilisation médiévale Xe–XIIe siècles*, 39 (1986), 101–12

Lancashire, Ian, 'Orders for Twelfth Day and Night *circa* 1515 in the Second Northumberland Household Book', *English Literary Renaissance*, 10 (1980), 7–45

Lapidge, Michael, 'Litanies of the Saints in Anglo-Saxon Manuscripts: A Preliminary List', *Scriptorium*, 40 (1986), pp. 264–77

Laqueur, Thomas, *Making Sex: Body and Gender from the Greeks to Freud*, 8th edn (Cambridge, MA and London: Harvard University Press, 1999)

Larsen, Ruth M., 'Expressions of Nobility: Conspicuous Consumption and Segregation in the Household of the Fifth Earl of Northumberland' (unpublished MA dissertation, University of York, 1998)

Larson, Wendy, 'Who is the Master of This Narrative? Maternal Patronage and the Cult of St. Margaret', *Gendering the Master Narrative: Women and Power in the Middle Ages*, ed. Mary C. Erler and Maryanne Kowaleski (Ithaca and London: Cornell University Press, 2003), pp. 94–104

Lauwers, Michel, 'L'Expérience béguinale et récit hagiographique: à propos de la *Vita Mariae Oigniacensis* de Jacques de Vitry', *Journal des savants*, 11 (1989), 61–103

Leclercq, Jean, 'Conversion to the Monastic Life: Who, Why and How?', in *Studiosorum Speculum: Studies in Honour of Louis J. Lekai O. Cist.*, ed. Francis R. Swietek and John R. Sommerfeldt (Kalamazoo: Cistercian Publications, 1993), pp. 201–32

Lefèvre, Jean-Baptiste, 'Gobert, seigneur d'Aspremont et moine de Villers (v. 1187–1263)', *Villers*, 8 (1998), 5–13

———, 'L'Abbaye de Villers et le monde des moniales et des béguines au XIIIe siècle', *Villers: Une Abbaye revisitée* (Villers-la-Ville: APTCV, Actes du colloque 10–12 avril 1996), pp. 183–230

L'Estrange, Elizabeth, *Holy Motherhood: Gender, Dynasty and Visual Culture in the Later Middle Ages* (Manchester: Manchester University Press, 2008)

Lettenhove, Baron Kervyn de, ed., *Istore et croniques de Flandres d'après les textes de divers manuscripts*, 2 vols (Brussels: F. Hayez, 1879)

Lewis, Katherine J., 'Becoming a Virgin King: Richard II and Edward the Confessor', in *Gender and Holiness: Men, Women and Saints in Late Medieval Europe*, ed. Samantha J.E. Riches and Sarah Salih (London and New York: Routledge, 2002), pp. 86–100

Lochrie, Karma, Peggy McCracken and James Schultz, eds, *Constructing Medieval Sexuality* (Minneapolis: University of Minnesota Press, 1997)

LoPrete, Kimberly A., 'Adela of Blois: Familial Alliances and Female Lordship', in *Aristocratic Women in Medieval France*, ed. Theodore Evergates (Philadelphia: University of Pennsylvania Press, 1999), pp. 7–43

———, 'The Gender of Lordly Women: The Case of Adela of Blois', in *Pawns or Players? Studies on Medieval and Early Modern Women*, ed. Christine Meek and Catherine Lawless (Dublin: Four Courts Press, 2003), pp. 90–110

Luykx, Theo, *De Grafelijke Financiële Bestuursinstellingen en het Grafelijk Patrimonium in Vlaanderen tijdens de Regering van Margareta Van Constantinopel (1244–1278)* (Brussels: Paleis der Academiën, 1961)

Maddern, Philippa, 'Social Mobility', in *A Social History of England*, ed. Rosemary Horrox and W. Mark Ormrod (Cambridge: Cambridge University Press, 2006), pp. 113–33

Matter, E. Ann, 'Mystical Marriage', in *Women and Faith: Catholic Religious Life in Italy from Late Antiquity to the Present* (Boston: Harvard University Press, 1993), pp. 31–41

McCracken, Peggy, *The Curse of Eve, the Wound of the Hero: Blood, Gender, and Medieval Literature* (Philadelphia: University of Pennsylvania Press, 2003)

McDonald, Nicola F., and W. Mark Ormrod, *Rites of Passage: Cultures of Transition in Fourteenth-Century England* (Woodbridge: Boydell, 2004)

McGinn, Bernard, *The Flowering of Mysticism* (New York: The Crossroad Publishing Company, 1998)

McGuire, Brian Patrick, 'Self-Denial and Self-Assertion in Arnulf of Villers' *Cistercian Studies Quarterly*, 28 (1993), 241–59

McInerney, Maud Burnett, *Eloquent Virgins from Thecla to Joan of Arc* (New York: Palgrave Macmillan, 2003)

_____ ,'Rhetoric, Power and Integrity in the Passion of the Virgin Martyr', in *Menacing Virgins: Representing Virginity in the Middle Ages and Renaissance*, ed. Kathleen Coyne Kelly and Marina Leslie (London: London Associated University Presses, 1999), pp. 50–70

McNamara, Jo Ann, 'An Unresolved Syllogism: The Search for a Christian Gender System', in *Conflicted Identities and Multiple Masculinities: Men in the Medieval West*, ed. Jacqueline Murray (New York: Garland Publishing, 1999), pp. 1–24

_____ , and Suzanne Wemple, 'The Power of Women through the Family in Medieval Europe, 500–1100', in *Women and Power in the Middle Ages*, ed. Mary C. Erler and Maryanne Kowaleski (Athens, GA: University of Georgia Press), pp. 83–101

Mertes, R.A. Kate, 'The Household as a Religious Community', in *People, Politics and Community in the Later Middle Ages*, ed. Joel Rosenthal and Colin Richmond (Gloucester and New York: Sutton, 1987), pp. 123–39

Michalsky, Tanja, *Memoria und Repraesentation. Die Grabmäler des Königshauses Anjou in Italien* (Göttingen: Vandenhoeck & Ruprecht, 2000)

Michaud, M., *Histoire des Croisades* (Paris: Furne et Cie, 1854)

Miller, Helen, *Henry VIII and the English Nobility* (Oxford: Blackwell, 1986)

Mills, Robert, '"Whatever you do is a delight to me!" Masculinity, Masochism, and Queer Play in Representations of Male Martyrdom', *Exemplaria*, 13 (2001), 1–37

_____ , 'A Man is Being Beaten', *New Medieval Literatures*, 5 (2002), 115–53

Minieri-Riccio, C., *Notizie Storiche Tratte da 62 Registri Angioini Dell'archivio di Stato di Napoli* (Naples: R. Rinaldi & G. Sellitto, 1877)

Monson, Craig, *Disembodied Voices: Music and Culture in an Early Modern Italian Convent* (Berkeley: University of California Press, 1995)

Mooney, Catherine M., ed., *Gendered Voices: Medieval Saints and their Interpreters* (Philadelphia: University of Pennsylvania Press, 1999)

_____ , 'Imitatio Christi or Imitatio Mariae? Clare of Assisi and her Interpreters', in *Gendered Voices: Medieval Saints and their Interpreters*, ed. Catherine M. Mooney (Philadelphia: University of Pennsylvania Press, 1999), pp. 52–77

_____ , 'Francis of Assisi as Father, Mother and Androgynous Figure', in *The Boswell Thesis: Essays on Christianity, Social Tolerance and Homosexuality*, ed. Mathew Kuefler (Chicago: University of Chicago Press, 2006), pp. 301–32

Mooney, Linne R., 'Lydgate's *Kings of England* and Another Verse Chronicle of the Kings', *Viator*, 20 (1989), 255–89

Moulton, Ian F., ed., *Reading and Literacy in the Middle Ages and Renaissance* (Turnhout: Brepols, 2004)

Mounsey, Chris, *Presenting Gender: Changing Sex in Early Modern Culture* (London: Associated University Presses, 2001)

Muir, Carolyn Diskant, 'Bride or Bridegroom? Masculine Identity in Mystic Marriage', in *Holiness and Masculinity*, ed. Katherine J. Lewis and Patricia Cullum (Cardiff: University of Wales Press, 2004), pp. 58–78

Mulder-Bakker, Anneke B.,'Jeanne of Valois: The Power of a Consort', in *Capetian Women*, ed. Kathleen Nolan (New York: Palgrave, 2003), pp. 255–69

Mulvey, Laura, *Visual and Other Pleasures* (Basingstoke: Macmillan, 1989)

Murray, Jacqueline, ed., *Conflicted Identities and Multiple Masculinities: Men in the Medieval West* (New York: Garland Publishing, 1999)

_____ , 'Mystical Castration: Some Reflections on Peter Abelard, Hugh of Lincoln and Sexual Purity', in *Conflicted Identities and Multiple Masculinities*, ed. Jacqueline Murray (New York: Garland Publishing, 1999), pp. 73–110

_____ , '"The law of sin that is in my members": The Problem of Male Embodiment', in *Gender and Holiness: Men, Women and Saints in Late Medieval Europe*, ed. Samantha J.E. Riches and Sarah Salih (London and New York: Routledge, 2002), pp. 9–22

_____ , 'Masculinizing Religious Life: Sexual Prowess, the Battle for Chastity and Monastic Identity', in *Holiness and Masculinity*, ed. Katherine J. Lewis and Patricia Cullum (Cardiff: University of Wales Press, 2004), pp. 24–42

Musacchio, Jacqueline Marie, 'Weasels and Pregnancy in Renaissance Italy', *Renaissance Studies*, 15 (2001), 172–87

_____ , *The Art and Ritual of Childbirth in Renaissance Italy* (New Haven and London: Yale, 1999)

Musto, Ronald, 'Franciscan Joachimism at the Court of Naples, 1309–1345: A New Appraisal', *Archivium Franciscanum Historicum*, 90 (1997), 419–86

_____ , 'Queen Sancia of Naples (1286–1345) and the Spiritual Franciscans', in *Women of the Medieval World: Essays in Honor of John H. Mundy*, ed. Julius Kirshner and Suzanne F. Wemple (Oxford: Blackwell, 1985), pp. 179–214

Neal, Derek, *The Masculine Self in Medieval England* (Chicago: University of Chicago Press, 2008)

Nelson, Janet L., 'Monks, Secular Men and Masculinity c. 900', in *Masculinity in Medieval Europe*, ed. Dawn M. Hadley (London: Longman, 1999), pp. 121–42

Newman, Barbara, *From Virile Woman to WomanChrist: Studies in Medieval Religion and Literature* (Philadelphia: University of Pennsylvania Press, 1995)

Newman, Martha, *The Boundaries of Charity* (Stanford: Stanford University Press, 1996)

_____ , '"Crucified by the Virtues": Monks, Lay Brothers and Women in Thirteenth-Century Cistercian Saints' Lives', in *Gender and Difference in the Middle Ages*, ed. Sharon Farmer and Carol Braun Pasternack (Minneapolis and London: University of Minnesota Press, 2003), pp. 182–209

_____ , 'Real Men and Imaginary Women: Engelhard of Langheim Considers a Woman in Disguise', *Speculum*, 78 (2003), 1184–213

Nicholas, Karen S., 'Countesses as Rulers in Flanders', in *Aristocratic Women in Medieval France*, ed. Theodore Evergates (Philadelphia: University of Pennsylvania Press, 1999), pp. 111–37

Noell, Brian, 'Expectation and Unrest Among Cistercian Lay Brothers in the Twelfth and Thirteenth Centuries', *Journal of Medieval History*, 32 (2006), 253–74

Nolan, Kathleen, ed., *Capetian Women* (New York: Palgrave, 2003)

Oakley, Ann, *Sex, Gender and Society* (San Francisco: Harper Collins, 1972)

―――― , 'A Brief History of Gender', in *Who's Afraid of Feminism: Seeing Through the Backlash*, ed. Ann Oakley and Juliet Mitchell (New York: The New Press, 1997), pp. 29–55

Orme, Nicholas, *From Childhood to Chivalry: The Education of the English Kings and Aristocracy, 1066–1530* (London and New York: Methuen, 1984)

―――― , 'The Education of Edward V', *Bulletin of the Institute of Historical Research*, 57 (1984), 119–30

Ormrod, W. Mark, 'Coming to Kingship: Boy Kings and the Passage to Power in the Fourteenth Century', in *Rites of Passage: Cultures of Transition in Fourteenth-Century England*, ed. Nicola F. McDonald and W. Mark Ormrod (Woodbridge: Boydell, 2004), pp. 31–49

Osborne, Peter, and Lynne Segal, 'Gender as Performance: An Interview with Judith Butler', *Radical Philosophy*, 67 (1994), 32–39

O'Sullivan, Sinéad, '*Aldhelm's De Virginitate* – Patristic Pastiche or Innovative Exposition?', *Peritia*, 12 (1998), 271–95

Paciocco, Roberto, 'Angioini and "Spirituali". I differenti piani cronologici e tematici di un problema', in *L'Etat Angevin: pouvoir, culture et société entre XIIIe et XIVe siècle* (Rome: Ecole française de Rome, 1998), pp. 253–87

Pantin, W.A., 'Instructions for a Devout and Literate Layman', in *Medieval Learning and Literature*, ed. Jonathan J.G. Alexander and Margaret T. Gibson (Oxford: Oxford University Press, 1976), pp. 398–422

Parker, Holt, 'The Magnificence of Learned Women', *Viator*, 38 (2007), 265–89

―――― , 'Women and Humanism: Nine Factors for the Woman Learning', *Viator*, 35 (2004), 581–616

Parsons, John Carmi, ed., *Medieval Queenship* (New York: St. Martin's Press, 1993)

Pasternack, Carol Braun, 'The Sexual Practices of Virginity and Chastity in Aldhelm's *De Virginitate*', in *Sex and Sexuality in Anglo-Saxon England: Essays in Memory of Daniel Gillmore Calder*, ed. Carol Braun Pasternack and Lisa M.C. Weston (Tempe: Arizona Center for Medieval and Renaissance Studies, 2004), pp. 93–120

Pearson, Andrea, *Envisioning Gender in Burgundian Devotional Art, 1350–1530: Experience, Authority, Resistance* (Aldershot: Ashgate, 2005)

Petrowiste, Judicaël, *A la foire d'empoigne. Foires et marchés en Aunis et Saintonge au Moyen Age (vers 1000 – vers 1500)* (Toulouse: CNRS-Université de Toulouse-Le Mirail, 2004)

Pettit, Emma, 'Holiness and Masculinity in Aldhelm's *Opus Geminatum De Virginitate*', in *Holiness and Masculinity*, ed. Katherine J. Lewis and Patricia Cullum (Cardiff: University of Wales Press, 2004), pp. 8–23

Phillips, Kim M., 'Bodily Walls, Windows, and Doors: The Politics of Gesture in Late Fifteenth-Century English Books for Women', in *Medieval Women: Texts and Contexts in Late Medieval Britain: Essays for Felicity Riddy*, ed. Jocelyn Wogan-Browne et al. (Turnhout: Brepols, 2000), pp. 185–98

Phillippy, Patricia A., 'Establishing Authority: Boccaccio's *De claris mulieribus* and Christine de Pizan's *Le Livre de la cité des dames*', *Romanic Review*, 77 (1986), 167–94

Poignant, Simone, *La Foire de Lille. Contribution à l'étude des foires flamandes au Moyen Age* (Lille: Chez Emile Raoust, 1932)

Polinsky, Maria and Ezra van Everbroeck, 'Development of Gender Classifications: Modelling the Historical Change from Latin to French', *Language*, 79 (2003), 356–90

Rabil, Albert, 'Laura Cereta', *Italian Women Writers: A Bio-Bibliographical Sourcebook*, ed. Rinaldina Russell (Westport, CT: Greenwood Press, 1994), pp. 67–75

Randolph, Adrian W.B., 'Gendering the Period Eye: *Deschi da parto* and Renaissance Visual Culture', *Art History*, 27 (2004), 538–62

—— , 'Renaissance Household Goddesses: Fertility, Politics, and the Gendering of Spectatorship', in *The Material Culture of Sex, Marriage and Procreation in Premodern Europe*, ed. Anne L. McClaren and Karen Rosoff Encarnación (New York: Palgrave, 2001), pp. 163–89

Rawcliffe, Carole, *Medicine and Society in Later Medieval England* (Stroud: Alan Sutton, 1995)

Richards, Mary P., and Jane B. Stanfield, 'Concepts of Anglo-Saxon Women in the Laws', in *New Readings on Women in Old English Literature*, ed. Helen Damico and Alexandra Hennessy Olsen (Bloomington: Indiana University Press, 1990), pp. 89–99

Riches, Samatha J.E., and Sarah Salih, eds, *Gender and Holiness: Men, Women and Saints in Late Medieval Europe* (London and New York: Routledge, 2002)

Riddy, Felicity, '"Women talking about the things of God": A Late Medieval Sub-culture', in *Women and Literature in Britain 1150–1500*, ed. Carol M. Meale (Cambridge: Cambridge University Press, 1993), pp. 104–27

Rieder, Paula M., *On the Purification of Women: Churching in Northern France, 1100–1500* (New York: Palgrave Macmillan, 2006)

Rigaux, Dominique, *A la table du Seigneur: L'Eucharistie chez les primitifs italiens 1250–1497* (Paris: Cerf, 1989)

Riley, Denise, *Am I that Name?* (Minneapolis: University of Minnesota Press, 2003)

Roberts, Anna, ed., *Violence Against Women in Medieval Texts* (Gainesville: University Press of Florida, 1998)

Robertson, Elizabeth, 'The Corporeality of Female Sanctity in the Life of Saint Margaret', in *Images of Sainthood in Medieval Europe*, ed. Renate Blumenfeld-Kosinski and Timea Klara Szell (London: Cornell University Press, 1991), pp. 268–87

Robin, Diana, 'Woman, Space, and Renaissance Discourse', in *Sex and Gender in Medieval and Renaissance Texts: The Latin Tradition*, ed. Barbara K. Gold, Paul Allen Miller and Chris Platter (Albany: State University of New York Press, 1997), pp. 165–88

——— , 'Humanism and Feminism in Laura Cereta's Public Letters', in *Women in Italian Renaissance Culture and Society*, ed. Letizia Panizza (Oxford: Oxford University Press, 2000), pp. 368–83

Roest, Bert, 'Rhetoric and Recourse in Humanist Pedagogical Discourse', in *Medieval and Renaissance Humanism: Rhetoric, Representation, and Reform*, ed. Stephan Gersh and Bert Roest (Boston: Brill, 2003), pp. 115–48

Rollason, David W., *Saints and Relics in Anglo-Saxon England* (Oxford: Blackwell, 1989)

Roisin, Simone, *L'Hagiographie cistercienne dans le diocèse de Liège au XIIIe siècle* (Louvain: Bibliothèque de l'Université, 1947)

Romano, Elena, *Saggio di iconografia dei Reali angioini di Napoli* (Naples: Fratelli Bergamo, 1920)

Rosenthal, Joel, and Colin Richmond, *People, Politics and Community in the Later Middle Ages* (Gloucester and New York: Sutton, 1987)

Rosenwein, Barbara H., and Lester K. Little, 'Social Meaning in the Monastic and Mendicant Spiritualities', *Past and Present*, 63 (1974), 4–32

Rublack, Ulinka, 'Female Spirituality and the Infant Jesus in Late Medieval Dominican Convents', *Gender and History*, 6 (1994), 37–57

Saint Genois, Baron Jules de, *Inventaire analytique des chartes des comtes de Flandre, avant l'avènement des princes de la Maison de Bourgogne* (Ghent: Vanryckegem-Hovaere, 1843–46)

Salih, Sarah, *Versions of Virginity in Late Medieval England* (Cambridge: D.S. Brewer, 2001)

Saul, Nigel, 'Richard II and the Vocabulary of Kingship', *English Historical Review*, 110 (1995), 854–77

Sautman, Francesca Canadé and Pamela Sheingorn, eds, *Same Sex Love and Desire Among Women in the Middle Ages* (New York: Palgrave, 2001)

Scattergood, John, 'Skelton's *Magnyfycence* and the Tudor Royal Household', *Medieval English Theatre*, 15 (1993), 21–48

——— , and Julia Boffey, eds, *Texts and their Contexts: Papers from the Early Book Society* (Dublin: Four Courts Press, 1997)

Schiller, Gertrud, *Iconography of Christian Art*, trans. Janet Seligman (Greenwich, CT: New York Graphic Society, 1971)

Schmitz, Philip, 'Conversatio Morum', in *Dictionnaire de Spiritualité, ascétique et mystique, doctrine et histoire*, ed. Marcel Viller et al. 16 vols (Paris: Beachesne, 1932–95), ii, cc. 2206–12

Scott, Joan W., 'Gender: A Useful Category of Historical Analysis', *The American Historical Review*, 91 (1986), 1053–75

_____ , 'Gender: Still a useful Category of Analysis', *Diogenes*, 225 (2010), 7–14

Schulenburg, Jane Tibbetts, *Forgetful of Their Sex: Female Sanctity and Society, ca. 500–1100* (Chicago: University of Chicago Press, 1998)

Sensi, Mario, 'Clarisses entre spirituels et observants', in *Sainte Claire d'Assise et sa postérité, Actes du colloque international organisé à l'occasion du VIIIe centenaire de la naissance de sainte Claire: U.N.E.S.C.O., 29 septembre–1er octobre 1994*, ed. Geneviève Brunel-Lobrichon et al. (Nantes: Association Claire Aujourd'hui, 1995), pp. 101–18

Seroux d'Agincourt, J.B.L.G., *Histoire de l'art par les monuments, depuis sa décadence au IVe siècle jusqu'à son renouvellement au XIVe* (Paris: Treuttel and Würtz, 1823)

Sharpe, Kevin, and Peter Lake, eds, *Culture and Politics in Early Stuart England* (Houndmills: Macmillan, 1994)

Shaw, Alison, 'Changing Sex and Bending Gender: An Introduction', in *Changing Sex and Bending Gender*, ed. Alison Shaw and Shirley Ardener (New York: Berghahn Books, 2005)

Sheppard, Alexandra, *Meanings of Manhood in Early Modern England* (Oxford: Oxford University Press, 2006)

_____ , and Garthine Walker, 'Gender, Change and Periodisation', *Gender and History*, 20 (2008), 453–62

Shorr, Dorothy C., 'Some Notes on the Iconography of Petrarch's Triumph of Fame', *Art Bulletin*, 20 (1938), 100–107

Simons, Patricia, 'Women in Frames: The Gaze, the Eye, the Profile in Renaissance Portraiture', *History Workshop*, 25 (1988), 4–30

Simons, Walter, *Cities of Ladies: Beguine Communities in the Medieval Low Countries, 1200–1505* (Philadelphia: University of Pennsylvania Press, 2001)

Skemer, Don C., 'Amulet Rolls and Female Devotion in the Late Middle Ages', *Scriptorium*, 55 (2001), 197–227

Smith, Julia M.H., 'Introduction: Gendering the Early Medieval World', in *Gender in the Early Medieval World: East and West, 300–900*, ed. Leslie Brubacker and Julia M.H. Smith (Cambridge: Cambridge University Press, 2004), pp. 1–19

Smith, Katherine Allen, 'Saints in Shining Armor: Martial Asceticism and Masculine Models of Sanctity, ca. 1050–1250', *Speculum*, 83 (2008), 572–602

Solignac, Aimé, 'Voies', in *Dictionnaire de Spiritualité, ascétique et mystique, doctrine et histoire*, ed. Marcel Viller et al. 16 vols (Paris: Beachesne, 1932–95), xvi, cc. 1204–206

Spargo, John Webster, *Virgil the Necromancer: Studies in Virgilian Legends* (Cambridge, MA: Harvard University Press, 1934)

Spiegel, Gabrielle, 'Introduction', in *Practising History: New Directions in Historical Writing After the Linguistic Turn* (London and New York: Routledge, 2005)

Stoertz, Fiona Harris, 'Young Women in France and England: 1050–1300', *Journal of Women's History*, 12 (2001), 22–46

Stone, Lawrence, *The Crisis of the Aristocracy, 1558–1641* (Oxford: Clarendon Press, 1965)

Strocchia, Sharon, 'Learning the Virtues: Convent Schools and Female Culture in Renaissance Florence', in *Women's Education in Early Modern Europe: A History, 1500–1800*, ed. Barbara Whitehead (New York: Garland Publishing, 1999), pp. 3–46

Strohm, Paul, 'Reading and Writing', in *A Social History of England, 1200–1500*, ed. Rosemary Horrox and W. Mark Ormrod (Cambridge: Cambridge University Press, 2006), pp. 454–72

Sweetman, Robert, 'Christine of St. Trond's Preaching Apostolate: Thomas de Cantimpré's Hagiographical Method Revisited', in *On Pilgrimage*, ed. Margot King (Toronto: Peregrina Press, 1994), pp. 411–31

Swift, Helen J., *Gender, Writing and Performance: Men Defending Women in Late Medieval France, 1440–1538* (Oxford: Oxford University Press, 2008)

Synnott, Anthony, *Re-thinking Men: Heroes, Villains and Victims* (Farnham: Ashgate, 2009)

Taylor, Andrew, 'Into His Secret Chamber: Reading and Privacy in Late Medieval England', in *The Practice and Representation of Reading in England*, ed. James Raven, Helen Small and Naomi Tadmor (Cambridge: Cambridge University Press, 1996), pp. 41–61

TeBrake, William, *A Plague of Insurrection: Popular Politics and Peasant Revolt in Flanders, 1323–1328* (Philadelphia: University of Pennsylvania Press, 1993)

Thiellet, Claire, *Femmes, reines et saintes (Ve–XIe siècles)* (Paris: Presses de l'Université Paris–Sorbonne, 2004)

Toews, John, 'Intellectual History after the Linguistic Turn: The Autonomy of Meaning and the Irreducibility of Experience', *American Historical Review*, 92 (1987), 879–907

Tougher, Shaun, 'Social Transformation, Gender Transformation?': The Court Eunuch 300–900', in *Gender in the Early Medieval World: East and West, 300–900*, ed. Leslie Brubacker and Julia M.H. Smith (Cambridge: Cambridge University Press, 2004), pp. 70–82

Treharne, Elaine, '"They Should Not Worship Devils…Which Neither Can See, nor Hear, nor Walk": The Sensibility of the Virtuous and the *Life of St. Margaret*', *Proceedings of the PMR Conference*, 15 (1990), 221–36

Turner, Denys, *Eros and Allegory* (Kalamazoo: Cistercian Publications, 1995)

Upchurch, Robert K., 'The Legend of Chrysanthus and Daria in Ælfric's *Lives of Saints*', *Studies in Philology*, 101 (2004), 250–69

—— , 'Virgin Spouses as Model Christians: The Legend of Julian and Basilissa in Ælfric's *Lives of Saints*', *Anglo-Saxon England*, 34 (2005), 197–217

van Dijk, Mathilde, and Renée Nip, eds, *Saints, Scholars, and Politicians: Gender as a Tool in Medieval Studies* (Turnhout: Brepols, 2005)

Vann, Theresa M., ed. *Queens, Regents and Potentates* (Dallas: Academia, 1993)

Walker, Greg, *Plays of Persuasion: Drama and Politics at the Court of Henry VIII* (Cambridge: Cambridge University Press, 1991)

Ward, Benedicta, *Harlots of the Desert: A Study of Repentance in Early Monastic Sources* (Oxford: Mowbray, 1987)

Warner, George F., and Julius P. Gilson, *Catalogue of the Western Manuscripts in the Old Royal and King's Collections*, 4 vols (London: Trustees of the British Library, 1921)

Warnkoenig, L.A., *Histoire de la Flandre et de ses institutions civiles et politiques jusqu à l'année 1309*, 5 vols (Brussels: M. Hayez, 1835)

Warr, Cordelia, 'The Golden Legend and the Cycle of the Life of Saint Elizabeth of Thuringia-Hungary', in *The Church of Santa Maria Donna Regina: Art, Iconography and Patronage in Fourteenth-Century Naples*, ed. Janis Elliott and Cordelia Warr (Aldershot: Ashgate, 2004), pp. 155–74

Watts, J., *Henry VI and the Politics of Kingship* (Cambridge: Cambridge University Press, 1996)

Watson, Nicholas, 'Desire for the Past', *Studies in the Age of Chaucer*, 21 (1999), 78–81

Weaver, Elissa, 'The Convent Muses: The Secular Writing of Italian Nuns, 1450–1650', in *Women and Faith: Catholic Religious Life in Italy from Late Antiquity to the Present*, ed. Lucetta Scaraffia and Gabriella Zarri (Cambridge, MA: Harvard University Press, 1999), pp. 129–43

——— , *Convent Theatre in Early Modern Italy: Spiritual Fun and Learning for Women* (Cambridge: Cambridge University Press, 2002)

Weinstein, Donald, and Rudolph Bell, *Saints and Society: The Two Worlds of Western Christendom* (Chicago: University of Chicago Press, 1982)

Weitzmann-Fiedler, Josepha, 'Zur Illustration Der Margaretenlegende', *Münchner Jahrbuch der Bildenden Kunst*, 17 (1966), 17–48

Whigham, Frank, *Ambition and Privilege: The Social Tropes of Elizabethan Courtesy Theory* (Berkeley, Los Angeles and London: University of California Press, 1984)

Williams, Sarah Rhiannon, 'English Vernacular Letters c. 1400–c.1600: Language, Literacy and Culture' (unpublished PhD thesis, University of York, 2001)

Wilson, Adrian, 'The Ceremony of Childbirth and its Interpretation', in *Women as Mothers in Pre-Industrial England: Essays in Memory of Dorothy McLaren*, ed. Valerie Fildes (London: Routledge, 1990), pp. 68–107

Wilson-Chevalier, Kathleen, ed., *Patronnes et mécènes en France à la Renaissance* (St-Etienne: Presse universitaire St-Etienne, 2007)

Winstead, Karen A., *Virgin Martyrs: Legends of Sainthood in Late Medieval England* (London: Cornell University Press, 1997)

Wogan-Browne, Jocelyn, 'Saints' Lives and the Female Reader', *Forum for Modern Language Studies*, 27 (1991), 314–32

——— , 'The Apple's Message: Some Post-Conquest Accounts of Hagiographic Transmission', in *Late Medieval Religious Texts and Their Transmissions*, ed. Alistair Minnis (Cambridge: D.S. Brewer, 1993), pp. 39–53

_____ , *Saints' Lives and Women's Literary Culture* (Oxford: Oxford University Press, 2001)

Woodward, William Harrison, *Vittorino da Feltre and Other Humanist Educators* (York: Zone Books, 1992)

Woolgar, Christopher M., *The Great Household in Late Medieval England* (New Haven and London: Yale University Press, 1999)

Žižek, Slavoj, *Looking Awry: An Introduction to Jacques Lacan through Popular Culture* (Cambridge, MA: MIT Press, 1992)

Index

CPSIA information can be obtained
at www.ICGtesting.com
Printed in the USA
BVHW042307210819
556452BV00004B/13/P